THE COMMENTARY
OF
FATHER MONSERRATE, S. J

ON HIS JOURNEY TO THE COURT OF AKBAR

THE COMMENTARY
OF
FATHER MONSERRATE, S. J
ON HIS JOURNEY TO THE COURT OF AKBAR

TRANSLATED FROM THE ORIGINAL LATIN BY

J. S. HOYLAND

ANNOTATED BY

S. N. BANERJEE

GYAN

Published by

Gyan Publishing House
5, Ansari Road
Daryaganj, New Delhi-110002
Phone: 011-47034999, 9811692060
E-mail: books@gyanbooks.com

Distribution Network
gyanbooks.com
India, USA, Canada, UK, Australia, France

ISBN : 978-81-212-3263-0 (PB)
First Published, London, 1922

2nd Impression 2020

Printed at: Gyan Press, Delhi.

The Commentary of Father Monserrate, S. J
Translated : J. S. Hoyland
Annotated: S. N. Banerjee

THE COMMENTARY

OF

FATHER MONSERRATE, S.J.

On his Journey to the Court of Akbar

Translated from the Original Latin by J. S. Hoyland, M.A., Hislop College, Nagpur, and annotated by S. N. Banerjee, M.A., Professor of History, Mahindra College, Patiala.

1922
HUMPHREY MILFORD
OXFORD UNIVERSITY PRESS
LONDON BOMBAY MADRAS CALCUTTA

PREFACE

This Translation and Annotation of Father Monserrate's Commentary on the first Jesuit Mission to Akbar owes everything to the careful editing of the Latin text carried through by Father H. Hosten, S.J., and published in the Memoirs of the Asiatic Society of Bengal (Vol. III, pp. 513-704).

Father Hosten's marginal notes and "apparatus criticus" have also proved of great value, and have been freely drawn upon.

The annotator wishes to take this opportunity of expressing his thanks to Mr. H. Beveridge for his notes in the Journal of the Asiatic Society of Bengal, which have been frequently consulted, and to Mr. S. Kumar, Superintendent of the Imperial Library, Calcutta, for help given in finding references.

The reader's indulgence is craved for faults of translation and proof-correcting, some of which have come to notice too late for correction.

It should be mentioned that in preparing the translation proper names have, in almost every case, been left in the form in which Father Monserrate wrote them. Exceptions are certain familiar and frequently recurring names, *e.g.*, Rudolf and Muhammad, which appear somewhat strange in their Latin form. Father Monserrate, by the way, is by no means consistent in his spelling of proper names, the same name often appearing in various guises on a single page of the Commentary.

S. N. BANERJEE,
JOHN S. HOYLAND,
Hislop College, Nagpur.

Aug. 15th, 1922.

CONTENTS.

Editors' Introduction.

AKBAR AND ASOKA.

Akbar's reign covered nearly half a century, from 1556 to 1605. In the long line of Indian sovereigns, the towering personalities of Asoka and Akbar stand high above the rest. They may be compared, and with profit. Akbar's greed for conquest and glory and his lack of sincerity form a marked contrast to Asoka's paternal rule, genuine self-control and spiritual ambition. The interest that each took in religious matters brings out the fundamental difference in their character. Having conceived an aversion for the illiberal sectarianism of the *Mullahs*, Akbar's analytical mind set itself to dissecting the various religious systems, with a view to discover the truth, and finally evolved an eclecticism, a 'hodgepodge of philosophy,' drawn mainly from Hinduism, Jainism and Zoroastrianism. Asoka, on the other hand, unhesitatingly and faithfully adopted the teachings of Gautama Buddha, and successfully wove them into politics. Akbar's wars were those of a true descendant of Timur, and had all the gruesome associations which this fact implies. Asoka's true conquest was the spread of the Law of *Dhamma*. The Great Moghal represented the reaction against the fanaticism of the orthodox Musalman divines—a reaction that was quickened and accentuated by theological discussions. The Maurya Emperor impersonates a revulsion, immediately caused by the Kalinga War, against the extreme Machiavellianism of the *Arthashastra*. The comparison can be pushed further.

The old notion that Akbar was a near approximation to Plato's philosopher-king has been dissipated by modern researches. His character with its mixture of ambition and cunning has now been laid bare. He has been rightly compared to 'a pike in a pond preying upon his weaker neighbours.' He was so 'close and self-contained with twists of words and deeds, so divergent one from the other, and at most times so contradictory, that even by much seeking one could not find a clue to his thoughts.'

Akbar's Eclecticism.

Three Missions from Goa were despatched at the request of the Emperor to his court, of which the last two are beyond the scope of this book. To the Jesuit missionaries Akbar was at first an encouragement, then an enigma, and ultimately, a bitter disappointment. They entertained high hopes and held many heated discussions, but the Emperor was never converted. An excerpt from the Jesuit reports to the authorities at Goa forms interesting reading in this connection: "The Emperor is not a Mahommedan, but is doubtful as to all forms of faith, and holds firmly that there is no divinely accredited form of faith, because he finds in all something to offend his reason and intelligence. Nevertheless he at times admits that no faith commends itself so much to him as that of the Gospel, and that when a man goes so far as to believe this to be the true faith and better than others, he is near to adopting it. At the court some say he is a heathen and adores the sun. Others that he is a Christian. Others that he intends to found a new sect. Among the people also there are various opinions regarding the Emperor, some holding him to be a Christian, others a heathen, others a Mahommedan. The more intelligent, however, consider him to be neither Christian, nor heathen, nor Mahommedan, and hold this to be truest; or they think him to be a Mahommedan who outwardly conforms to all religions in order to obtain popularity."

The fact is that Akbar was a keen and appreciative student of Comparative Religion. He invited to his court not only Christian missionaries, but Parsee and Jain teachers as well. By nature a curious and superstitious eclectic, he always eagerly enquired after some new cult, but was perfectly aware of how far he could gratify his curiosity without interfering with the safety of his tenure of the throne. He was no doubt a seeker after truth, but the search was circumscribed by, and secondary to, dynastic and political interests. He could not have became a Christian without provoking a general rebellion of his subjects, Hindu and Mahommedan, and demolishing the fabric of the Empire, the result of years of patient and painful effort. It is very doubtful how far he was sincere when he suggested that he might arrange to be baptised by travelling to Goa on the pretext of a pilgrimage to Mecca.

Secondly, an eclectic like Akbar, who found "in all religions something to offend his reason and intelligence," was reluctant to pin himself down to any one of the existing creeds, and was eager, in the true spirit of an autocrat, to establish and lead a new religion drawn from all.

Thirdly, it is legitimate to guess that the Emperor would not have allowed himself to be converted by missionaries who appeared to him as intolerant and uncompromising as Makhdum-ul-Mulk and Abdun-Nabi, and whose co-religionists were guilty of the horrors of the Inquisition at Goa, of which he must have heard. It is no refutation of this to say that Akbar was "far too sensible to attribute the Inquisition to the Christian religion."

Fourthly, the Emperor found the doctrines of the Holy Trinity and of the Incarnation a stumbling-block in the way of conversion.

Fifthly, he was 'seeking a sign like that of the fire-ordeal, but no sign was given him.'

Lastly, he was unable to give up his polygamous habits, for no importance need be attached to the bazaar gossip of the time that he once intended to distribute his wives among the grandees.

The above may be considered to have been Akbar's objections to conversion; and presumably the first four had great weight with him. But it is doubtful whether he ever seriously considered embracing the Christian faith. The Jesuit missionaries seem to have overestimated his favourable disposition towards their religion. Our present knowledge permits us to conclude that he invited the missionaries out of intellectual inquisitiveness. In a letter, dated Ajmir, the 30th October, 1616, Sir Thomas Roe notes this trait in his character: "Akbar Shah was by nature just, inquisitive after novelties and curious of new opinions." The *Din-i-Ilahi*, promulgated in 1582, gives very little evidence of his reputed penchant for the Christian faith. Zoroastrianism and Jainism had the most obvious influence on him. There were Parsee *mobeds* and Jain teachers at his court. His reverence for fire indicates his leaning towards the faith of Zarathustra. This once led him to order a poor lamp-lighter to be hurled down from the roof of the palace for showing what he considered to be disrespect for fire. Dastur Meherji Rana wielded much the same influence as Father Aquaviva, if not greater.

AKBAR AND HIS JAIN TEACHERS.

The names of six Jain instructors of Akbar have been handed down to us;—Hiravijaya Suri, Santichandra, Vijayasena Suri, Bhanuchandra Upadhyaya, Siddhichandra, and Jinchandra. From 1578 onwards to the end of the reign there always resided one or two Jain teachers at the court. Of the above-named teachers, the first may be called the Father Aquaviva of the Jains. He was invited in the usual manner, and the free-thinking Secretary, Abul Fazl, was placed in charge of the guest. The Emperor received instructions in the *Dharma* from Suri till his departure from Fatehpur in 1584. Santichandra stayed till 1587; he wrote a turgid encomium (*Kriparasa-Kosa*) on Akbar. The other teachers duly took their place at the court, and Bhanuchandra remained till 1605. We know very little of Jinchandra; but he is said to have "converted Akbar to the Jain religion." Conversion, actual and complete, there never was; but the Jain instructors have a better right to make such a statement than the Jesuits. Unfortunately the Jain teachers have left no Commentary. But a long Sanskrit inscription on the porch of the temple of Adiswara on the Satrunjaya hill (close to Palitana in Kathiawad) records the achievements of Hiravijaya Suri and Vijayasena Suri at the Moghal Court. It may be summarised as follows:

(1) Hiravijaya, who was called by Sahi Akabbara to Mevat, persuaded the Emperor in Samvat 1639 (A.D. 1582) to issue an edict forbidding the slaughter of animals for six months, to abolish the confiscation of the property of deceased persons, the *Sujijia* tax (the *Jizia*) and a *Sulka*, to set free many captives, snared birds and animals, to present Satrunjaya to the Jainas, to establish a Jaina library, and to become a saint like King Srenika (Bimbasara c. 582-554 B.C.) (2) Vijayasena, who was called by Akabbara to Ludhapur, received from him great honours, and a *phuraman*, forbidding men to slaughter cows, bulls and buffalo-cows, to confiscate the property of deceased persons and to make captives in war; who, honoured by the king, the son of Choli Vegama (Hamida Bano Begum), adorned Gujarat.

Akbar and the Sikh Gurus.

We have given some account of the Jain teachers. It may be remarked that the Hindu ladies of Akbar's zenana and his Hindu subjects, much more than Debi or Birbal, were his silent but effective instructors in Hinduism. Without straying into irrelevancies a few words about his relations with the Sikh Gurus, which historians generally omit, may be noted here. The tolerant Emperor had high opinions of the merits of Sikhism and restrained by his attitude any attempt at persecution. He is said to have visited Guru Amar Das (1552-74) at Goindwal, dined with him, and received a dress of honour. On one occasion the Brahmans whose ascendancy the Sikhs violently assailed, complained to him that the conduct of the Gurus in diverting the people from the prescribed religious and social customs was likely to lead to political disturbance. Consistently with his usual practice he wanted to confront the Guru with the Brahmans in a religious discussion, and was very much pleased with the arguments of the Guru's representative, Jetha (afterwards Guru Ram Das), who thus concluded: 'The Brahmans claim to be equal to God. The Guru maketh no such boast, for he knoweth that he is God's slave.' But to placate the Hindus, the Emperor diplomatically advised Guru Amar Das through Jetha to go on a pilgrimage to Hardwar, promising on his part to exempt the party from the pilgrim tax. This probably resulted in the total remission of the pilgrim tax, which is dated 1563. We are also told that the Emperor sent in a request to the Guru to pray for his success at Chitor (1567-8). Guru Amar Das was succeeded by his son-in-law Guru Ram Das (1574-81), who was held in high esteem by Akbar. The king granted him a Jagir, within the limits of which was excavated a tank called *Amritsar* or the pool of immortality. This since has developed into the religious capital of the Sikhs. A story is related of Guru Ram Das that owing to 'the long stay of Akbar with his retinue and camp followers at Lahore the price of food had risen greatly, and that when the court left the place, it was expected to fall and the rayats to suffer in consequence. He therefore begged the king to remit a year's rent to the poor rayats.' This was granted (Latif's *History of the Punjab*, p. 252). The suggestion may be hazarded that this was in the year 1581. The next pontiff, Guru Arjun (1581-1606), compiled the Granth Sahib; and it was represented to the Emperor that the Guru had compiled a book in which Mahommedan prophets and divines and Hindu incarnations and gods were spoken of with contempt. In consequence of this Bhai Budha and Bhai Guru Das were sent with the book to Akbar, who on hearing portions of it, thus gave his verdict: "Excepting love and devotion to God I so far find neither praise nor blame of any one in this

Granth. It is a volume worthy of reverence." The Emperor once at the request of Guru Arjun remitted the revenues of the Punjab for a year on account of a severe famine. This may be dated between 1595 and 1598.

THE FIRST JESUIT MISSION.

But to return to our topic. The first Jesuit Mission to the court of Akbar left Goa on November 17, 1579. On December 13 of the same yeai they left Daman for Surat, and on February 28, 1580, Fathers Aquaviva and Enriquez arrived at Fatehpur Sikri. Father Monserrate, having been taken ill at Narwar, reached the Moghal capital a week later, on March 4. The missionaries were warmly received at the royal court. Abul Fazl and Hakim Ali Gilani were asked to look to the comforts and health of the guests. Father Monserrate was shortly afterwards appointed tutor to the Emperor's second son Murad, who is also known by the name of Pahari, probably 'on account of his having been born on the low hills of Fatehpur.' Theological discussions were held with the Mahommedan divines and were marked by great bitterness; but the Fathers continued to share the royal condescension along with the Jain teachers. However, from the beginning of 1580 to the beginning of 1582 the times were troublous for the Emperor. His attempt to make himself the head of a new religion, his suspected rejection of Islam, and his close attention to the Jain, Parsee and Christian preachers alarmed his Mahommedan subjects. Troubles arose in the east, to which a religious colour was given by the *fatwa* of the chief Kazi of Jaunpur; and discontented orthodoxy employed Mirza Mahommad Hakim as an instrument for vexing Akbar's peace. In consequence of the unrest there must have been, as is stated by Father Monserrate, some perceptible coldness, however temporary, in the Emperor's attitude towards the Christian missionaries.

By 1582 however the disturbances were quelled and the murmurings silenced, and Akbar felt secure enough to proclaim the *Din-i-Ilahi*. His repudiation of Islam was now open and avowed. As Badaoni says, 'not a trace of Islam was left in him.'

FRICTION WITH THE PORTUGUESE.

The missionaries, seeing the futility of continuing any more at court, requested permission to go back to Goa, but were asked to stay on. Besides the religious attitude of Akbar, they had other reasons for wishing to leave the court. Political complications had come to a head which threatened to strain the relations between the Emperor and the Portuguese on the west coast almost to the breaking point. Since the incorporation of Gujarat in the Empire in 1573, the possibility of friction had become very great. To the Moghals the Portuguese at Daman and Diu were mere intruders. Moreover the 'Portugalls' claimed dominion over the sea, intercepted the pilgrim ships to Mecca, and subjected the pilgrims to indignities. The sea route was then the only route to Mecca, as the overland route was rendered extremely unsafe by the hostility of the Qizilbashis. But in order to take this sea route the pilgrims had to obtain costly passports with the pictures of Mary and Jesus stamped on them. Without these the Portuguese would not give the pilgrim ships a safe-conduct. The use of such passports must have been considered idolatry by some Musalmans, but the pious duty of a pilgrimage to Mecca could not be foregone. Thomas Coryat relates an incident which throws a flood of light on the relations between the Musalmans and the Portuguese, and which is supposed to refer to this period of the reign of Akbar. "Ecbar Shaugh was a very fortunate prince and pious to his mother. And never denyed her anything but this, that she demanded of him, that our Bible might be hanged about an asses necke and beaten about the towne, for that the Portugals having taken a ship of theirs at sea, in which was found the Alcoran amongst the Moores, tyed it about the neck of a dogge and beat the same dogge about the towne of Ormuz. But he denyed her request saying that if it were ill in the Portugals to doe so to the Alcoran, being it became not a king to requite ill with ill, for that the contempt of any religion was the contempt of God, and he would not be revenged upon an innocent book." (Foster's *Early Travels in India*, p 278).

There was a party at court opposed to the introduction of Christianity, and it was backed by the whole harem; for as Peruschi writes, 'Akbar's numerous wives, afraid of being repudiated, adopted an attitude of hostility towards the Christian religion." The opposition of this party stiffened after the return, early in 1582, of Hamida Bano Begum (Akbar's mother) and Gulbadan Begum (Akbar's aunt) from Mecca. These two causes produced a state of tension that soon broke into open hostility; and Father Aquaviva was recalled (February 1583), Father Monserrate having already left with the Embassy to Europe (April 1582).

Akbar's Embassy To Europe.

Reference will be found in the body of this book to the Embassy to Europe sent under Sayyid Muzaffar. The letter which the envoy conveyed was, according to some, addressed to the *Danyan-i-Farang*, *i.e.*, to the scholars of Europe, or, in the opinion of others, to the *Riwa-i-Farang*, *i.e.*, to the ruler of Europe. It is almost certain that it was a letter to Philip II of Spain intended to pave the way for his help against the Turks, but sent under the pretext of arranging for a fresh mission of Christian priests to the Moghal court. The letter, filled with heavy rhetoric and wearisome verbosity, does not form very interesting reading. A full English translation of it will be found in the *Indian Antiquary*, April 1887, p. 135 ff. It points out the importance of international alliances for the purpose of establishing peace and harmony on earth, and does not omit to enumerate, in a subtle way, Akbar's conquests, power and position. "It is not concealed," runs the letter, "and veiled from the minds of intelligent persons who have received the light of divine aid and are illuminated by the rays of wisdom and knowledge, that in this terrestrial world, which is the mirror of the celestial, there is nothing that excels love, and no propensity so worthy of cultivation as philanthropy, because the peace of the world and harmony of existence are based upon friendship and association; and in each heart illuminated by the rays of the sun of love the world of the soul or the faculties of the mind are by them purged of human darkness; and much more is this the case when they subsist between monarchs, peace among whom implies the peace of the world and of the denizens thereof. Considering these things we are with the whole power of our mind earnestly striving to establish and strengthen the bonds of love, harmony and union among the population, but above all with the exalted tribe of princes who enjoy the noblest of distinctions in consequence of a greater share of divine favour, and especially with that illustrious representative of dominion, recipient of divine illumination, and propagator of the Christian religion, who needs not to be praised or made known; and this decision is on account of our propinquity, the claims whereof are well-established among mighty potentates and acknowledged to be the chief conditions of amicable relations. But as weighty obstacles and great hindrances have delayed personal intercourse, an interchange of messages and correspondence is the best substitute for it. Intelligent and shrewd men, having considered it fit to take the place of oral conversation, we entertain hopes that the portals of correspondence will be continually kept open on both sides, whereby we may inform each other of various affairs and pleasant hopes. It will be known to your enlightened mind that by the unanimous consent of the adherents of all religions and Governments, regarding the two states, namely, the religious and secular—the visible and the invisible world—it is believed and considered fully proved that in comparison to the next the present world is of no account. What laudable efforts the wisest men of the period, as well as the great princes of every country, are making to ameliorate the present perishable outward state! But they are nevertheless spending the essence of their lives, and the best of their time, in the acquisition of mundane objects, striving for and being fully absorbed in the enjoyment of pleasures, and the indulgence of appetites which must soon vanish! Allah, the Most High, has, however, by His eternal favour and unceasing guidance—despite our multifarious occupations, drawbacks, connections and dependence on external circumstances—graciously inspired us with a longing after Him; but although we have brought the dominions of several great princes under subjection—the administration and amalgamation whereof engrosses our intellect, because we are bound to promote the happiness and welfare of all our subjects—nevertheless, Allah be praised, the purpose of all our activity, the head and front of all we do, is a desire to meet with divine approbation and to discover that which is true." The conclusion of the letter is significant. "Sayyid Muzaffar, who is endowed with many excellent qualities, loyal, and distinguished by enjoying our special favour, will orally communicate to you certain matters and may be trusted. Please always keep open the portals of communication."

But the trusted envoy did not trust his master. He concealed himself in the Deccan. Father Monserrate and Abdullah Khan reached Goa. Abdullah afterwards returned to Fatehpur without ever sailing for Europe. The letter thus did not reach its destination. In 1607 Jahangir expressed an abortive desire to send a similar mission to Europe.

FATHER MONSERRATE.

The first mission then failed in its object, in the sense that from the missionary point of view no tangible result was achieved. But the historian of the mission has enriched (by his Commentary) the historical literature of the Mahommedan period of Indian history. Our information about the early life of Father Monserrate is meagre. When the Great Plague devastated the city of Lisbon in 1569, he was a member of the monastery of S. Martha and exhibited conspicuous zeal in tending the sick and caring for the destitute. While he was with the Moghal Emperor, whether at Sikri or on the march to Kabul, he combined the earnestness of a missionary with the observant shrewdness of a historian. In February 1581, Akbar marched against his half brother, Mirza Muhammad Hakim, King of Kabul, who had invaded the Punjab. Father Monserrate accompanied the Emperor in his suite as far as Peshawar, and afterwards proceeded with the rear-guard of the Moghal army to Jalalabad. On his return from this expedition Monserrate remained at the then capital. But the shifty conduct of the Emperor and the promulgation of the Divine Faith irritated him, and preferring to be with his charge Murad he repaired to Agra. In April 1582, Akbar sent an embassy to Europe, as noted above, and Father Monserrate was allowed to accompany it as far as Goa. In accordance with the order of the Provincial of Goa, Father Monserrate had written up his notes on the Emperor and the Empire of India. After his return to Goa, he was engaged in arranging and amplifying the materials when he was ordered to Abyssinia (1588). Thus the work must have lain in abeyance for a number of years. He took the MS. with him in the hope of finishing it. While coasting round Arabia the vessel was seized by the Arabs, and he was thrown into prison at Dhafar and subsequently removed to Sanaa. However, he was allowed facilities to complete his book, which he did in his prison at Sanaa on the feast of S. Damasus in December 1590. Ransomed in August 1596, he returned to Goa in December, bringing back with him the MS. The troubles of these years had broken his health, and he was sent to Salsette, where he died in 1600.

The Commentary.

For some reason or other Monserrate's Commentary was never sent to Lisbon or Rome. Somehow "the MS found its way to Calcutta in the beginning of the last century, and after passing successively through the Fort William College, the Metcalfe Hall, and the Imperial Library, it was discovered in 1906 by the Rev. W. K. Firminger in St. Paul's Cathedral Library, Calcutta." The Latin Text was published in 1914 by the Asiatic Society of Bengal, in its Memoirs, Vol. III, No. 9.

Unfortunately the Commentary lacks its first pages. It abruptly begins with Father Pereira at the Moghal court. But the importance of the document as an original historical authority cannot be exaggerated. It sheds new light upon the character and reign of Akbar, who was by far the greatest of all Musalman rulers of India. It serves as a useful corrective alike to the fulsome laudations of Abul Fazl and to the spiteful cavillings of Abdul Qader. It shows a great ruler and a great soldier, who was also profoundly interested in the spiritual world, and greedily eager to gain any information, whether authentic or the reverse, about that world. It throws a hundred sidelights upon different aspects of the Emperor's character: his grim severity: his humour: his munificence: his penuriousness: his keen and critical insight: his credulity and superstition. Some of the brief incidents recorded are worth a hundred dry facts and dates, as, for instance, the Emperor's causing his treacherous brother's envoys to be brought before him in the midst of a bison-fight, and his sending them away again with a gift of old clothes; or his pardoning of the condemned wretch on account of the witty fashion in which he explained his inability to substantiate the claim to mercy which he had based on the plea that he was a sweet singer.

Its Style.

Father Monserrate's Latin style is frequently exceedingly involved and obscure, and the translator of this document would be the first to acknowledge the doubtful authenticity of his interpretation of a large number of passages. At times, however, Monserrate can give a clear and concise account of some special topic with which he has evidently made himself thoroughly acquainted. Instances may be found in his description of the Moghal feudal army, and in his account of the Tibetans. He was evidently by no means a master of Greek; for though in accordance with the custom of his age he loved to interlard his Latin with a sprinkling of Greek expressions, these are very often wrongly spelt. He is extremely careless in his spelling of names.

At times the author shows a vein of dry and caustic humour; but unfortunately this is generally reserved for the bitter attacks upon Islam which fill his journal. Some of these attacks have been slightly toned down by the translator; but he has not felt free to omit them altogether, since without them it would be impossible to comprehend the spirit in which the mission went to the Moghal court and the manner in which it was received there. Readers will realise that Monserrate speaks in the terms of religious controversy belonging to the sixteenth century; and that the fact of his religious bigotry adds to the value of his witness to the greatness and glory of the Moghal civilization. For if an observer so prejudiced and bigoted against the bases of that civilization gives a picture so rosy-tinted, the reality must have been even more gorgeous than the picture.

The last part of the journal consists of a series of ill-authenticated tales which Monserrate had collected regarding the ancestors of Akbar, especially Timur. As these have no bearing on the first mission to the Moghal court they have been taken out of their place and put in an Appendix.

In a few cases of common names (*e.g.* Mahommadans) Father Monserrate's terminology and spelling have been abandoned, but in the great majority of instances the names are given as he wrote them.

S. N. BANERJEE (*Annotator*)
JOHN S. HOYLAND (*Translator*)

Hislop College,
Nagpur, C. P.

Father Monserrate's Introduction.

To **P. Claudius Aquaviva, head of the whole Society of Jesus, Antonius Monserratus, priest of the same Society, sends greetings.**

The men of antiquity were so exact and diligent that, when they were making a journey, they entered the happenings of every single day in their journals, with the most minute carefulness. Alexander, when he made his expedition into Asia, gave the charge of this important matter to Eratosthenes the Macedonian, whilst Antiochus Nicator, the son of Seleucus Nicator, gave it to Artemidorus. But Julius Cæsar himself undertook this task and wrote Commentaries on the wars he waged. The Persian kings, as is mentioned in the book of Esdras, used to do the same. For the recorders of events, as they were called, were ordered by royal command to note down every event that occurred.

Many have since followed the example of this diligence, both by land and sea; and thus, in their devotion to Geography, marine Exploration, and History—those most weighty subjects of study—have enriched the republic of letters with generous provision.

For this and other reasons it has become a rule in the Society of Jesus that a record should be kept of all events. This rule dates from the blessed memory of our Father Ignatius (Loyola), who first pronounced it.

At the time when we were setting out for the court of Zelaldinus Equebar[1], King of the Mongols, the saintly Roderic Vincentius, Superior of the Society in the province of India, being unwilling to break this excellent rule, laid upon me the charge of recording everything that happened both on the journey and during our residence with the King. It was my duty,

---

[1] Jalal-ud-din Akbar.

in accordance with the discipline under which I live, and with the rules of the Society, to obey this behest with the greatest exactitude. I therefore set myself, for full two and a half years, to write down every evening all the events of the past day. In this daily task of conscientious record-keeping, I embraced every new experience or fact which the day's journey or events had brought before my notice—for example the rivers, cities and countries which we saw: the customs, temples and religious usages of their inhabitants: and, after we arrived at the King's court, the devotion which he showed (though indeed it was but a pretence) towards the religion of Christ. I recorded also his kindness towards Rudolf, to whom had been given charge of that most weighty business, and towards his companions, (though indeed that kindness was but counterfeit, and assumed for selfish reasons). The zeal, prudence and skill of Rudolf himself was another of my topics, as also were the debates with the Musalmans concerning the Christian religion, and the Afghan war, in which Zelaldinus defeated and put to flight Hachimus, by the exercise of the greatest determination and the most remarkable military skill. Finally, I recorded the triumphant reception of Akbar himself by his subjects.

After my return I read these rough and casual notes of mine, just as I had hurriedly jotted them down, to certain members of our Society, who were distinguished for their experience, wisdom and skill in letters. They heartily advised me to write out again what I judged to be the more important parts, setting them in sequence and due order. Having been accustomed to follow the excellent counsel and opinion of these men in other matters of greater moment, I was by no means willing to abandon it in a matter which must be afterwards referred to your testing, and either approved or rejected in accordance with your most weighty judgment.

This is now the eighth year since I first set my hand to this task. For in the sixth year after it was begun (*i.e.* in 1588) I was sent by Peter Martin, Superior of the province of India, to Africa: and was compelled, by the fact that the season for navigation had already arrived, to stop the work, eager though I was to go on with it. I got no time or opportunity to return to my task till I was captured by my enemies the Musulmans near Dofar[1] in Arabia (that is, Sabaea) close to the city of Atramitis,[2] where frankincense is found. I was sent away to Eynanus;[3] but the Musalman king Ommar allowed my slender baggage and my books to be preserved and returned to me. He also permitted me a considerable degree of freedom, though I was still held in custody. For I was granted four months of leisure, in which I was able to make the necessary corrections and additions to what I had written. For, by the singular goodness of God, I had to bear none of the bitternesses of captivity except the mere fact of being a prisoner. My chief solace was the companionship of Father Peter Paesius (to whom I used to make confession); and next to this I took comfort from holy books and from a breviary of the morning and evening prayers.

However, after that four months' leisure, I had once more to lay aside my literary weapons, for I was ordered to proceed to Sanaa, where a Turkish Viceroy resides. He was an Albanian by race (an Albanian is commonly called an Arnautes by the Turks, and an Allanesian by the Portuguese, both names being derived from the name of the principal town of that tribe[4]). He pretended to treat me with the same kindness and ordered (my) books to be given to me; whereupon I returned to my task, and yet further revised, corrected and added to my records, and freed them from blemishes.

It will be for you to decide whether I have written in the approved style and fashion of the Society, and

---

1 It is now known as Mir Bat (Jarret II 51.)

2 Hadramaut.

3 Ainaud, 207 miles N-E. of Aden.

4 *i.e.* Alessio.

whether readers will gain anything from my records. For my part—unless I am deceived by self-love—I believe that some attention given to Indian History will not prove to be without its use to students of Geography and the Classics, and especially to those of us who are devoted to the study of learned and polite writers.

Everything relating to the journey of the Fathers, to their stay at the King's court, and to the Afghan campaign, I have written down exactly as it happened, and as I saw it with my own eyes. But whatever pertains to digressions from the direct course of my narrative (for instance the references at the end of the first book to Cinguiscanus, Temurbegus, the Scythians, the Mongols, etc.), I have gathered primarily from King Zekaldinus himself, or else from a diary of travel written by a certain ambassador[1] sent by King Henry the Fourth of Castile to Timur, or lastly from many other writers whose authority is to be relied upon.

Finally, I have divided my work into two books, of which this first forms an account of the first journey to the court of the King of the Mongols, whilst the second is, as it were, an appendix and commentary upon the first; in this I have collected facts bearing on the condition and natural history of India (within the Ganges), of its ancient aborigines and present-day inhabitants.

In the two remaining books which I have added to those already mentioned, I have written in the same fashion a record of my journey to Ethiopia and a brief account of the condition and natural history of Arabia. In these books I have endeavoured (if I may say so without arrogance) to correct, explain and reconcile—in as seemly and moderate a manner as possible—many passages in those Geographers and Historians who have written about India and Arabia: and this I have done as a service to the teachers and lecturers in our own schools.

---

1 Ruy Gonzalez de Clavijo.

I trust that my work may have been done to the glory of the divine Name and to the benefit of men's minds—a benefit which should not only be earnestly desired but sought after with all one's might. If my double work appears, in your most weighty judgment, to achieve these two aims, I believe that it will be amply satisfying to you.—Farewell.

Sanaa,
January 7th, 1591.

ABBREVIATIONS.

A. G. ... *The Ancient Geography of India* by Major-General Alexander Cunningham.

Ain. ... *Ain-i-Akbari* of Abul Fazl translated by Blochmann (Vol. I) and Jarret (Vol. II and III).

Al-Badaoni. ... *Muntakhab-ut-Tawarikh* by Abdul Qader Al-Badaoni, commonly known as *Badaoni* or *Al-Badaoni*. The first two volumes have been translated by Lowe and Ranking. The second volume contains an account of Akbar.

A. N. ... *Akbar-Nama* by Abul Fazl, translated by H. Beveridge. So far as published.

A. R. ... *Archæological Reports.*

Badaoni. ... Same as *Al-Badaoni.*

B. G. ... *Bombay Gazetteer.*

Blochmann. ... *Ain-i-Akbari* Vol. I, translated by Henry Blochmann.

Campos. ... *A History of the Portuguese in Bengal* by Campos, Vols. 2.

Danvers. ... *The Portuguese in India* by F. C. Danvers. Vols. 2.

D. R. E. ... A misprint for E. R. E. which stand for *Encyclopaedia of Religion and Ethics* edited by James Hastings.

E. D. ... *The History of India as told by its own Historians*, edited by Sir H. M. Elliot and Prof. J. Dowson, Vols. 8.

Elphinstone. ... *A History of India* by the Honourable Mountstuart Elphinstone, with notes and additions by E. B. Cowell.

I. G. ... *Imperial Gazetteer.*

Irvine. ... *Moghul Army and its organisation* by W. Irvine.

Jarret.	... Vols. II and III of Abul Fazl's *Ain-i-Akbari* translated by Jarret.
J A. S. B.	... *Journal of the Asiatic Society of Bengal.*
J. B. B. R. A. S.	... *Journal of the Bombay Branch of the Royal Asiatic Society.*
Ptolemy.	... *Ancient India as described by Ptolemy* by J. W. McCrindle.
Smith.	... *Akbar the Great Moghul* by V. A. Smith.
Strabo.	... *The Geography of Strabo* translated by H. C. Hamilton and W. Falconer. Vols. 3.
Von Noer.	... *Emperor Akbar* by Frederick Von Noer translated by Annette Beveridge. Vols. 2. In some places in the notes this author's name is misprinted Von Neor.

MONSERRATE'S COMMENTARY.

Akbar's Invitation.

* * * was compelled to go before the King. When he[1] came before him, the King talked to him about religion and asked him whether there were many priests amongst us. He replied that there were large numbers and that very many of them were much more learned than he was himself.

He made especial mention of the priests of the Society (of Jesus), about whom he had already heard both from Ismail[2] and from Tauarius.[3] For this reason he decided to summon them as speedily as possible to his presence, and in the year 1579 A.D. he sent envoys

---

1 Francis Julian Pereira (Vicar-General in Bengal stationed at Satgaon) whom, at the request of Pietro Tavares, Akbar in 1578 had invited to his court, in order to learn from him something more about the Christian faith (Campos). Pereira was a 'man of more piety than learning,' and having acquainted Akbar with the tenets of Christianity, asked him to send for more learned priests from Goa. From this resulted the First Jesuit Mission to Akbar. Bartoli gives his full name as Egidio Anes Pereira. He was still at the Court when the First Mission arrived in February 1580.

2 He may be identified with Ismail Quli Khan (Blochmann *Ain*. Vol. I. p. 360 No. 46). Akbar used also to send his trusty servants to Goa to collect European curiosities and probably to report on the political and naval power of the Portuguese.

3 Pietro Tavares who has been described as a 'man well-versed in politics and state-affairs,' was Captain or Commandant of the port of Hugli. He came to the Imperial Court in 1576, and had many interviews with the Emperor who gave him many presents and a *firman* granting full freedom of conscience to the Portuguese in Bengal with permission to preach and convert as well as to build churches. He also obtained a *firman* exempting the Portuguese merchants in Bengal from all customs duties up to 1579. Akbarnama mentions one Partap Bar the Feringhi as having been at Akbar's Court for some time. Beveridge identifies Partap Bar with Tavares (*J. A. S. B.* 1888, p. 34).

to the Viceroy of India[4] and to the Archbishop of Goa asking, amongst other weighty matters of state, that two of the Society's priests should be sent to him. He sent despatches also of the same type and with an identical request to the Superior of the Society in that province. These despatches ran as follows :—'The commandment of Zelaldinus the Great, King by God constituted. Know, O chief Fathers of the Order of St. Paul,[5] that we are very well disposed unto you. We are sending unto you Ebadulla[6] our envoy, and Dominicus Petrius[7], that they may communicate to you in our own words our desire that two learned priests should be sent unto us, to bring the chief books of the Law and the Gospel, in order that we may learn the Law and its full meaning and perfect truths in every respect. For I earnestly desire thoroughly to learn that Law. Let them not hesitate therefore to set out with the same envoys when they leave Goa on the return journey; and let them bring the books of the Law with them. Let the priests understand that I shall receive them with all possible kindness and honour. Their arrival will be a great delight to me : and when I have learnt what I long to know about the law and its perfection and the salvation it offers, they shall be allowed to return as soon as they like. I shall send them back again dignified with very many honours and gifts. Let them have no fear in coming. For I take them under my own protection and guarantee. Farewell !'

---

4 The Portuguese Viceroy at Goa at this time was Luis de Athaide who was Viceroy from 1568 to 1571 and again from 1578 to 1581.

5 This refers to the Jesuits.

6 Abdullah Khan. V. A. Smith is inclined to identify him with Sayyid Abdullah Khan (Blochmann's *Ain*. Vol. I. p. 465 No. 189.) He served in the First Gujrat War, and fought under Munim Khan, Khan Alam and Aziz Kokah. He was a faithful Imperialist ; died in 1589.

7 Dominic Peres was an Armenian Christian at the Court of Akbar. He married an Indian wife in Sept. 1582 (*J. A. S. B.* 1896, Vol. LXV. p. 57.) He was the interpreter of the Embassies of 1578 (Dec.) and of 1594, to Goa.

The good faith of this letter was supported by the testimony of letters from Ægidianius[8] who had already spent a year and a half with him[9], and from Tauarius, the governor of the port,[10] who said that confidence should be placed in the good-will of the King and in his genuine desire to see the Fathers. However, the Viceroy, the Archbishop, the Superior of the Province and other individuals of every rank, received the letter with great hesitation. Wherefore Ludovic Athaidius the Viceroy, a man very remarkable both for his statesmanship and for his wisdom, decided to lay the matter before the Council of Bishops[11], who were then at Goa, and the Portuguese nobles and lawyers. Every man gave his opinion. Most of them stated their belief that no confidence should be placed in the promises of an Agarenus.[12] But all were agreed that the matter under discussion, since it referred to religion, should be left to the decision of the Archbishop and the other Bishops.

The Mission.

Henry of Tauora, the Archbishop, then held a council with the Bishops : and the decision was unanimously arrived at that the King's invitation should be accepted, and two priests of the Society sent to him as he asked.

In view of this decision of the Fathers, the Viceroy had no occasion for further hesitation. He forthwith summoned Roderic Vincentinus, the Superior of the Society : announced to him the decision of the Bishops, and said that he himself agreed with it. This greatly delighted the Superior. For his mind was greatly inclined to meet the King's wish, and he had the keenest

---

8 See note 1.

9 Akbar.

10 See note 3.

11 The Bishops referred to here were D. Frey Leonardo De Sa (Bishop of China), D. Frey Matheos (Bishop of Cochin), and D. Joao Ribeyro Gayo (Bishop of Malacca)

12 The word that Father Monserrate uses for a Musalman is Agarenus. The term is derived from Hagar, mother of Ishmail.

desire to satisfy his pious wishes (for so they seemed). Therefore when he received from the Viceroy the report of the Bishops' decision, he referred it to those priests with whom by the constitution of the Society he must take counsel. Then he put Rudolf Aquaviva[13] in charge of the Mission, and promised to give him two companions.

I should like to describe the pleasure, nay the inordinate delight, with which Rudolf received this commission, from the mouth of the Superior as though it were a direct divine command. But I intend to commemorate his many virtues in another place.

When the Viceroy heard from the Superior that Rudolf had been put in charge of the Mission, he approved the choice and ordered him to be supplied with transport and supplies for his journey. When Rudolf came to take leave of him, the Viceroy bade him God-speed in an address full of missionary zeal.

The Start.

The Superior appointed as one of Rudolf's companions a man[14] who had an excellent knowledge of Persian; and, the season for navigation having by now arrived, himself accompanied Rudolf the eight days' voyage from Goa to Xeulus[15] and thence to Daman, where he appointed

13 Father Aquaviva, a Neapolitan and a younger son of the Duke of Atri, entered the Society of Jesus against the wishes of his parents. He was a zealous missionary and had a morose contempt for the arts and pleasures of life. He came to Goa in Sept. 1578 and was then selected the head of the First Mission to Akbar's Court where by his diligence, learning and earnestness he won the respect of the Emperor. He returned to Goa in 1583 and went to Salsette where he was murdered at Cuncolum by a mob.

14 Father Francis Henriquez was a Persian convert from Mahomedanism. He returned to Goa from Fatehpur Sikri sometime in 1581 either 'secretly as one authority states or with permission as stated by another.' Though a member of the Mission, he was a man of slight importance.

15 Chaul. It is situated in 18° 34′ N. 72° 55′ E. and is 30 miles south of Bombay. It is a place of great antiquity. It figures in Hindu legends under the names of Champavati and Revatikshetra. In the 16th century it was a fortified place with a good harbour and famous for trade. C. Joppen calls it one of the doors of communication between India and the non-Indian world.

Rudolf's third companion.[16] After waiting four days at Daman, Rudolf and his companions set out again. The Superior, other priests, and the inhabitants of the fortress, accompanied the Fathers to the first mile-stone out of Daman, and then one by one took their leave of them, not without signs of mutual love, which was clearly testified to by the many tears shed on either side. They spent the night at a village called Oroar near the boundary of the territory of the two kingdoms.

On the next day they entered the dominions of Zelaldinus, crossing the river of Mount Nera, which is called in the vernacular 'Paharnera,' and divides the territory of the Mongols from that of the Portuguese. Thence they came to Balsar,[17] a name signifying in the vernacular 'Bucephala' or the ox's head. On the next day they reached Nausarinum; and on the third day from Daman they came to Surat.

Nausarinum[18] is the chief seat of certain men who

---

16 Father A. Monserrate (See *Introduction.*)

17 Bulsar is 40 miles south of Surat and is situated in 20° 37' N. and 72° 50' E.

18 Naosari is now the headquarters of a prant or district of the same name in the Baroda State. It is situated in 20° 57' N and 27° 56' E, and is 147 miles from Bombay.

The Zoroastrians (the followers of Zarathushtra or Zoroaster or Zardusht), persecuted by the Mahomedans who conquered Persia, emigrated first to Diu in Kathiawad (766 A. D.) and thence in 785 A.D. to Sanjam (60 miles north of Bombay), then a Hindu state under Jai Rana. The first Parsi emigration to Naosari took place in 1142 when one Kamdin Zarthost with his family settled there. At the end of the 15th century one Changah Asa of Naosari was appointed Desai, i.e. farmer of large territories—a position which was held thenceforward by Parsi families under successive Mahomedan and Marhatta rulers. His wealth made him the leader of his community. "He renewed and spread the true religion, and gave to the needy Parsis the sacred shirt and girdle, the symbols of their faith by which they were distinguished. He brought to Naosari the sacred fire and caused a building to be built (1516) for its installation." Thus Naosari throve and prospered and became one of the principal centres of Zoroastrianism. "Naosari at the end of the 16th century was a prosperous place among the 31 Mahals of the Sarkar of Surat,

Parsis. call themselves Persians,[19] or Jezeni,[20] from the city of Jeze[21] in Persia. By race they are Gabraeans[22] whom the Portuguese call Cuarini. In colour they are white, but are extremely similar to the Jews in the rest of their physical and mental characteristics, in their inclination for hard work, in their dress and in their religion. Indeed they are often called Jews by the Portuguese, nor do they themselves entirely disavow the name. For they acknowledge that they are descended from Abraham, and for this reason practise the rite of circumcision, as do the Hebrews. They correctly calculate the date of the coming of Christ from their ancient documents. The peculiar mark, by which they are conveniently distinguished from other races, as if by a token of religion, is a garment[23] made of linen, of cotton, or of muslin (?), which hangs down to the thigh. The edges of this garment are stitched together; and its two ends are sewn up. It covers the head, and the ends are tied together over the chest, leaving a square-shaped fold about four inches wide,

---

being 19th in point of area as well as in point of the revenue that it brought to state. Its area was 17,353 bighas and its revenue 297,720 dams (40 dams=1 Tanka.) It was noted for a manufactory of perfumed oil found nowhere else."

19 Parsis, as the Zoroastrian settlers in India were denominated (See *Note* 22.)

20 Zoroastrians.

21 Father Monserrate's information does not seem to be correct. "According to the *Avesta,* Airyanum Vaejo, on the river Daitya, the old sacred country of the gods, was the home of Zoroaster and the scene of his first appearance." Zarathushtra, according to Jackson, was a native of Western Persia (Atropatene or Media) and belonged to the Median tribe of the Magi; he flourished about the middle of the 7th Century B.C. and died in 583 B.C.

22 After the conquest of Persia by the Mahomedans, the Zoroastrians who still remained there in their native land were called Gabers by the conquerors. The word 'Gabar' (popular Turkish *Kiavur*) is derived from the Arabic *Kafir* or Infidel.

23 An eminent author writes "To European travellers the Parsis were distinguished from the surrounding population only by the *Surdah* and *Kusti* (sacred shirt and girdle.)"

which seems to correspond to the Theraphis, as it is called, of the Jews. They are forbidden by their religious prejudices to put anything into this fold. They tie round this garment a woven woollen girdle of a considerable length, so that it goes round the body several times. They are under a religious obligation to wear this girdle at all times. They are polluted if they touch a corpse. They do not carry out their dead through the front part of the house, but break a hole[24] through the back wall. The dead moreover are not borne away on men's shoulders, but their feet are tied together and they are dragged along the ground on their backs. They neither burn nor bury corpses, but let them down into a place[25] surrounded with high walls to prevent wild animals entering, as though it were better to be torn and devoured by birds of prey or scorched by the heat of the sun, than to be consumed by the flames, or covered with earth and so disposed of! They pour out any water that has been left in the house, and no one may use the articles which the dead man has used. These religious customs not only resemble, but definitely reproduce, those of the Jews.

But though these people are bound by so many Jewish religious usages, still they worship Fire and the Sun, and build temples to Fire. They appoint priests, temple-guardians and soothsayers, and feed the sacred fire with fresh *ghi* or with precious sweet-smelling oil. If they are compelled to establish some statement by oath, they make water upon burning coals, which they

24 This is laid down in *Zend.* VIII. 10; but it is not followed in practice.

25 The *Dakhma* or as it is known to the Europeans the Tower of Silence. The corpse is left naked in the *Dakhma* so that it may be completely devoured by the vultures, 'Nature's scavengers.' If the Zarathushtrian community be too small or poor to maintain a *Dakhma* the corpse is left on some hills or mountains. Burning or burying is prohibited because of the purity of fire and earth. The corpse is unclean because, according to Parsi ideas, the corpse-demon takes possession of it after death.

regard as the most sacred form of oath. If they refuse to do this, no faith can be put in their word.

On their feast days they pray in the morning, with a very loud voice and in a strange tongue. They have their own writing script. The scriptures of their religion are contained in a single volume,[26] which only those who know the language in which it is written can understand. This volume has three parts, dealing with religious observances, the wisdom and legal enactments of the ancients, and the lore of the Magi (who are regarded by the Persians as a class of sages) regarding prophecy and divination.

The diet of these people consists of milk, *ghi*, oil, vegetables, pulse and fruit. They drink no wine. They are allowed to divorce their wives at will. They cut off the noses of unchaste women, and permit them to become prostitutes.

In conclusion, their character is so wild and savage that they seem to differ not at all from other heathen. For if any disaster happens to them they commit suicide in a horrible fashion.

These are the customs of these Persians.

Surat.

The Fathers were compelled to stop at Surat[27] for almost a month. For the ambassador was unwilling to begin his journey before the

---

26 The Zend-Avesta or the Gatha.

27 Tradition ascribes the prosperity of Surat to Gopi a rich Hindu trader who settled on its present site in the 16th century. It has further been transmitted that Gopi in consultation with a certain astrologer, named the place Suraj or Suryapur ('the city of the Sun'). But the Mahomedan overlord of the district, Sultan Muzaffar Karim, orthodox and politic, changed the Hindu name by simply substituting 't' for 'j', and decreed that the city should thenceforward be called Surat—"a name surely free from all objection, since identical with the word employed to designate each chapter of the glorious Koran." But it would be an anachronism to date the prosperity of Surat to Gopi; for the Portuguese traveller Duarte Barbosa (1514) describes it as 'a city of great trade in all classes of merchandise.' But it is just possible that the original Hindu name was Suraj or Suryapur. (*J.B.B.R.A.S.* 1908, p. 245 et seq; *I.G.* Vol. XXIII 153-57).

moon should have reached a favourable state. It is the custom of the Musalmans to take the auspices before they start upon any undertaking, and for this purpose to observe whether the moon shows herself to the sun after his rising. If she does so, they regard her as in an auspicious state.

However this delay was neither useless nor unoccupied. For while the Musalmans rested idly, the Fathers applied themselves with diligence to the study of the Persian language. Very many visitors came to their lodgings to call upon them, inspired by curiosity and by the desire of seeing men of strange aspect, dress, speech and religion, who had been summoned on account of their reputation for wisdom and piety, to his court by that King whom they thought most powerful of all. The Fathers showed these visitors pictures of Jesus Christ and of the Virgin Mary, by which they were so much impressed that they not only kissed them devoutly, but placed them reverently upon their heads. So true is it that all men naturally regard as worthy of reverence that which is truly excellent, although many are frequently deceived in their judgment of excellence, or through obstinacy and prejudice rashly and insolently refuse to honour and worship it.

In this connection a wonderful, nay almost a miraculous, event occurred. For one of the Gabraeans, whom I regard as Jews or Samaritans, was obstinately opposing the Fathers in controversy. Meanwhile Rudolf chanced to open a casket in which were preserved certain relics of St. Stephen the Protomartyr, and of several other saints. The Gabraean immediately became terrified, uttered a loud shriek, started back, and exclaimed as though he had gone mad. "If there are bones of dead men here, I cannot stay, unless I tear off these garments in which I am clothed, and rend them to pieces." Rudolf answered him quietly, wisely and in the true spirit of Christianity,—"We do not carry about the bones of the dead, but of the living." Forthwith he shut up the casket. And the

Gabraean, recovering from his terror, started again upon the interrupted controversy.

Surat stands on the river Taphaeus, which enters the sea six miles from the town. The citadel is in a naturally strong position, is well fortified, and is guarded by a garrison of two hundred mounted archers. The town is adorned by a lake,[28] which is much the largest and the most beautiful (by reason of the pains which have been taken to embellish it artificially) of all the lakes that are to be seen in India. For the eye is delighted by the flights of marble steps which surround this lake in a broad sweep. These steps are two hundred feet wide, and are divided into several sections. In the centre rises a finely built tower which is reached by boat whenever the citizens resort thither to amuse themselves. The place is also dignified by the tomb of Qhoja Sopharis,[29] who is frequently mentioned by our writers for his treachery and abandoned character. This tomb is rather an extraordinary structure, but is elaborately and expensively decorated. Close by is the grave of another worthless fellow,[30] an

---

28 Does the priest allude to the Gopi Talao?

29 Khawaja Zafar (otherwise known as Safar Aga) was according to some, a Greek, and according to others he was born of a Turkish mother and a Christian father in the island of Chios. Beveridge calls him Rumi Khan and says that he was known as Khawaja Sophar because of his colour or his Greek origin; and he further distinguishes him from another Rumi Khan who had the title of Khudawand Khan. But according to Nizamuddin Rumi Khan was Governor of Surat, the fort of which he constructed in order to strengthen it against the frequent attacks of the Protuguese. When Bahadur Shah was killed in 1538 at Diu, the Khawaja fell into the hands of the Portuguese who, recognising his capacity, treated him well and even placed confidence in him. But he seems to have repaid it with ingratitude and desertion. He was killed in the second siege of Diu in June 1546, and was buried at Surat (Danvers I. 426, 429, 468-70; *A. N. Errata and Addenda*, p. XV, Notes. 100, 112, 114; Whiteaway's *Rise of the Portuguese Power*, p. 250).

30 Does this refer to Cide Meriam who was killed in September 1562? (Danvers I. 524).

Æthiopian renegade from, and enemy of Christianity, who was the leader of Qhoja Sopharis' troops. The common people revere him as a saint, solely because he was executed by Garsia of Tauora, Governor of Daman. The women bring wreaths and garlands of flowers to his tomb.

Surat is thronged with merchants, and the near-by port is full of ships: for it is a safe anchorage, since the river extends deep and broad from the sea right up to the city.

At last the ambassador, having got favourable auspices from the moon, led his company out of Surat, and pitched his camp outside the town near the gates. Camels and other means of transport had been provided to carry provisions and merchandise. On the next day, *i.e.* January 24th, they set out, greatly to the delight of the Fathers, who did not approve of this delay and its superstitious cause, and were inexpressibly eager to reach the King's court; for they were confident that he would embrace Christianity. Having moved one mile, across the river Mophis (*i.e.* the Taphi), to a spot near Rhaenerum,[31] the company encamped. This Rhaenerum, which is commonly called Raynel by the Portuguese, is a celebrated military fortress opposite Surat, to which it bears the same relation as Abydos does to Sestos. Its citizens have frequently defended themselves most manfully against the Portuguese, although they have been overcome.[32]

On the next day the travellers set out from this place, whereupon two of the Fathers and the rest of the Christians fell into no small danger. One of the

---

31 Rander or Reyner (called Ranal by Barbosa, 1514) is situated in North lat. 21° 13', East long. 70° 51'. It was at first a Jain city, then it passed into the hands of the Moors under whom it was highly prosperous. Its prosperity however declined owing to the rise of Surat to importance.

32 E. G. In 1530, after sacking Surat, the Portuguese General Antonio de Sylvera attacked it and ultimately bore down all opposition of the citizens. The city seems to have suffered much on account of its proximity to Surat.

priests was being carried in a litter, as he was ill. His bearers, eager to get rid of their burden, had gone on at a rapid pace far ahead of the rest of the company. The governor of Surat met them, surrounded by a band of guards. The priest saluted the governor, who asked him what party was coming behind. Meanwhile the governor's followers went on ahead, and perceiving the foreign appearance of the rest of the company fell upon them savagely, with intent to kill them all, shouting 'Franks, Franks.'

However the governor and the ambassador whipped up their horses, reached the spot from opposite directions, and by the mercy of God succeeded in quelling the riot before a single Musalman had been slain by the Portuguese. If one had so perished, we should all have been killed. The two Fathers who had been in such danger thought that the one who had gone on ahead must certainly have been killed. When they caught him up they embraced him as though he had been restored to them from heaven.

On the next day they came to a fort built out of the debris of some Hindu temples which the Musalmans had destroyed. Such destruction would have been a praiseworthy action if many of their other actions had not been so abominable.[33] The camp was pitched on the bank of the Taphi. On the same day the Hindus expatiate their sins of the past years in the following manner. A cocoanut shell is scraped out and filled with oil. A wick inserted and lighted. The Hindu then strips off his clothes and enters the river with the lighted lamp on his head. He slowly submerges himself till the lamp, caught by the current, is carried away. They regard themselves as purified from sin by this process. This festival is called by the Hindus the Satamia[34] because it is held on the seventh day of the

33 Father Monserrate often displays his fervent orthodoxy in such a manner as to detract, to a certain extent, from the value of his book.

34 Probably the *Ratha Saptami*.

moon in the eleventh month, which in their reckoning is January.

The Satpura Range.

Leaving the bank of the river the company reached Sultanpurum[85] (*i.e.* King's town) on the ninth day form Surat. This was the day on which the Musalmans perform their sacrifices. A three days' halt was made at Sultanpurum, as the ambassador desired to wait there on account of this festival. Thence they crossed the Avazus range and reached Cenduanum[86] four days later. The Avazus extends for 75 miles eastward from the sea, and is 16 miles wide. It is crossed by a narrow and difficult track. The camels have to be led in single file; and the carts are carried on men's shoulders. The jungle on each side is exceedingly dense, and the ground broken and rough. There one of the ambassador's guards was killed by robbers, and no revenge could be taken. The inhabitants[87] of these mountains worship ghosts. They are ruled by three kings, of whom one is the master of the other two and is as it were their emperor. They are constantly at war with the Mongols. When one of their tribes is pacified, and a treaty made with the Mongols, the other two tribes carry on the wild and savage warfare, and frequently defeat their great enemy. Occasionally these battles are drawn; but the Mongols can never inflict on the mountaineers a decisive defeat. These mountaineers are wild, barbarous and degraded. They are addicted to brigandage, and have no weapons except bows made of bamboo and short arrows with rusty points. Yet they are exceedingly fierce, intractable, greedy of spoil, and headstrong. They have no cavalry and no artillery, but are vastly aided by the

---

85 Malik Naib Kafur on his way to the Deccan, 1306, halted at this site and called it Sultanpur after Sultan Allaudin Khalji. Jaswant Rao Holkar in alliance with the Bhils, is said to have destroyed this town. It is now in W. Khandesh District and is situated in 21° 38' N. and 74° 35' E.

86 Sindwa.

87 The Bhils.

nature of their country, which is remarkable for its deep jungles and precipitous crags. They fortify these natural strongholds with intrenchments and stockades. They assail the enemy from ambuscades, which they lay in thickets and thorny places. Their attack may be open or concealed ; but they hesitate to come to close quarters. The extreme narrowness of the tracks, and the steep cliffs on either side, enable a very few of them easily to hold the enemy at bay. If in spite of this a determined attack is made upon them which they cannot withstand, they successfully conceal themselves in the dense and craggy jungle.

The principal town of this tract of country, in which the emperor of these mountaineers himself resides, is called Avazus, just as the mountains are. The circuit of its walls is indeed great, but its huts are very mean and wretched.

At last, having crossed the mountains and penetrated the defiles along a rough and dangerous track, we reached Surana. While we were there, at 11 P.M. on January 31st, there was an an eclipse of the moon. In the following year we learnt that at that very time the pious and devout King Henry of Portugal, the royal pontiff, had passed away. This exalted and mighty monarch died on his own birthday. Many people also regard it as a portent that, on the day when he was born, the district of Ulyssipon was whitened with snow; for it is very unusual for it to snow in that province, on account of the mildness of the climate. At any rate on the day of his death the moon suffered eclipse. In regard to the life and character of King Henry, he was a signally pious and devout man. This eclipse may also be reckoned to have foreshadowed the trials and griefs[38] which came upon Portugal after the death of King Henry.

---

[38] Father Monserrate alludes to the evils following the union of Portugal with Spain in 1580. Portugal remained so incorporated till the diplomacy of Richelieu secured its emancipation in 1640.

Not very far from Surana the river Nerbada is crossed, which after passing Amadabaea[39] flows into the sea at Barocium.[40] In the stormy season the very wide and deep bed of this river is filled with rapidly-flowing muddy water, so that it can only be crossed by means of a bridge or a boat. But in the summer, when the water of the rains has subsided, it can be crossed on foot. It is full of fish, and its water is so clear that the fish (?) and turtles, and even the smallest pebbles, can be counted. Its banks are covered with thick reed-beds, and with the health-giving herb marjoram.

Mandu.

Two days after crossing the Nerbada we reached the great city of Mandho,[41] the former importance of which, in the days of its prosperity, is indicated by the huge circuit of its walls, the vastness of the buildings which remain standing, and the ruins of those which have fallen. The walls are still perfect in those places which are not defended by precipitous crags; their total circuit is nearly 24 miles. The city stands on the level top of a hill, and is everywhere defended by

---

39 Ahmedabad. This chief city of Gujrat was founded by Ahmed I (1411-53.)

40 Broach. To a Hindu the city is of special interest as containing the site of Bali's sacrifice and the temple of Bhrigu. In the 16th century it was a flourishing seaport and as such attracted the Portuguese plunderers who 'admired its magnificence and its weavers who produced the finest cloth in the world.' The original name was Bhrigu-Kaccha or shore of Bhrigu; its Greek name was Barugaza.

41 Father Monserrate gives such a detailed description of Mandu that all of his references cannot possibly be accurately explained. The old capital of Malwa was Ujjain, but the seat was transferred to Mandu by Hushang (1406-34) who may be said to be founder of Musulman Mandu. The great palace mentioned in the text probably refers to the Hindol Palace; the half finished royal tomb to that of Sultan Hushang (though it is said that it was completed by Mahomed Khilji about 1440); the temple built like a Christian church to the Tower of Victory built by Mahmud Khilji in 1443 to commemorate his victory over Rana Kumbha of Chitor (Elphinstone, pp. 768-9; Malcolm's *Central India*, pp. 29, 40; *J. B. B. R. A. S.* Vol. XXI, 355-91; *B. G.* Vol. I. Part I. 352-84)

deep gorges and inaccessible cliffs. It has only one very narrow entrance. It can never lack water, as there are many tanks and springs in it, as well as never-failing wells of abundant and sweet water. In that quarter where the single entrance to the town is situated there are five walls placed one above the other at the head of a steep approach, so that the city is impregnable and can only be subdued by lack of food. No one can tell with any degree of certainty by whom and at what time this great city was founded; for the Musalmans, whose nature is indeed that of barbarians, take no interest in such things: their chronicles being scanty and unreliable, and full of old wives' tales. However, judging from the structure of the walls, one may venture a confident conjecture that the town is fairly modern and was built by Musalmans. I was told that its builders were Mongols, of a different tribe from that which has become so celebrated in our own time. For it is said that two hundred years ago the Mongols, being in search of a fresh country to occupy, left their ancestral encampments, invaded India, and settled at Mandho, both because it is by nature very easily defended and also because it is the most fertile part of the district, and indeed of the whole province of Malwa. These Mongols, however, were afterwards crushed by the Pathans in a number of battles, were driven into the single stronghold of Mandho, were besieged there for seven years, and finally, having been compelled to submit, were destroyed. For the Pathan King, who was in command of the besieging army, after many vain attempts to storm the city, fully perceived that it could only be subdued by compelling it to surrender through hunger. He therefore summoned masons, smiths, contractors and workmen, and ordered them to build walls, defences and houses for the soldiers to live in—indeed a whole city—in the very place, close to the gate in the walls, where his camp was at that time pitched. He gave strict injunctions also that all provisions intended for the city should be intercepted by his cavalry, who occupied all roads to the town and especially one path which approached the city from behind and was so rough and precipitous that soldiers could scarcely climb it even on their hands and knees. Finally he captured the city and ordered it to be razed to the ground.

Inside the city is to be seen a fragment of a huge iron gun which for some superstitious reason or other the heathen revere and worship. It is smeared with oil and coloured red. There is also a great palace, the home of the ancient kings, in which the governor of the province now lives. There is an excellently fortified citadel, and a half-finished royal tomb, which I suppose will never be completed; but it is worth seeing for its architecture and huge size. It stands in the middle of a square platform, which is raised five cubits above the ground, is eighty feet wide at the top, and is everywhere surrounded below by arches and colonnades. The tomb itself, which is crowned by a dome, measures twenty feet across, forty feet from the floor-level to the base of the dome, and forty feet from that point to the top of the dome. At the four corners of the platform rise minarets, seven storeys high and octagonal in shape. Each storey of these minarets is five cubits high. They have windows directed towards the four winds, out of which the Musalman call to prayer is pronounced. Opposite this tomb is another great building of similar magnificence and costliness. In the tomb are buried three Mongol kings, and also the tutor of one of these kings. Each sepulchre is embellished with mosaics, bass-reliefs and inlaid work. In front of these sepulchres are preserved the gilded thrones of the three kings, these being regarded as the emblems of royal rank, just as we regard the crown and sceptre as such emblems.

There is also a temple built like a Christian Church. Beneath, one on each side of the building, are two shrines with arched roofs, in which altars might be placed. Above these are two rooms, also with arched roofs, opening into each other and thus forming a passage towards the sanctuary of the High Altar. Probably it will appear to many an incredible traveller's tale when I declare that outside the walls of the city is a graveyard six miles long. This may sound an exaggeration ; but no one who knows with what magnificence and costliness the Musalmans are wont to build tombs will wonder at it. For, believing as they do that those whose life here is ended can only be admitted amongst the saints of Heaven through the name of Muhammad, they therefore honour their dead with elaborately built tombs, which, as they esteem, are worthy of those who are now holy saints in Heaven. Indeed in this respect—namely their belief that fitting honours should be paid to heavenly saints and seemly tombs made for the dead—these Musalmans are wiser and better than certain abandoned creatures of our own age.

Ujjain.

The above is a description of Mandho. The party arrived at Usena,[42] near the river Machipara,[43] on the second day after leaving this vast city. The founder of Usena is said to have been Birbitcremas,[44] who is venerated as a God, and as the inventor of all the mechanic arts, by the people of the whole of Gedrosia[45] and the neighbouring provinces. This superstition may probably be accounted for by Birbitcremas' interest and skill in such arts. For he was a very

---

42 Ujjain was not founded by Birbitcremas (Chandragupta II Vikramaditya cir. 375-413 A.D.) It was the capital of the foreign Sakas from whom the Gupta King wrested Malwa about 395 A.D.; it was "one of the most ancient cities of India, the principal depot for the commerce between the ports of the west and the interior (of Northern India), famous as a seat of learning and civilisation, and also notable as the Indian Greenwich from which longitudes were reckoned." The conquest of Ujjain by Chandragupta II Vikramaditya and the Brahminical reaction under him led to the traditional association of the city with the name of the Gupta King.

43 Machiwara.

44 See note 42.

45 Gujrat.

powerful and wealthy king, and the designer of many great works, which he left as a memorial of his glory, and which are still to be seen in the shape of numerous ancient temples. If one comes across an ancient temple of this type anywhere in this part of India and asks who was its builder, the reply is sure to be 'Birbitcremas.' And if a builder or carpenter is asked whom he honours and worships as his god, he will surely answer 'Birbitcremas.' The said Birbitcremas' style of architecture possesses a distinctive character of its own, and is not unpleasing to the eye, though it is infinitely inferior to the glories of the Roman workmanship.

While the party was at Usena, the Hindus carried to the pyre an old man who had died and whom they regarded as a god. The bier was gaily painted and gilded. The funeral procession took place at night, and was conducted with such exact observance that even tiny pieces of chaff and straw were removed from the path by which the bier was to be carried. Incense and sweet-smelling spices were placed in censers around the bier and there burnt. How extraordinary it is that the heathen should pay these honours to men whom they mistakenly regard as saintly, while wicked renegades from the Christian Faith refuse such honours to true saintliness!

Sarangpurum[46] was reached in two days from Usena. On the way a river was crossed flowing westward. This town is the seat and residence of the King's viceroy in that province. After three days' rest at Sarangpurum the river Paharbatium[47] was crossed and three days later the party passed through Pimpaldarus,[48] which is situated on the tropic of Cancer.

---

46 Sarangpur is situated on the east bank of the Kali Sindh river in 23° 34' N. and 76° 30' E. Numismatic evidence points to the great antiquity of the place. But its present name was derived from Sarang Singh Khichi under whom in the closing years of the 13th century it rose to importance. The place is associated with the romance of Rupmati, 'the Cleopatra of Malwa' and there is a small tomb known as *Rupmati ka Gambaz*.

47 River Parbati.

48 Pipaldhar.

Sironj.

Next Siuranges[49] was reached. This town suffers from a most unhealthy climate, as a consequence of which the cracks and dark corners of the houses are infested with all manner of poisonous vermin, which are found here in great quantities. At night also the beds are beset by scorpions, whose sting brings on horrible agony. In the neighbouring marshes certain lizards are found (although indeed they are just as much at home in dry places as in marshes), whose bite is fatal. In bushes and thickets the many-coloured Regulus is found, which kills by the glance of its eye. The middle part of its body is red towards the head—a more brilliant red even than scarlet,—but elsewhere it is orange-coloured, varying towards dark-brown. It attracts the eyes of all who see it by reason of the beauty of its colouring. However, the mercy of God has decreed that its nature shall be such that, if a man see it first, the Regulus—like the wolf, if one may believe the common tale—is compelled to retreat precipitately to some hiding-place, where it conceals itself. But if some unfortunate man, who in ignorance of his danger is doing something else, is seen by the Regulus (which like other creatures of this class is very proud of its own beauty) some little time before he sees it, then he is bound to perish miserably, at least so the inhabitants of that region stoutly declare. One of the Fathers unwittingly ran a risk of perishing in this way; for seeing the little creature, and being attracted by its beauty, he tried to catch it and followed it till the Regulus hid itself in a thicket. When he returned to his quarters and asked the inhabitants of that place what sort of lizard it was that he had seen, they were no less surprised at his having escaped the glance of the Regulus than were the inhabitants of Malta at Saint Paul's remaining unharmed by the bite of the snake. This creature is roughly the size of a dormouse, and resembles the

49 Sironj.

lizard called 'chamaeleon' which feeds on air and disguises itself with the colour of whatever object is nearest.

Many of the inferior classes in this town live in small round huts. Indeed nowhere else in that region are such miserable hovels to be seen. They live by agriculture, though the land which can be worked is scanty and poor. Their fields are everywhere surrounded by rocky hills, from which I suppose come the swarms of noxious beasts, and especially of scorpions.

Narwar.

Three days of difficult and even dangerous travelling brought the party from Siuranges to Naroaris;[50] for after the town of Cyperinum[51] is passed the country is uninhabited and mountainous, and many narrow defiles and streams are met with. This district is called after the neighbouring town; its savage inhabitants, knowing that they can commit robberies with impunity, are wont to attack travellers from ambush and to carry off their goods as plunder.

The town of Naroaris is situated at the foot of a hill, the levelled top[52] of which is occupied by a fort. Fierce storms and violent whirlwinds are so frequent there that not a house in the town would be able to retain its roof, had not God himself solved this difficult problem by supplying a natural abundance of marble slabs, which are used for roofing. Whilst the party was at this place, about the 15th day of the month of

---

50 Narwar is probably derived from the classical name, Nalapura, the home of Naila or Naisadha. Major-General Cunningham identifies the place with the great ancient city of Padmavati, the scene of Bhababhuti's drama Malati-Madhava (*A. R.*1862-5, Vol. II pp. 307-28). During the Mahomedan period it was a well-known place, standing next in importance to Gwalior in Northern Malwa.

51 Sipri, situated in 25° 26' N and 77° 39' E.

52 William Finch who visited Narwar in 1610 records that the fortified summit was 5 or 6 kos in circuit.

February the Musalman nine-days' festival[53] began. At the same time the Hindus held their Idaean[54] festival. The former is held in honour of Asson and Hossen, grandsons of Muhammad by his daughter Fatima. Their father was Halis. They are said to have been conquered by the Christians in a war which they had undertaken in order to establish and spread their grandfather's religious system. They were thereupon cruelly tortured by the unbelievers (as the Musalmans call us) and were compelled to walk with bare feet over hot coals. For this reason the Musalmans fast for nine days, only eating pulse; and on certain of these days some of them publicly recite the story of the sufferings of Asson and Hossen from a raised platform, and their words stir the whole assembly to lamentation and tears. On the last day of the festival funeral pyres are erected and burnt one after the other. The people jump over these, and afterwards scatter the glowing ashes with their feet. Meanwhile they shriek 'Asson Hossen' with wild and savage cries.

Nor is the Idaean festival of the Hindus less savage and degraded. For during a space of fifteen days they are at liberty freely to cast dust upon themselves and upon whoever passes by. They plaster with mud their own bodies and those of any persons they may meet. They also squirt a red dye out of hollow reeds. Having thus degraded themselves they come at length, on the fifteenth day, to the most abominable part of the whole festival. On this day they dedicate a tree, of a species somewhat similar to the palm, to that Mother of the Gods, who is called by many names, (the ancient Romans knew her as Cybele and the Great Mother and

---

53 Muharram. It begins on the first day of the month of that name and is continued for ten days and is held by the Shias in commemoration of the martyrdom of Ali who was assassinated in the mosque of Cufa (660 A.D.), Hussain who was slain at Karbela in 680 A.D. and Hassan who was poisoned by his wife. The tenth day is held sacred by the Sunnis also.

54 Holi Festival.

'Idaea'). Such superstition is indeed senseless and absurd. When the tree has been dedicated, they make offerings to it as though it were a god. At last, having vowed that they will dedicate another tree the following year, they build up huge piles of logs, as high as towers, in front of the houses, in places where three ways meet. When night comes they pace round these piles singing: and finally burn to ashes the consecrated (or rather most execrable) tree.

Gwalior.

The party came to Goaleris[55] in two days after leaving Naroaris. This city is embellished by a very strong fortress on the top of a rocky hill, on which there is also a royal palace; the city itself stands at the foot of this hill. There is only one path up to the fortress, and that a rough and difficult one. In front of the gates is seen an immense statue of an elephant.[56] In steep parts of the crag are underground temples and houses. The Fathers were astonished to see, carved in the wall of the vestibule of one temple,

---

55 The hill on which the fortress of Gwalior is situated was originally called Gopachal or Gopagiri. It was named Gwalior after a hermit Gwalipa who lived there. Cunningham thus relates the story: "Gwalior was founded by a Kachhwaha chief named Suraj Sen, the petty Raja of Kuntalpuri or Kutwar. Suraj Sen was a leper and one day while thirsty with hunting near the hill of Gopagiri, he came to the cave of Gwalipa and asked for water. The hermit gave him water in his own vessel and no sooner had he drunk it than he was cured of leprosy. The grateful Raja then asked what to do for the holy man and he was directed to build a fort on the hill"; and the fort was called Gwali-awar or Gwalior as it is written. The fort, however, in Mahomedan Indian history had the evil reputation of being the state prison for the confinement of near kinsmen of the reigning kings; and the prison of a prince was often very near his grave.

56 The statue of an elephant was just outside the gate called the Hathiya Paur or Elephant Gate. It was built by the Tomara chief, Raja Man Sing, who reigned from 1486 to 1516; on its back were also two figures (which, it so appears, did not exist at the time when Father Monserrate wrote) viz., the Raja and the driver. Babar mentions the statue in his *Memoirs* and Abul Fazl in *Ain* (Jarret II p. 181).

thirteen rude statues,[57] of half length only; the middle one of these is (judging by the style and position) that of Christ: six are to the right and six to the left of this, and appear to represent the Apostles. But it cannot definitely be proved whom the statues are intended to represent, since they lack the characteristic insignia of Christian sacred images. It is clear, however, that they were not placed there by Musalmans, as these show no reverence for such images, but ill-treat and break them. I am well aware of the fact that three hundred years ago this district was inhabited by Christians, who were, alas, defeated in various battles by the Musalmans, and so effectively crushed that all memory of Christianity has perished from the minds of men. The Musalmans might readily learn to expiate this sin (if only they were wise enough) from observing the fact that they are everywhere made fools of by the wiles, deceptions and lying tricks of worthless rascals. For a few years ago there lived in this very city a certain villain named Baba Capurius,[58] a follower of Muhammad, who

---

57 These statues were Jain sculptures executed between 1440 A.D. and 1473 A.D. during the reign of the Tomar chief Danger Singh. Cunningham thus writes on this point "Father Monserrate was assured by respectable persons that there were thirteen figures in basso-relievo, scultpured on the Gwalior rock. The middle figure being higher than the rest, the group represented Our Saviour and his twelve disciples. When a grave and educated missionary can write thus of the stark naked statues of Gwalior, we need no longer wonder at the marvellous travellers' tales that were brought to Europe by illiterate adventurers." Had Major General Cunningham read the original—for the archæologist derived his information from Wilford's *Asiatic Researches*—he would have found the good Father's account of India bristling with such tales; his sound historic sense would have been shocked to read of the Christian Kings at Delhi before the advent of the Moghuls.

58 Baba Kapur. Shaikh Kipur Majzab of Gwalior, a Hussaini Sayyid, was at first a soldier, but his later life he devoted to the philanthropic mission of supplying water to widows and the poor. He was a native of Kalpi and his real name was Abdul Gafur. Abul Fazl in his classification of the learned men of the time, puts him under the second category as being one of those who pay less attention to the external world, but in the light of their hearts acquire vast knowledge. He died in 1571 A.D.

revived the fast disappearing habit of drinking intoxicating liquors, and discovered a certain new drink, made of poppy pods steeped in water. The damnable fellow believed that perfect happiness consists in the absence of all feeling and in insensibility towards the ills of the flesh and the troubles of the mind: though in reality one is more liable to be tortured by the incitements of the senses when in a state of semi-insensibility. He had noticed that his object could be effected by means of opium, but that those who are addicted to this drug run an imminent risk of early death. So he devised his poppy-pod drink which is made in the following manner. The juice is first drained from the pods, which are split up for the purpose; these are then allowed to mature; then the seeds are removed, and the pods thrown into water, in which they are kept immersed until the liquid assumes the colour of wine. It is allowed to stand for a little longer, and is then passed off into another vessel through a strainer made of the finest linen. After impurities have been removed, the makers of this drink themselves eagerly quaff it off in cupfuls. They eat no meat, onions, garlic or anything of that kind. They even abstain from fruit, and are particularly careful never to take any oil, which is fatal after opium or this drink. They eat only cooked pulse and any sweet food. Then they put their heads between their knees, and sleep as heavily as did Endymion.

One would have thought that Baba Capurius would have been heartily blamed for snoring his days away in this fashion, and for such disgraceful idleness. However he firmly belived that he would be honoured for his wonderful chastity, and held up to admiration rather than to blame. Nor was this hope ill-founded, as it proved, benighted though his mind truly was. For the nature of this drink is such that it numbs and freezes the impure desires of the flesh. Whence it has come about that this man has been so honoured for his sanctity as to be given a grand tomb and even a temple in this city. At least thirty of his followers are always on watch at this tomb, or rather are constantly asleep there, with no care for the morrow. This new leader of the Epicureans has countless admirers and followers, amongst whom are many princes and even the great king Zelaldinus himself. All these consider themselves to be honoured by the name Postinus, which is given to them from the drink, which is commonly known as post.[59]

After leaving Goaleris the river Sambalus[60] was reached, which passes near Daulpurum[61]. This is the boundary between the province of Malwa and that of Delinum, or rather of Indicum. The passage of the river has been excellently fortified both by nature and also by the careful labour of men. For in times gone by, before Malwa and Delinum were combined under one emperor, this river was the stoutest bulwark of Delinum, just as Goaleris was of Malwa. The nature of the place is such that cavalry can here achieve nothing worthy of warlike praise. For though the ground apears to those who look at it from a distance to be far-reaching, level and open, it is in reality so cut up and rugged, with such sudden defiles and deep gullies, that if anyone wanders from the path, he runs a grave risk either of only being able to return to it by a wide detour along rough and exceedingly narrow tracks, or of falling into the hands of the enemy or of brigands.

Daulpurum will be the 'White City' in Latin. The Sambalus is a large river and flows westwards towards the coast of Gedrosia It is equidistant (*i.e.* a two days' journey) from Agara, which is the capital of the empire, and from Fattepurum where the great King

---

59 *Post* means poppy-seed.

60 The river Chambal.

61 Dholpur. Its strategic importance has been sufficiently clearly pointed out by Father Monserrate. The reader might recall to mind the war between Dara and Aurangzeb, and the march of the latter from Dharmat to Samugarh (1657). See Sarkar's *Aurangzeb* Vol. II.

resides. The Fathers were conducted by the ambassador to the latter city.

In commenting on the journey that was thus brought to a conclusion, one may notice in the first place that the country from the coast northward rises, as it were, in a series of terraces, such as are seen in gardens placed on a slope. The mountain-ranges represent the walls of these terraces. Secondly it should be observed that the religious zeal of the Musalmans has destroyed all the idol temples[62], which used to be very numerous. But the carelessness of these same Musalmans has on the other hand allowed sacrifices to be publicly performed, incense to be offered, oil and perfumes to be poured out, the ground to be sprinkled with flowers, and wreaths to be hung up, wherever—either amongst the ruins of these old temples or elsewhere—any fragment of an idol is to be found. Thirdly, in place of the Hindu temples, countless tombs and little shrines of wicked and worthless Musalmans have been erected, in which these men are worshipped with vain superstition, as though they were saints. This moved the Fathers to deep pity, not unaccompanied by tears and heart-felt grief. For who would not deeply pity these who—to the destruction of their souls—give reverence to vices instead of virtues, to crimes instead of miracles, to abandoned wretches instead of holy saints ?

Fatehpur.

When the Fathers perceived from afar the city of Fattepurum, they gave hearty thanks to the Eternal God who had brought them safe to their destination. They then began to gaze with the keenest delight upon the great size and magnificent appearance of the city. On entering the city they became the cynosure of all eyes on account of their strange attire. Everyone stopped and stared

---

62 The persons whose names stand out conspicuous in this business of destruction were Allauddin Khalji (and also Malik Naib Kaper who had all the fiery zeal of a neophyte), Sikandar Lodi and Babur.

in great surprise and perplexity, wondering who these strange-looking, unarmed men might be, with their long black robes, their curious caps, their shaven faces, and their tonsured heads.

First Interview with Akbar.

At length they were taken before the King, who having looked at them from his high dais, ordered them to come nearer to him, and asked them a few questions. Thereupon they presented to him an Atlas, which the Archbishop of Goa had sent as a present. This he graciously received. He was greatly pleased to see them, but was not too warm in his greeting, and shortly afterwards withdrew, partly in order to hide his true feelings and partly to preserve his dignity. Having retired for a short time into an inner apartment, he ordered them to be conducted to him there, (*i.e.* to the hall which is known as Capur Talau), in order that he might exhibit them to his wives. Then he took them to another courtyard called the Daulatqhana, where he seized the opportunity presented by a sudden rain-storm and put on Portuguese dress[63]—a scarlet cloak with golden fastenings. He ordered his sons also to don the same dress, together with Portuguese hats. This he did in order to please his guests. He also ordered 800 pieces of gold to be presented to them; but the Fathers replied that they had not come there to get money. Nothing that he could say would persuade them to accept the present, whereupon he expressed admiration at their self-control, and ordering the money to be distributed to certain attendants of Tavarius, who had remained behind, he retired to the inner part of the palace.

The Fathers were delighted at the King's kindly reception and were conducted rejoicing to their quarters. For they were persuaded that these signs foretold the speedy conversion of the king to the true religion and the worship of Christ.

---

63 Akbar used to don Portuguese dress on suitable occasions. He put it on for the first time probably in the course of his negotiations with the Portuguese through Antonia Cabral in 1573.

Meeting With Father F. J. Pereira.

On the next day we were most kindly entertained by the priest* who had been summoned by the king from Gangaris (as has been mentioned above), and who was then in residence at Fattepurum. As it was Lent, the diet was simple, fish only. After dinner we enquired from our host what was the state of the King's mind regarding Christianity. He replied that Zelaldinus reverenced Christ and the Virgin, and was not far from paying divine honours to Christ. Moreover he not only approved, but warmly praised those portions of the Gospel story which he (Pereira)* had recounted to him. He was astonished that Christians paid so much attention to chastity of life as to forbid a man to have more than one wife and to enjoin complete celibacy on their priesthood. But, as the King himself said, his judgment was dulled and clouded, as it were, when he heard that there are three persons in one God, that God had begotten a son from a virgin, had suffered on the Cross, and had been killed by the Jews. He might, however, be led to acknowledge the truth of these doctrines if they could persuade him that the Gospel had indeed come from God. He listened gladly to the story of Christ's miracles, and believed in them. His sentiments with regard to Muhammad were very different; for he believed him to have been a rascally impostor, who had deluded and infatuated men by his lies. In his dining-hall he had pictures of Christ, Mary, Moses and Muhammad; when naming them he showed his true sentiments by putting Muhammad last; for he would say 'This is the picture of Christ, this of Mary, this of Moses and that of Muhammad.' In brief, this priest's description of the king's state of mind enlightened the other Fathers as to the necessity for a more thorough investigation regarding the course they must adopt.

Before the coming of the Fathers, Aegidius—for

---

* L. E. Pereira, see *Note* 1.

that was the name of this priest—had made zealous attempts to instruct the King, and in this he had been greatly assisted by the King's own decided leanings towards Christianity. However, he had been prevented from making much progress by the ignorance of his interpreter, and had hence been induced several times to make a resolute offer to undergo the ordeal of fire, in order that he might thus establish the truth of his faith and avoid the difficulties of theological debate.

Description of Fatehpur.

Fattepurum[64] (that is the city of victory) had been recently built by the King on his return to his seat of government after the successful termination of his Gedrosian war. It is placed on a spur of the mountain range which in former times was called, I believe, Vindius, and which stretches westwards for a hundred miles towards Azmiris.[65] The site is rocky and not very beautiful, near to an old town which for this reason is called Purana Siquiris,[66] (for Purana means 'old' in the vernacular, and Siquiris is the name of the place). In the past nine years the city has been marvellously extended and beautified, at the expense both of the royal treasury and of the great nobles and courtiers, who eagerly follow the King's example and wishes.

The most noteworthy features of Fattepurum are, firstly, the King's audience chamber, which is of huge size and very beautiful in appearance, overlooking the whole city: secondly, a great building supported on arches, around which is a very spacious courtyard: thirdly, the Circus where elephants fight, gladiatorial displays take place, and a game is played, on horseback, with a wooden ball which is hit by hammers also of

---

64 For a short history of the growth of Sikri and the causes of the transfer of the capital, see *Note* on Agra. The place came to be called Fatehpur Sikri when Akbar halted here on his return from the Gujrat campaign, 1573. (*Von Neor* Vol. I. pp. 306; Jarret II. 180).

65 Ajmir. (See *Note* 220).

66 Sikri.

wood: fourthly, the baths: fifthly, the bazaar, which is more than half a mile long, and is filled with an astonishing quantity of every description of merchandise, and with countless people, who are always standing there in dense crowds.

To supply the city with water a tank has been carefully and laboriously constructed, two miles long and half a mile wide. The work was performed, by the King's directions, in the following manner. Across the end of a low-lying valley which was filled with water in the rains, (although the water afterwards drained away or dried up), a great dam was slowly built. By this means not only was a copious supply of water assured, but the discomfort of the climate was mitigated. For when the sun gets low in the sky, the heat, which in Fattepurum is very great, is tempered by a cool and pleasant breeze blowing over the tank. Besides this the King descends to the lake on holidays, and refreshes himself with its many beauties.

Passing over the other remarkable features of Fattepurum, I must mention that the citadel is two miles in circumference and embellished with towers at very frequent intervals, though it has only four gates. The Agarena gate is to the east, the Azimirina to the west, that of the Circus to the north, and that of Daulpurum to the south. The most striking of these is the Circus gate, through which the King frequently descends to the Circus. For there stand in front of this gateway, which they seem to guard, two statues of elephants, with uplifted trunks, and of life-size. These statues are so majestic and so true to life, that one might judge them to be the work of Phidias. Close to the Circus rises a pyramid from which are measured the distances for the mile-stones (or rather half-mile-stones, for such they are), which have been placed after the Roman manner along the roads eastwards to Agara and westwards to Azimiris.

While Zelaldinus was residing at Agara, he decided to remove his court to Siquirinum in accordance with the advice of a certain philosopher[67] (member of a class professing both wisdom and piety) who was then living in a small hut on this hill.

Agra. Agara[68] is a magnificent city, both for its size and for its antiquity. It stands on the river Jomanes. In it Zelaldinus the Great was

---

67 Shaikh Selim Chisti. He was the most celebrated of the Sikri Shaikhs and Akbar had a great respect for him. The Shaikh settled at Sikri as a hermit in 1537-8 (944 A. H.), and in the following year constructed a monastery and school-house to which soon after a small mosque was attached. Nizamuddin may be quoted: "Shaikh Selim Chisti, who resided at the town of Sikri, twelve cos from Agra (23 miles to the west of Agra), had gladdened Akbar with the promise of a son. The Emperor went to visit the the Shaikh several times and remained there 10 or 20 days on each occasion. When one of the Emperor's wives became pregnant, he conveyed her to the dwelling of the Shaikh and left her there." This was Marium-uz-Zamani (daughter of Behari Mull of Amber) mother of Selim who was born at the Shaikh's house on the 30th August 1569. The Shaikh had a great reputation as a saint, and Blochmann has the following notes (p. 267): "Tying knots or bits of string or ribbon to the tombs of saints is considered by barren women a means of obtaining a son, and the tomb of Selim Chisti in Fathepur Sikri, in whose house Jahangir was born, is now-a-days visited by Hindu and Mahomedan women who tie bits of string to the marble trellice surrounding the tomb." In Abul Fazl's classification of the learned men of the time, the Shaikh is put in the second class. Father Monserrate however stigmatises him as vicious and wicked. He died in 1571 A.D.

68 Originally Agra was a village dependant on Bianah. It was during the reign of Sikander Lodi (1488-1518) that Agra first emerged into prominence and was fixed upon as the place for Royal residence. But it suffered badly from the effects of an earthquake (July 1505.) The account of the naming and foundation of the city as given by Niamutullah is very interesting: "In the same year (1504 A.D.) the heat of the air became so intense that almost all the people fell grievously sick of fever. It had for a long time occurred to the Sultan to found a town on the banks of the Jumna which was to be the residence of the Sultan, and the head quarters of the army, and to serve to keep the rebels of that quarter in awe and deprive them of further opportunity of growing refractory, for frequently the Jagirdars, government servants and the peasantry in general in Sarkar Bianah had complained of the violence to which they were subject. With this view he commissioned in 1505 A.D.

some judicious and intelligent persons to explore the banks of the river and to report upon any locality they might consider to be the most eligible. They arrived at and selected the spot where Agra now stands and communicated their selection to the Sultan. Whereupon he left Delhi and as he approached the site indicated, he observed two elevated spots which seemed suitable for building and enquired of Mihter Mulla Khan, who was called Naik and commanded the royal barge, which of these mounds appeared to him the most suitable. He replied "That which is *Agré* or in advance is the preferable one." The Sultan smiled and said "The name of this city then shall be Agra." Agra thus established, gradually grew in size and beauty. But "the old Agra of the Lodhi dynasty lay on the left bank of the river Jumna where traces of its foundation still exist. The modern city is on the right bank and is the work of Akbar. The fort was built in 1566 A.D." (*Ain.*: Jarret II. p. 180 n. 3). Father Monserrate is substantially right in ascribing the removal of the seat of royal residence to Sikri by Akbar to the death of his sons; but for the first time we read that the death of the sons was due to the cruel spite of the evil spirits that haunted the buildings at Agra (not the fort, for he had left the place before the red sandstone fort was completed). So the reason lay in the point of contrast between Agra and Sikri, the one had killed his sons and the other blessed him with sons. Sikri was a lucky place for the Emperor in as much as—to quote Abul Fazl—"his exalted sons (Selim and Murad) had taken their birth in Sikri and the God-knowing spirit of Shaikh Selim had taken possession thereof and hence his (Akbar's) holy heart desired to give outward splendour to this spot which possessed spiritual grandeur." How the 'fairy city,' which has been truly called the offspring of faith, grew up may be gathered from some passages of the *Tabkat-i-Akbari*. "The Emperor having visited Shaikh Selim Chisti several times, commenced a fine building there on the top of a hill, near the Shaikh's monastery. The Shaikh also commenced a new monastery and a fine mosque which at the present day has no equal in the world, near the royal mansion. The Amirs also built houses and mansions for themselves. Then was born Selim, and the Emperor made Sikri a royal abode, raised a stone fortification round it, and built some splendid edifices, so that it became a great city."

born and brought up, and first proclaimed king[69] upon the terrible death of his father. For while his father, whose name was Emaumus[70] was walking upon the roof of his hall[71] at Delinum leaning upon a stick, he came too near the edge; his stick slipped, and he was precipitated into the garden below. This sudden and terrible fall proved fatal. He was devoted to literary studies, and was a great patron of the learned, but was not keen and active in war. Zelaldinus on the contrary, who is uneducated, has become famous for his war-like skill and courage. Hence Zelaldinus on being acclaimed King changed the seat of government from Delinum, where it had been established since the time of the Christian kings,[72] to Agara, where he himself had been born; and built there a palace and citadel which are in themselves as big as a great city; for he included in the confines of the citadel the mansions of his nobles, the magazines, the treasury, the arsenal, the stable of the cavalry, and the shops and huts of drug-sellers, barbers, and all manner of common workmen. The stones of these buildings are so cunningly fitted that the joints are scarcely visible, although

---

69 This is a deviation from the acknowledged facts of history. Humayun was a fugitive under the shelter of Rana Pershad of Umarkot when Akbar was born (Thursday, 23rd November 1542). In November, 1555, Akbar was appointed governor of the Punjab and sent (along with his *Ataliq*, Bairam Khan) against Sekunder Sur who, after his defeat, had taken refuge in the Siwaliks Humayum died at Delhi on January 27th, 1556. Akbar was formally enthroned king in a garden at Kalanaur in the Gurdaspur district of the Punjab, on 14th February, 1556, though his succession had been proclaimed three days before at Delhi.

70 Humayun.

71 This was the Sher Mandal constructed by Sher Shah, which was the library of Humayun. " At sunset he had ascended to the roof of the library. The muazzin cried aloud the summons to prayer and the Emperor reverently sat down on the second step. When he was getting up again his foot slipped and he fell from the stairs to the ground." (*E.D. v.* 239-40.) As regards his love for literature and arts, see Von. Neor, Vol I. pp. 102-4.

72 One of the Father Monserrate's pet theories which have no relation to facts.

no lime was used to fix them together. The beautiful colour of the stone, which is all red, also produces the same effect of uniform solidity. In front of the gateway are statues of two petty kings,[73] whom Zelaldinus himself shot with his own musket; these are seated on life-size statues of elephants on which the kings used to ride when alive. These statues serve both as trophies of the King's prowess, and as monuments of his military victories.

If all had happened as he wished, Agara would indeed have formed a fitting memorial of the King's wisdom. For it has the advantage over almost all other cities of that region in respect of its mild climate, of its fertile soil, of its great river, of its beautiful gardens, of its fame spread to the end of earth, and of its large size. For it is four miles long and two broad. All the necessaries and conveniences of human life can be obtained here, if desired. This is even true of articles which have to be imported from distant corners

---

73 These were the statues of Jaimal and Potta who bravely though fruitlessly resisted Akbar's siege of Chitor. Both were killed before the fort could be taken. Jaimal previously had been in command of the fort of Mirtha which was taken by the Moghuls in the beginning of 1562. When Akbar besieged Chitor in October 1567, the cowardly Rana Uday Singh fled leaving the fort in command of Jaimal Rathor of Bednor. It was Akbar's shot from his favourite gun Sangram (Blochmann, p. 617) that killed the hero (Feb. 1568). Potta of Kailwa, who died in the gallant defence of the fort, was only a lad of 16. The conduct of Potta's mother and wife was no less heroic. After having urged on the son the need of sacrificing life for the national cause she, surpassing the Spartan mother of old, descended the rock accompanied by her daughter-in-law, fought, and illustrated her precept by example. Akbar had the statues constructed and placed in front of the gate-way not as a trophy but as a mark of respect to the memory of the martyrs whose conduct he approved and considered worthy of imitation. On the shifting of the capital from Agra to New Delhi by Shah Jehan, these statues were also removed and placed at the entrance of the fortress of the capital, as it appears from the account of Bernier (Smith's Edition, p. 256). Aurangzeb however in his coquetry with iconoclasm ordered the removal of these statues.

of Europe. There are great numbers of artizans, iron-workers and gold-smiths. Gems and pearls abound in large numbers. Gold and silver are plentiful, as also are horses from Persia and Tartary. Indeed the city is flooded with vast quantities of every type of commodity. Hence Agara is seldom visited by dearth of food supplies. In addition to this its central position (for it is, as it were, the navel of the whole kingdom) enabled the King, whenever he had the occasion, easily to go himself in any direction, or to summon his subjects to meet him. However, as so often happens in human affairs, the event proved different from what he had hoped. For, when the work of building was completed, and the King went to reside in his new fortress and palace, he found (for such was God's good pleasure) the place overrun with ghosts, which rushed to and fro, tore everything to pieces, terrified the women and children, threw stones, and finally began to hurt everyone there. Perhaps these drawbacks might have been put up with, if the thing had stopped there. But the cruel spite of the Evil One began to wreak itself on the children of the King, who were slain a day or two after birth. Two or three[74] were thus destroyed. Wherefore, greatly moved by this terrible loss, and fearing that he would be left without descendant, the king betook himself to the sage whom we have already mentioned as living in solitude on the hill of Siquiris, and told him all that he had suffered from the Evil One. The wise man bade him remove his dwelling immediately from Agara to Siquiris. The King obeyed at once, and ordered a country-house—small indeed but of royal magnificence—to be erected as swiftly as possible. This was shortly afterwards enlarged into a palace.

Gift of a Bible.

When the Fathers had refreshed themselves for a short time from the fatigue of their journey, they were again summoned before the King. Whereupon they set their hands

[74] The reference is to the twin sons Hassan and Hussain who were born, according to Smith, on 9-10-1564. They lived only a month.

to the work on behalf of which they had undertaken so long and tedious a journey. For this purpose they made the following opening. On the 3rd of March they took to the audience chamber a copy of the Holy Bible, written in four languages and bound in seven volumes; this they showed to the King. In the presence of his great nobles and religious leaders Zelaldinus thereupon most devoutly not only kissed the Bible, but placed it on his head. He then asked in which volume the Gospel was to be found. When he was shown the right volume, he showed yet more marked reverence to it. Then he told the priests to come with their Bible into his own private room, where he opened the volumes once more with great reverence and joy. He shut them up again very carefully, and deposited them in a beautiful bookcase, worthy of such sacred volumes, which stood in the same private room, where he spent a great deal of his spare time.

Religious Discussion.

As a result of this an opportunity was given for a discussion, which was held at night, and in which the priests met the religious teachers and doctors and debated keenly with them the question of the accuracy and authority of the Holy Scriptures, on which the Christian religion is founded and that of the vanity and lies of the book in which the Musalmans put their faith treating it as though it had been given by God—although (to disregard other points) Muhammad stuffed it with countless fables full of futility and extreme frivolity. It was pointed out that the most ancient books of Moses and the Prophets bear testimony to the Gospel; and that Alcoranus itself, although it contends with the Gospel, and contains teachings so different from and indeed contrary to those of the Gospel, cannot avoid testifying, not only to the truth, but also to the sanctity of the Gospel. For Alcoranus says in more than one place that the Most High God gave the Gospel to Christ, although the author of Alcoranus most foolishly affirms that God gave the Gospel in a complete and finished state to Christ, just as He gave the Torah (that is the law) to Moses, the Zabur (that is the Psalms) to David, and to himself Alfurcanus—for I shall be excused if I mix up so many barbarian names. But indeed no one gave testimony to the truth of Alfurcanus; and so by the grace of God it came about that the opponents of the Fathers were reduced—their arguments against the Gospel having been refuted—to an inability to prove the very points by which they were attempting to defend their own book from attack. Thus, being thrown into confusion by observing the look on the King's face, they retired from the debate, and finally became entirely silent.

After the debate was finished the King retired, taking the priests with him, and said to them, "You have proved your case entirely to my satisfaction, and I am well pleased with the religion contained in your law; but I should advise you to be cautious in speech and action, for your opponents are unscrupulous villains. Now I want more enlightenment on these points—how the Most High God can be both three and one, and how He can have a son, a man born of a virgin. For these ideas are entirely beyond my comprehension." The Fathers replied, "We will be cautious as regards the Musalman religious leaders, as you advise,—not because we are afraid of them for ourselves, but because we wish to obey you. With regard to the other point, about which you ask for information, pray for enlightenment on it from God, who hath abundance and giveth generously to all men; then humbly wait to hear His answer to your prayer."

The King was greatly impressed firstly with the fact that, although the Holy Bible is written in so many languages, yet no contradiction can be detected in it, but every language found in it expresses one and the same truth; and secondly with the fact that the Fathers were as well acquainted as their Musalman opponents with the Latin translation of Alfurcanus, which we owe to the great diligence and accuracy of Saint Bernard. The Musalman leaders were exceedingly mortified and chagrined by this fact. In addition to this the Fathers agreed together in their arguments but the Musalmans were by no means all of one mind in their defence of Alfurcanus. The King was greatly displeased by this.

This was what happened at the first discussion with the Musalman religious leaders. Three days later a second discussion was held, about heavenly bliss, which Muhammad most wickedly and lyingly asserted to consist in feasting and impure delights, and in other things absolutely the reverse of the teachings of the Holy Scriptures.

Some days later the haughty pride of Muhammad provided the matter for a third discussion. For in Alcoranus he writes that Christ was righteous and without fault, was born of a virgin who conceived him by the Holy Ghost, and had no earthly father. On the other hand Muhammad records that he himself had been a sinner and a worshipper of idols, and moreover that he had never performed miracles. Nevertheless he shamelessly and arrogantly claims to be greater and more powerful than Christ. The Fathers maintained, first, that a man, who in his own defence used his own testimony against himself, must of necessity be both shameless and ridiculous, (for proof of any matter must be sought elsewhere than from the one whose interests or claims are being defended): second, that mighty testimony is born to Christ, both by the Prophets, famous men who foretold his coming, and by the Gospel itself which narrates his virtues and his wonderful works, and was not, moreover, written by Christ himself, as Alfurcanus was patched together by Muhammad: thirdly, that Muhammad is the only witness to himself, the only writer about himself, the only authority for his own wonderful experiences—there is no one but himself. The Musalmans were beaten and discomforted; whereupon they appealed to an ordeal. 'Let us put it to the test,' said they, 'which Holy Book is true. Let a pyre be constructed and kindled. Then let one of you, carrying the Gospel, and one likewise of us, carrying the

Syndagma, ascend the burning pyre. The book which comes out safely together with its bearer, shall be judged true.' The King urged the same course upon the priests, who briefly replied that there was no need of miraculous ordeals in order to demonstrate the truth of Christianity. The King answered that he had had enough of argument, whereupon everyone cried 'Peace be to the King.' This was the end of this third discussion.

Proposal for an Ordeal.

Now Rudolf, whose leadership his companions gladly followed, was full of religious zeal and fervour, and eagerly sought any opportunity of facing death for Christ's sake; moreover, he always earnestly sought to obey the dictates of his religious duty; and hence, if he had been convinced of its necessity, would never have shrunk from the proposed ordeal. But he was in doubt as to its rightness at present, and hence had made no attempt to clinch the matter. However, in order to avoid the appearance of cowardice in refusing the ordeal, he took the first opportunity of making the following proposal to the King—a proposal in which his companions had already agreed. "Since, O King," he said, "you desire, with regard to the proposed ordeal, to put to the test the constancy of myself and my companions in the Faith and Religion of Jesus Christ, which we received from our ancesters and drank in with our mother's milk, in which we have been nurtured, and to which we are utterly devoted, we will, with a cheerful heart, and fortified by the help of God, most readily ascend not one but a thousand pyres. Nor do we hope or wish to be miraculously kept from harm, although we are servants of the same God who preserved the three Hebrew children harmless in the furnace, and brought them out of it again without any injury from the flame. Trusting in divine aid, we have no fear of elephants, lions, panthers, leopards, precipices, crosses, stripes, and all manner of tortures. You can prove by immediate experiment, O King, if you so please, whether or no this is true. Let no longer delay intervene than the few moments that are needed to summon hither our comrade who is sick; and him, we believe, the joy of such a prospect would immediately restore to health. But if you propose this ordeal of fire in order that you may behold a miracle—as though any one of us were held so dear by God that He would not suffer the fire to do him any harm—we freely confess that, though our trust in God is unbounded, we have frequently fallen into wrong-doing in other respects, and still continue so to fall; for we are sinners, and hence are kept back by grave religious scruples from daring to expect for ourselves miracles, especially since we are ignorant whether God holds us dear or regards us as stumbling-blocks in His way. Moreover to make trial by fire as to whether or no the Bible is from God, according as to whether or no it and its bearer are burnt, is at variance with the teaching and example of Christ, whom you, O King, honour and esteem. For you will not willingly allow yourself to become one of those miracle-hunters, of whom he said 'An evil and adulterous generation seeketh a sign' (by which name he rebuked the Jews). Again, when the Evil One made the suggestion to him, 'If thou art the son of God, cast thyself down,' he replied, 'Thou shalt not make trial of the Lord thy God.' When Herod demanded to be shown miracles, he replied to him no single word; and when he was nailed on the Cross and the Jews were asking for a miracle and saying, 'If thou art the son of God, come down from the Cross and we will believe in thee,' even then he paid no attention. As regards ourselves, all those who have suffered torments on behalf of the Faith (whom we call martyrs) have been better men than we are: and yet many of them have been burnt. As regards our Book, many Churches and houses containing copies of the Gospels have been burnt by the enemies of our religion: and also many Musalman Mosques containing their sacred volumes: and hence the proof by fire must needs be doubtful and uncertain. Now—not to neglect the proposal of the Musalmans,—if you definitely order us to undergo the ordeal, we demand that you should release them from their dangerous share in the compact, though indeed, we do not believe that a single one of them would be so faithful to his religion and his Prophet, or so utterly foolish, as to submit himself to such a risk. Indeed their nature is such that they demand miracles; but if a miracle were to be performed by some upright follower of our religion, they would say that it had been brought about by magic and sorcery. As such an one emerged from the fire, they would strike him down with spears or would stone him to death: and in the last resort they would endeavour to conceal the truth and sanctity of the divinely-wrought miracle. This indeed actually happened forty years ago in the case of Andreas Spoletanus,[75] a Franciscan. A similar ordeal had been proposed by the Musalmans at Marrhoqium[76] in Africa. They falsely declared that they would become Christians if he came out of the fire unharmed. They beheld Andreas walking about in the middle of the flame and lifting up his hands and eyes towards heaven; but when the Christian people who were held in captivity there and were present to see the ordeal began to clap their hands for joy, together with the rest of the common people who were astonished by the novelty of the affair, forthwith the leaders of the Musalmans and of the Jews, who were also spectators, buried both Andreas and his pyre beneath a hail of stones, lest it should be said that the flames had spared him. His relics—of which the flesh is still as healthy as that of a living man—were taken to Portugal to Queen Catherina of Austria by a certain captive who was exchanged out of his captivity."

To this speech the King replied, "God forbid that I should have summoned you hither in order that you might suffer any calamity. But there is in my Court

75 Friar Andrew of Spoleto.
76 Morocco.

a certain religious preceptor,[77] who boasts that he is a holy man—though indeed he is befouled with many and great crimes,—and who has written a new and original commentary on Alcoranus. I am desirous of punishing him, and wish to use your help in the matter."

"In this," replied Rudolf, "we cannot help you; for priests are forbidden not only to kill a man, but also to make any attempts to bring about a man's execution or death, even in a case where express permission is granted by the ruler."

The King replied, "I do not wish you to undergo the ordeal; I only desire that you should say you will undergo it." "We cannot do even that, O King." "At least agree to this—I myself will loudly announce that you will ascend the pyre: you yourselves shall be silent." "If you make this announcement publicly, O King," replied Rudolf, "we shall as publicly declare that we will do no such thing. And indeed if this man deserves punishment, what need is there of adopting this round-about and disingenuous course in committing him to the flames?" The nobles who heard this clear and straight-forward declaration on the part of Rudolf, applauded it with remarkable enthusiasm.

Such was the course of the first meetings and debates with the King and his religious preceptors.

Address to Akbar.

The priests had not forgotten the King's impulsive saying that he wanted no more arguing; but they preferred to interpret this declaration as having been uttered on purpose to satisfy his courtiers. However, in order to test his state of mind, they decided to lay the following considerations before the King,—"It is needful that he who desires thoroughly to learn the divine doctrines of Christianity should ponder especially two matters

---

77 This might refer to Shaikh Kutubuddin of Jaleswar who is described by Badaoni as wicked yet pretending to be attracted by God (Al-Badaoni II. p. 308), a description that tallies with what Akbar is reported here to have said. (See also Blochmann I. p. 91.)

—as (Christ) himself very frequently testified,—in order that the mind of such an one may be disposed to drink in the divine light with the eyes of his soul, and to let as it were the gentle rain of (God's) gifts soak into and thoroughly permeate his heart. In the first place he must endeavour with the greatest earnestness to avoid those sins which divide the soul from God. For, taught by the Holy Spirit, Solomon declared that wisdom will not enter a soul that is full of evil wishes, nor dwell in a body that is given up to sins. And one of the prophets speaking for God himself says, 'Turn unto me and I will turn unto you, saith the Lord.' Moreover John the son of Zacharias, who was the forerunner of Christ, desiring to prepare the hearts of the children of Israel for faith in Christ, repeatedly urged them to repent and to make ready and smooth a road for him who was to come. Nay more, Christ himself in the beginning of his Gospel ministry exhorted men to penitence; he even declared that his disciples, who were sent out to teach and preach must perform the same duty (of repentance). I believe that he wished to teach the same lesson—the lesson of the necessity of fleeing from sin—when, before raising from the dead the daughter of the leader of the synagogue, he drove out the musicians and the unruly crowd. For nothing is so successful as sin in arousing that tumult in the soul which can prevent the acceptance of Christ, who is the God of peace and calm; nothing can so take away the sight of the eyes and prevent a man beholding that light of faith which Christ himself brings with him; nothing can so shut up a man's heart and prevent its drinking in the heavenly showers with which God floods it. The example indeed of masons and workmen may moreover admonish us in this matter. For if a house is to be built, it is necessary, in order that the foundation may be laid on which the whole house is supported, that the earth should be dug out and cast away, so that room may be found for the great stones on which the house is built. Again, if we wish to fill with oil a vessel which is already full of water, we must first of all pour out the water. If you wish to put on a clean garment, you must first take off the dirty one. Hence St. Paul tells us all to put oft the old man, that is, not to follow the sins of Adam and our own evil tendencies to wrongdoing, in order that we may be able to put on the new man, that is, Christ himself.

Wherefore let such a man know that he can keep only one wife, the first, namely, whom he married. The rest are all courtesans and adulteresses, whom by the commandment of God and Christ it is wickedness to retain. Firstly therefore this man must repent of his past sins ; secondly he must put away all his paramours; thirdly he must give himself up to fasting and acts of penance, must pour out prayers to God, give generous alms, and perform other pious acts. For all these things render the Most High God kindly and propitious. Claudius the centurion merited the mercy of God towards himself by such actions, and was rewarded by an angelic message and by the administration of baptism at the hands of Saint Peter, who was the first of the Apostles, and acted as the representative of Christ.

Moreover such a man will find it advantageous, and indeed essential, that he should abstain from all unnecessary employments, and appoint a day and time, at which, quite alone (or if he wishes with only a few religious preceptors, in whom he can confide), and without a vestige of the spirit of controversy, he shall listen to us as our pupil. It will be legitimate for him to draw attention to any matter which is not clear in what is said. We learn from one of Christ's parables that seed which is sowed near to the path is caught up and devoured by the birds of the air. By the path Christ means the hearts of those men who are approachable and accessible to all, like a road, distracted from spiritul influences by the interference of all manner of other thoughts, immersed in troublesome and unprofitable business. Such men cannot cover the seed with (the good soil of) careful consideration and meditation; so that Christ cannot spring up in their hearts and minds. They are far different from those husbandmen who harrow in the seed as soon as it sown, so that it is covered by the soil. The birds which take away the seed are in Christ's meaning, the evil ones who induce many men of this type to forget righteousness. The same teaching is given in the ancient Law when God rejects from his sacrifices, and forbids his people to use for their food those animals which do not chew the cud. This is the reason why many wander away from the worship and knowledge of the true God, for their laziness has led them to abandon the practice of meditation. The pure and holy Virgin, whom the King himself reverences, received the messenger of God at a time when she was meditating in solitude in the inner room of her house, with no one near at hand, about the liberation (as it is said) of the human race, and was praying and desiring that she might be the handmaiden of that virgin who (as is foretold by Isaiah, whose book it is believed she was reading at the time) should be the mother of God made man. Again Philip, the disciple of Christ, met the eunuch of Candace, Queen of Ethiopia, at the time when the eunuch was meditating upon the book of Isaiah: and, having been instructed by Philip, he was forthwith baptized in a stream, and became a Christian; whereupon Philip, greatly to the wonder of the eunuch and his followers, was caught away by an angel and carried to Azotus. But indeed if we desire to learn any art or science, we must abandon our other occupations and devote our minds to that alone: and this is above all needful in learning about the things of God. Nicodemus, a man who was eagerly desirous of true piety, came by night to the house in which he had heard that Christ was staying and spent the night in listening to his teaching. In our own days the kings of Japan are imitating this example, for they frequently visit the humble houses of the priests of our Society, that they may learn the precepts of the true faith. We do not ask that of you; but we are ready to come to the palace and to labour night and day in teaching the Christian religion. We only expect that our pupil should be free from the cares of business and should show himself teachable, attentive and eager to learn. But if we carry on this enterprise without due respect given to the divine words, we come under a curse, and fear that (having forgotten the heavenly warning 'Woe to that man who performeth carelessly the work of God') both we and the king himself will be punished in hell."

Rudolf watched for an opportunity of laying these matters before the King. A few days later the priests went to the palace, where the King saw them, summoned them, withdrew with them into an inner room, and of his own accord declared that it was his desire that Christians should live freely in his empire, and build their churches,[78] as he had heard was the case in Turkey. No one could think this an innovation, since he allowed the idolators to live in and build their temples in his empire. He made this declaration with plain signs of great love and kindliness. Hence Rudolf thought the above speech should not be delivered on that occasion. However, two days later he spoke to the King about the points already mentioned one by one—or about those of them which seemed suitable to the occasion,—and advised him to prepare for the future, and to decide immediately upon some plan and process by which he might become a Christian without causing an upheaval or risking his life. For the King desired to be instructed in the faith in such a way that there might be no danger of stirring up the bitterness of his enemies, or of his being compelled to desist through fear of the consequences. For it would be bad policy to begin to build, or to undertake a war, and then to abandon the work before completion. And if he himself were killed, his dynasty would be lost and his empire destroyed.

---

[78] But the written order to preach and convert feely was not obtained till 1602—that, too, after much difficulty. (*J.A.S.B.* Vol. LXV. p. 86).

The King answered briefly, "These things are in the hand of God, who grants to those who ask plain paths from which they cannot stray. I myself have no desires. I reckon wives, children, empires, as of no account. If there is no other way of my becoming a Christian without rousing a tumult, I will pretend that I wish to go on pilgrimage to Mecca, and will go to Goa to be baptised."

Easter.

When they heard this, the Fathers were vastly encouraged. On Easter Saturday, in the company of certain Portuguese guards who had remained behind after Tauarius had left, they went to pay their respects to the King in order that they might congratulate him, and pray for his welfare in accordance with the Easter custom. Having acknowledged their good wishes the King ordered them to tell him the religious significance of that day. Furthermore he gave them quarters inside the palace precincts, in order that he might have them ready to hand whenever he wished for instruction. Then he sent away his followers and the great nobles who were in attendance, and spent much of the night in private conversation with the Fathers. He asked about the methods and merits of prayer; and Rudolf gave him brief instruction on these points. On the next day he sent them a dinner from his own table. After Easter the Fathers moved from their inn, which was crowded and inconvenient, to the house which the King had offered them in the precincts of the palace. When the King heard of their arrival he came alone to their house, and proceeded straight to the chapel, where (having laid aside his turban and shaken out his long hair) he prostrated himself on the ground in adoration of the Christ and his Mother. He then began to talk about divine things. A week later he brought three of his sons[79] and several nobles to see the chapel. He himself and all the others took off their shoes

79 Selim, Murad and Danyal.

before entering. He told his sons to do reverence to the pictures of Christ and his Virgin Mother. One of the nobles exclaimed with emotion that she who was sitting on her throne in such beautiful garments and ornaments was in truth the Queen of Heaven. The King himself accepted with the greatest delight a very beautiful picture of the Virgin, which had been brought from Rome and was presented to him by the Fathers in the name of the Superior of the Province.

Study of Persian.

All these events filled the priests with the greatest joy. An unwonted enthusiasm was kindled in them. A new spirit was, as it were, born in their hearts: and they applied themselves anew to their work, with thanks to God and great spiritual advantage, being determined to carry their task successfully through to a conclusion. To this end they requested the King to give them a teacher who would instruct them in Persian, the court-language, which is well suited to debate and discussion. The King gave this task to a certain young man,[80] of a keen and capable mind, by whose careful help Rudolf, who had very considerable intellectual ability, made such progress, that in three months he could easily make himself understood in Persian, although he could not indeed speak as yet in a polished or fluent manner. Persian is a very beautiful language, and its vocabulary is well suited to the use of those who are devoted to learned and philosophical studies. Another[81] of the priests, who had been born at Ormuz, recovered the use of his mother-tongue (Persian), which he had almost

80 Abul Fazl. He was at this time aged 30 years and a few months. We read in Sir Edward Maclagan's article (*J.A.S.B.* 1896 LXV. p. 51) that 'in matters of difficulty the Emperor bade the priests consult Abul Fazl and confide their troubles to him as they would to himself; in any case the Fathers received many favours from him (Abul Fazl), as also from the Emperor's physician (Hakim Ali of Gilan); Abul Fazl also sought instruction from them (priests) regarding the faith.'

81 Francis Henriquez. He was a Persian convert from Mahomedanism and was the interpreter of the Mission.

forgotten. Rudolf's quickness in learning not only gave him a great reputation for cleverness and wisdom, but even roused the admiration of the whole court. They were astonished that a stranger and foreigner could learn so easily an unknown language. Even his foreign accent pleased them. When the priests had attained sufficient profficiency in Persian safely to translate the Gospel records and the teachings of the Faith, they began to turn into Persian the chief passages of Gospel history, and afterwards to write very careful comments and explanations on those points which the Musalmans generally used to call in question. They handed to the King everything that they wrote, in order that he might have it read to him carefully at his leisure, and in order to avoid the frequent mis-interpretations, which were wont to take place through the malice of their opponents when the Fathers were conversing with the King. In addition to this they were anxious to avoid the suspicion that they, being foreigners, were being unduly favoured by the King's granting them too many confidential conversations.

Debates.

The Fathers and the religious leaders of the Musalmans held frequent debates concerning an infinite variety of points—the Trinity, God the Son, his death, Muhammad, Alcoranus, the day of judgment, death, resurrection, and various philosophical and political subjects. However, be it recorded without pride or boasting that, by the help of God, the Fathers so effectually silenced their opponents that they frequently demanded miraculous portents as proof of the truth of Christianity, and constantly appealed to the ordeal by fire, which I have already mentioned. I have no doubt that their purpose in so doing was to avenge themselves for the injuries which had been inflicted by the Fathers on Islam during the discussions. For they have religious scruples against permitting the rules of their faith to become a subject of controversy (as Muhammad himself warned them), and against allowing the honour of the false prophet to be impugned in their presence. This latter is with them a very grave offence, and one that was expressly condemned by the founder of their faith. Moreover they were chagrined and embittered by being beaten with their own weapons in public discussion. For the priests made use, as far as possible, of arguments and quotations drawn from the Musalman scriptures instead of from the Bible; and the Musalmans were astonished at their having the teaching of their own religion so much at their fingers' ends that their opponents appeared mere infants beside them. The chief indeed of all the Musalman religious leaders,[82] who laughed at the system of Muhammad (and for this reason was regarded with great favour by the king), was always on the side of the priests. Whenever in the course of discussion the question arose whether such and such a quotation really occurred in the Quran, he awaited their opinion in silence; and when the matter was referred to him, he always agreed with the Fathers' view of it. For he had constantly found, when the scriptures were brought for reference, that our party had given the most careful study to the Quran, and indeed that they never made a mistake in their quotations; and of his opinion regarding this he made no secret, though he did not actually express it in so many words.

A School Established.

The King himself was the Fathers' advocate, umpire and friendly arbitrator in every discussion. If any argument came up which favoured the case of the priests, he publicly and eloquently drew attention to it. Nor did he let any opportunity pass of applauding them, so that they were even put to the blush by his extravagant praise. Most of all did he approve and commend the Fathers' zeal for poverty and chastity. He affirmed that his mind was strongly attracted to a life of devotion and to the renunciation of all worldly affairs; for he could well understand that a man was specially dear to

[82] Abul Fazl (1551-1602) (See Note 85).

God who abjured the pleasures of the world, wife, children and all possessions. He trusted the priests so completely that he handed over his second son[83] to them for education and training, and ordered them to be given money which they might bestow as alms upon the poor. However, the Fathers succeeded in avoiding this latter responsibility. They agreed to undertake the education of the prince, both because they had vivid expectations of success, and because the work of education is the peculiar function of the Society, though indeed, with the characteristic humility of Jesuits, they would willingly have declined so great an honour. On the day when the prince's education began, the King gave his son's teacher a golden coin weighing five sestertia (?) for this is the custom of the country. But the teacher refused to accept the gift, at which both the King and the other nobles expressed unbounded admiration and unqualified praise for such disregard of money. The prince's education was conducted as follows—at the beginning of each lesson he called devoutly upon the names of Jesus and Mary[84] as is the Christian custom; then he made the sign of the Cross on his forehead, face and breast; finally he paid reverence to the picture of Christ which was in his book. The same practice was observed by the prince's schoolmates, who had been chosen by the King from the children of the higher nobility.

The children were taught Christianity out of a little book of Christian doctrine, and their copy-books contained pious sentiments as the examples they had to copy. The young prince was an ideal pupil as regards natural ability, good conduct and intellectual capacity. In all these respects it would have been hard to find any Christian youth, let alone a prince, surpassing him.

---

83 Murad. He was born on June 8, 1570; he was also known, as Pahari, 'because of his being born on the low hills of Fatehpur' (*J.A.S.B.* 1896 Vol. LXV. *P.* 50 N. 4), Before this appointment, the task of instructing Murad had been entrusted to Faizi.

84 Badaoni also says the same. (Al-Badaoni II. pp. 267-8).

He was obedient to his teacher, and so submissive that he sometimes did not even dare to raise his eyes to his teacher's face when he was reproving him. Before three months were up he had learnt to read, and could imitate his tutor's handwriting so cleverly that he might easily have been thought to have spent a year at that task. All this greatly pleased the King, his father, who had bidden him to recite before himself every day whatever he had learnt, either by heart or from reading stories. With this incentive the boy worked hard. For the King's nature was such that, though he loved his children very dearly, he used to give them orders rather roughly whenever he wanted anything done; and he sometimes punished them with blows as well as with harsh words. He gave the prince's tutor authority to punish his pupils if they committed any offence. When the young prince found out that this authority had been given to the priest, he stood in the utmost dread of him, until the kindly words of his tutor reassured him. For the Father told him that he need fear nothing from himself, since it was not the custom of the Portuguese to allow princes to be beaten by anyone except their own parents and, in their infancy, their nurses; and in addition to this, it was not fitting that a stranger (although the custom of that country allowed it) should chastise the son of so great a ruler. The tutor also told the prince that the King's gracious permission and confidence in this matter indeed rather prevented his chiding and punishing his pupil than enabled him to do so; and the King in his great wisdom had not overlooked the fact that he would not avail himself of this privilege. This assurance and the rest of the master's treatment, which was very different from that of other masters, so endeared him to the hearts of the prince and his two brothers, that they all three became the closest friends of the Fathers. The prince's name was Pahari which means "mountaineer."

Abul Fazl.

The authority of the chief of the Musalman religious preceptors, who was also the Prime Minister, and who always treated the Fathers in a friendly way, increased the favour of the King towards them. The name of this man was Shah Abdulfasilius,[85] and the priests used to call him the King's Jonathan. He was the son of an exceedingly pious old

---

85 Shaikh Abul Fazl. An account of Abul Fazl and his elder brother Abul Faiz (usually known by his nom de plume of Faizi) and of their father Shaikh Mubarak, is, I think, necessary. The family had originally come from Sindh and had settled at Nagor, northwest of Ajmir. But Shaikh Mubarak migrated to the left bank of the Jumna opposite Agra where his two sons were born. The tenth century of the Hijra Era saw the birth of a religious ferment known as the Mahdawi movement, which eagerly awaited the appearance of Imam Mahdi, "Lord of the Age" who would 'restore the sinking faith to its pristine freshness.' The common features of the movement were that its preachers (e.g. Mir Sayyid Muhammad of Jaunpur and Shaikh Alai of Bianah) were men of condition and oratorical powers which enabled them to sway the multitude; and secondly that the preachers and their followers made the place-hunting Court Ulamas the objective of their attack. Shaikh Mubarak professed Mahdawi ideas and as such incurred the life-long enmity of Mukhdum-ul-Mulk (Maulana Abdullah Ansari of Sultanpur), the most influential divine from the time of Sher Shah to the first twenty years of the reign of Akbar. The downfall of the Afghan power and the restoration of Humayan witnessed a lull in the persecution of the Mahdists. But when it was again taken up after the fall of Bairam Khan, Shaikh Mubarak whose scholarship and breadth of views had already made him famous was marked out as their victim by Abdun Nabi and Makhdum-ul-Mulk, from whose clutches however the Shaikh was saved by the generosity of Akbar's foster-brother Mirza Aziz Koka. But the fame of Mubarak and his two precocious sons grew; and Faizi for the first time presented himself before the Emperor in 1567 during the siege of Chitor; and Abul Fazl was introduced by his elder brother to court in 1574. The inherited comprehensiveness of their views and the persecution to which they were subjected in their life contributed in no small measure to the hatred of religious intolerance which formed the basis of Akbar's friendship with them. Faizi was made Poet Laureate in 1588. And Abul Fazl, though a commander of only two thousand five hundred horse, exercised unbounded influence over the Emperor and was his trusted minister; but it is doubtful whether he was ever formally appointed as his Vakil (Prime Minister). Abul Fazl led the court party in its wranglings with the orthodox Mullas, and by adroitly shifting the disputes from one point to another exposed their narrow sectarianism and bigotry. As the ultimate result of these

man,[86] who was devoted to the study of religious commentaries and of books of religious meditation, and who had little faith in Muhammad and his book. All his sons followed this old man's example, and openly declared that the Quran contained many impious, wicked and highly inconsistent passages, and that hence they were convinced that it had not been sent by God. The priests were astonished at this old man's wisdom, authority and friendliness to Christianity. He was wont devoutly to kiss the Gospel, and to place it on his head. He looked upon the

disputations, a document (drafted by Shaikh Mubarak) was signed by the orthodox divines which gave the spiritual leadership to the Emperor (Sept. 1579). Mubarak and Faizi did not play any considerable part after this—the former died in 1593 and the latter in 1595. But Abul Fazl continued to be the Emperor's most intimate friend and adviser. Abul Fazl's first experience of active service was in the Deccan in 1597, where his honesty and loyalty stood out in strong contrast with the intrigues and treachery with which military operations were generally conducted. When a bride was offered to him by Bahadur Shah, the King of Khandesh, he replied "The favour of the Emperor has extinguished every desire in me of accepting gifts from others." His end was tragic. On his way to Agra, from the Deccan, he was murdered (Aug. 1602) by Raja Bir Singh, a Bundela chief of Orchha, at the instigation of Selim, who suspected, without any reason, that the minister had been using his influence against his succession. This was the unkindest cut that the rebellious son ever gave to the aged father, who on knowing the circumstances exclaimed, "If Selim wished to be emperor, he might have killed me and spared Abul Fazl."

Mahommedan historians attribute the apostacy, if not the religious fantasies, of Akbar to the evil influence of the two brothers. But if they led him away from the prescribed path, they helped, if not awakened, him to a true sense of duty towards his subjects, composed as they were, of diverse races. In few other countries has a Mahomedan ruler had to solve the problem of controlling composite and antagonistic elements. The freethinking friends of Akbar showed the right way of enthroning the policy of toleration above the rigid law of the Koran. The Khan Khanans, the Khan Azams and the Khan Jehans, fought battles and won victories for him, but the King's Jonathan evolved the right policy that reconciled the conquered to the foreign yoke, and placed the Empire on a broad and stable basis.

86 Shaik Mubarak (1503-93), See note on Abdul Fusilius.

priests as angels, and used to declare that their young interpreter[87] was an exceedingly fortunate fellow, since he constantly enjoyed their company. In his private conferences with the King he held it his most precious privilege to extol the learning and humility of the Fathers. These latter had made an arrangement with Abdulfasilius that before any public discussion he should listen to their view of the position which they were defending or attacking, and to their arguments, so that he might answer their opponents more fully and elaborately (than they could do themselves). This office he performed in many discussions and especially in one, in which his attitude was so praiseworthy that he seemed to be almost a Christian. Saturday[88] was the day assigned for these discussions. However, owing to bad news[89] having come from Bengal—that Pathan deserters had overcome and killed the King's Viceroy[90] in that province—and owing also to a rumour having spread that the King was too much

---

87 Francis Henriquez. One authority states that he withdrew to Goa secretly without permission from the other two members of the mission.

88 The reference here is not to the discussions held in the Ibadat-Khana, where originally the four classes (Shaiks, Sayyids, Ulamas and Amirs) and schools of Islam used to meet on Thursday evenings, which in the Mahommedan Calendar are reckoned as part of Friday, the Mahommedan Sabbath. But after the signature of the document which made Akbar the supreme Mujtahid there was no wrangling, for the Emperor's will was law in ecclesiatical matters as well (Sept. 1579). Theological discussions were continued, not in the Ibadat-Khana but in the hall of private audience or in some other premises, and probably these discussions with men of all classes were on Saturdays.

89 The revolt of Bengal and Behar in 1580. It was mainly due to strict military regulations and reduction of allowances to soldiers. It was also partly caused by the rumoured rejection of Islam by Akbar, and Mulla Muhammad Yazdi Kazi of Jaunpur made matters worse by issuing a fatwa justifying rebellion against the innovating Emperor (1580).

90 Muzaffar Khan Turbati, Governor of Bengal, who was captured and killed by the rebels with all sorts of tortures (Ap. 1580).

attracted to Christianity, Zelaldinus[91] somewhat relaxed his zeal for religious discussions and for a time did not grant audience to the priests[92]. Seizing the opportunity thus afforded, the Fathers devoted themselves to translating parts of the Gospel into Persian. The King ordered these passages to be publicly read to him in the presence of some of his religious preceptors, whereupon a discussion was opened concerning the Son of God, and the manner and purpose of his divine generation. At this time Abdulfasilius seemed to be inspired by a divine earnestness, so clearly did he demonstrate how we believe that God has a Son. The Fathers themselves were greatly astonished as they listened to him. Rudolf not only agreed with his expressions, but also upon opportunity being given for a fuller statement of our position complimented Abdulfasilius upon what he had said; so that some of our opponents declared that they could believe in God's having a Son in the manner thus expounded. When the debate turned to the death and passion of Christ, and it was asked why he had allowed himself to be killed by

---

91 Jelaluddin Muhammad Akbar. The name given to him on his birth was Badr-uddin Muhammad Akbar. The first word means 'Full moon of Religion' (because he was born on the night of the full moon), the second, word is sacred being the name of the Prophet, and the third word, signifying 'very great,' had a reference to the name of his maternal grandfather, Shaikh Ali Akbar Jami. On the recapture of Kabul in 1545, the circumcision ceremony was performed and the name and the date of his birth were changed. "His relatives," says Dr. V.A. Smith, "who believed firmly in all the superstitions of their time, sought to protect him against the perils of malignant sorcery by concealing the true date of his nativity and so frustrating the calculations of hostile astrologers. The circumstances of his birth in the desert ensured the advantage that very few people in Kabul knew exactly on what date he had first seen the light." So his name was changed from Badruddin to Jelaluddin—a word similar in form and not too remote in meaning. So also the date of birth was moved back from November 23, to October 15, 1542 (See Smith's *Akbar* pp. 18-19).

92 Just to allay the suspicions of the Mahommedans (See *J.A.S.B.* 1896 Vol. LXV p. 53).

that kind of death, another of those who were present[93] inspired by the same divine spirit, said that Christ underwent that death because of the goodness and mercy which belonged to his nature, although, if he had wished, he could have saved us in many other ways. Rudolf then entered upon a careful argument concerning the two natures co-existing in Christ. The King expressed his agreement and applauded; and our opponents were reduced to a gloomy silence. Abdulfasilius was so attracted to Christianity that, whenever he entered the little chapel, he declared that he was deeply moved in his mind, but that the reverse was the case when he entered a mosque. He said that he was persuaded that there was something heavenly and divine in our places of worship.

Christmas.

The common report of the King's extraordinary kindness towards the priests prevented their meeting him, and they hence began to plan to remove their quarters into a house which was actually built against the palace wall, so that by making a door through this wall a secret means of meeting might be devised. When they told the King of this plan and its purpose, he immediately ordered the ointments, perfumes and very numerous jars of scented water to be conveyed out of that house into another; for the house (which the priests wanted) was used for the manufacturing and storing of ointments and perfumes, whence it was called the Storehouse of Perfumes.[94] The priests were reminded of the saying, 'We are Christ's sweet perfume.' When the place had been cleared out, slightly repaired in accordance with their request, and furnished with

93 According to the Author's notes, he was one of the physicians, that is to say, one of the three important personages, Hakim Ali of Gilan, Hakim-Ul-Mulk, and Hakim Abul Fath (For the names of other physicians see Blochmann I pp. 542-4). I think the allusion here is to Hakim Ali of Gilan.

94 Coxbinqhana (Khosbai-Khana) i.e. house of pleasant perfume—*Author's Note.*

couches, they moved into it; and the King announced that he would speedily come to visit them there. Since Christmas was at hand, the Fathers asked him to come on that day. They adorned their chapel[95] with rich silken curtains. They made models of the grotto where Christ was born, of the crib in which his mother laid him, and of the mountain on which the shepherds watched. The people were represented by tiny statues, and all was made true to life. The King, and a few of his intimate friends, whom he brought with him, were greatly delighted by this spectacle. He examined everything, and began to talk about the birth of Christ. Whereupon Rudolf asked the Musalman religious teachers how two conflicting texts in Alcoranus could be reconciled. In one it is written that Christ was not really killed by the Jews, but someone else instead of him, as the Nestorians also believe: and in the other, that God promised that he would be gracious to him in his birth, death and resurrection. If he was not going to die why did (God) look forward to his death? But if he died, he gained what a certain prophet foretold, viz. 'If he shall lay down his life, he shall see his seed long-enduring, and the will of God shall be directed by his hand.' Again if he did not die, he certainly was not raised from the dead; but if he did not rise from the dead, the promise of God was vain and empty. Christ therefore must have been raised from the dead in order that the promise might not be meaningless. And if he was raised from the dead, he must for some time at least have been dead. But if he died, their prophet was inconsistent; for at one time he said that Christ died and at another time he denied it; and it followed of necessity that the statement was false that another was killed instead of Christ and that Christ himself was not killed at all. If then their prophet was detected in a lie, he was not to be regarded as the prophet of God.

95 The domestic chapel was known as *Bibi Mariam Ki-Kothi*, Bibi Marium referring to the Virgin Mary.

This reasoning of Rudolf's rendered those wretched Musalmans so desperate that they would pass on to no other point; nor could they find any answer to his arguments even when they fetched Alcoranus and several commentaries on it. In addition to this Rudolf cast in their teeth the fact that their precious prophet in one passage (which he quoted) permitted the practice of unnatural and abominable vice. The volume was consulted, and the accusation found to be true; for some had denied it. When this fact was discovered the Musalmans reddened with shame. Some were astonished; others said that what the prophet taught was enough for them and should not be objected to. One clever fellow said that the passage ought to be understood figuratively; but Rudolf met this by declaring that there was nothing in that passage which could be rightly called a figure of speech, since the same phrase was used just above in its literal meaning. "If these lusts are indulged," said he, "in the abode of the blest, the bliss therein is not perfect."

The same evening the king sent his sons to see the crib. They were greatly delighted with it.

The priests' new quarters were rendered very noisy on account of their nearness to the scribes, who were continually thronged by crowds of clients. The King, therefore, as a sign of favour to the priests and without their knowledge, ordered these scribes to move away. The fame of the beautiful statue of the blessed Virgin had been spread so widely that crowds of Musalmans and Hindus (the latter bringing offerings) came to the chapel. When they beheld the statue, they lifted their hands to heaven and did reverence before it. In other respects they may be no better than those Christian revolutionaries, the 'iconoclasts;' but in this respect at least they are certainly their superiors.

Gladiatorial Contests.

I have already mentioned the high opinion which the King had conceived of the Fathers' wisdom and integrity. Lest this opinion should turn out to be ill-founded, they felt it to be their duty to mention freely to him anything which was blameworthy. Hence they very frequently pointed out to him his carelessness and dilatoriness in learning divine things. This they did gently, and after testing the state of his mind. When he invited them to see a gladiatorial contest, they replied that they could not comply. He forthwith excused their attendance at the contest, but asked why they would not come. They replied that it was absolutely contrary to the Christian discipline and moral standard to organise, or even to look on at, human carnage: and that he who was responsible for the holding of gladiatorial games committed a terrible crime. If he wished to amuse himself with mimic war, he should have the edges of the swords dulled, and make the gladiators wear breastplates and helmets, and let them carry small shields on the left arm, with which they could catch the blows without risk to their lives. The King approved of this advice and wondered at the holy mercy of the Christian religion. It is the custom at the gladiatorial combats of the Mongols for the various signals to be given by four pairs of drums; of which the first pair leads the music of the others, the second gives a low deep note, the third a gentle sound, and the fourth a high note in contrast to the low one given by the second pair.

Sati.

The wives of the Brachmans—a famous class of nobly-born Hindus—are accustomed, in accordance with an ancient tradition of their religion, to burn themselves on the same pyres as their dead husbands. The King ordered the priests to be summoned to see an instance of this.[96] They went in ignorance of what was to take place; but when they found out, they plainly indicated by their saddened faces how cruel and savage they felt that crime to be. Finally Rudolf publicly reprimanded

---

96 I do not think Akbar ever countenanced the inhuman practice of Sati.

the King for showing openly by his presence there that he approved of such a revolting crime, and for supporting it by his weighty judgment and explicit approbation, (for he was heard to say that such fortitude could only come from God). Such was Zelaldinus' kindness and favour towards the priests that he showed no resentment; and a certain chief,[97] a great favourite of his, a Brachman by birth, who held the office of Superintendent of sacred observances, could no longer persuade him to attend such spectacles. The wretched women are rendered quite insensible by means of certain drugs, in order that they may feel no pain. For this purpose opium is used, or a soporific herb named bang, or—more usually—the herb 'duturo,' which is known to the Indians, although entirely unfamiliar alike to modern Europeans and to the ancients. Sometimes they are half-drugged: and, before they lose their resolution, are hurried to the pyre with warnings, prayers and promises of eternal fame. On arriving there they cast themselves into the flames. If they hesitate, the wretched creatures are driven on to the pyre: and if they try to leap off again, are held down with poles and hooks. The nobles who were present were highly incensed at the Fathers' interference. They did not dare to gainsay the King; but they grumbled loudly amongst themselves, saying, 'Away with you, black-clothed Franks.' The whole city was filled with praise and admiration when news was brought that the Franks had dared to rebuke the King regarding this affair.

On one occasion the Fathers met a crowd of worthless profligates, some of those who dress and adorn themselves like women. The priests were rightly disgusted at this, and took the first opportunity of privately complaining to the King (since he was so favourable to them) about this disgraceful matter. They declared with the greatest emphasis that they were astonished at his permitting such a class of men

97 Raja Bhagwan Das (See note 213.)

to live in his kingdom, let alone in his city, and almost under his eyes. They must be banished, as though they were a deadly plague, to his most distant territories; even better, let them be burnt up by devouring flames. They never would have believed that such men could be found in the court itself and in the royal city, where lived a king of such piety, integrity and prudence. Therefore let him give orders that these libertines should never again be seen in Fattepurum, seeing that his remarkable prophet had guaranteed that good men should never suffer for their good actions. The King laughed at this piece of sarcasm and retired, saying that he would attend to the matter.

Furthermore they warned him that some day he would be punished, because he knew well that the Musalman teaching was pernicious to the minds of men, and yet he allowed his two sons[98]—boys of great natural ability and intellectual power—to be educated by certain old men,[99] whose minds were filled with Muhammad. He replied that he had given orders that these tutors should only teach the history of the reigns of his own ancestors.

Akbar's kindness.

Not to go into too many details, the Fathers frequently and freely admonished the King; but their conscientious readiness in doing this never lessened, still less put an end to, the kindly friendship of the King towards them. Nay more, when the King perceived that it was the sincerity of their hearts that led them to feel themselves free to correct him, he took it in such good part that he always seemed not only to favour them, but to heap honours upon them in his desire to show his affection towards them. For when they saluted him, which they did with uncovered heads, he answered with a nod and a bright smile. He did not allow them to keep their heads uncovered

98 Selim and Danyal.

99 Kutubuddin was for sometime tutor to Selim and Said Khan to Danyal. (See note 286).

when they were in his presence. When a council was being held, or when he summoned them to his private audience-chamber for familiar conversation, he used to make them sit beside him. He shook hands with them cordially and familiarly. He frequently left the public audience-chamber to converse with them in private. Several times he paced up and down with his arm round Rudolf's shoulders. Once, when he was in camp, he desired another of the priests, in the middle of a crowd of his nobles, to help him fasten on his sword, which service the Father performed, amidst the envy and wonder of all the courtiers. He wished the priests to be sharers of his inmost thoughts, both in good and ill fortune—no common mark of love and kindness. He ordered his door-keepers to grant them entrance, whenever they wished, even into the inner courtyard of the palace, where only the most distinguished nobles had the right of entrance. He sent them food from his own table—a mark of distinction which he is said never to have conferred upon anyone before. He visited one of the Fathers when he was ill, and greeted him in Portuguese as a sign of respect. There would have been no end to his gifts, had the Fathers not frequently told him that all they needed was food and clothing, and these of the most simple description. This reply pleased him so much that he repeated it publicly: and each month sent them as much money, under the guise of alms, as he thought would be sufficient for their daily expenses.

Conspiracy of Shah Mansur.

This kindness of the King towards the Fathers greatly confirmed and increased the rumour that he had abjured Muhammad; so that it was publicly reported that he wished to become a Christian. It happened that he was not in the habit of saying the customary Musalman prayers at the times appointed by Muhammad, and did not observe the month's fast which is called Ramadan. He frequently made jokes at the expense of Muhammad, especially at his being thrust out of doors without shoes or breeches on account of his licentiousness. All this enraged many Musalmans and especially one[100] whom the King had raised from a low and abject condition to the highest dignity and honour, and had made chief guardian of his resources. This man, feeling that he himself and the other Musalmans could no longer brook the insults which, in his view, were being heaped upon their prophet, was stirred to treason by his religious feelings (for it is commanded that those who disbelieve and slander the prophet shall be destroyed). He persuaded many to join in his

---

100 Khwaja Shah Mansur (Xamansurus as Father Monserrate puts his name). He began his career as an accountant in the Perfume Department (*E.D.V. 401*) and in 1575 A.D. became Vizier and filled the post with ability till his execution on 28th February 1581. About his capacity as a financier there can be no question. Abul Fazl says, "But there is seldom found such an acute accountant and one so laborious, so discriminating." (A.N. III p. 504-5). Tahir Muhammad in his *Ranzat-in-Tahirin* writes that he was an incomparable Vizier. Regarding his execution there is difference of opinion. To Blochmann it is a foul murder; to Von Noer it is a judicial murder; and to Beveridge it is a sad story throwing lurid light on the morals of Akbar's officers; but to Smith it is the just nemesis of long-continued and well-proved treason, and this verdict is based as the author writes, on Father Monserrate and Abul Fazl—the other Mahomedan historians all declare the Vizier to be innocent. It appears to me that Abul Fazl, whom Smith draws to his support, attributes the execution more to the rigour of Mansur's administration than to treason. Before quoting Abul Fazl, I may say that the Long-tailed Star, as Mansur was derisively called after the appearance of the comet (which passed its perihelion on 26th Oct. 1577; *J.B.B.R.A.S.* Vol. XXI, 146) on account of the tail of turban hanging down his back, was the most unpopular figure in Akbar's Court. His stern policy of retrenchment, his meticulous inquisition into the financial matters of his department, and his want of sympathy had all contributed to his unpopularity (Bloch. I. 430). Abul Fazl writes, "From love of office and cupidity he was always laying hold of trifles in financial matters and displaying harshness. Sympathy with debtors never touched the hem of his heart. His whole idea was to fill his own house. He advanced his business by fair speeches while behaving badly. * *. For his own advantage he destroyed a number of poor people. He did not read the signs of the times and did not distinguish between the season of conciliation and that of strictness.

If he had had a little piety to God, a little loyalty to the lord of the Universe (Akbar), some kindness to the people and a little absence of cupidity and injuriousness, he never would have come to this end from the wrath of the Shahim Shah, nor have been caught in this illustration of Divine Anger." The historiographer also quotes the political maxims of renowned kings to show that the execution of Shah Mansur was an illustration of them: "Whoever with the idea of flattering us (kings) leaves the highway of truth and lets drop the reins of right consideration and promotes our prosperity by harsh dealings with the soldiers and subjects, and seeks by improper means and incorrect statements to increase the treasures of dominion will assuredly cause the stewards of destiny to turn our hearts from him and will receive condign punishment. The case of the Khwaja is a fresh instance of this." Other Mahommedan historians, notably, Abdul Kader and Nizam-uddin Ahmad, write that letters were forged to prove the Khwaja's persistent treason; but it may be noted that the latter historian is of opinion that only the last batch of letters, on the strength of which the Vizier was hanged, was forged. The *Maasir* states that Akbar was unwilling to put the Vizier to death but he was induced by Birbal and others. Clearly then there was a plot against his life. Some historians state that Todar Mal engineered the plot, as he envied the Vizier's capacity and the royal favour that the latter enjoyed, or probably he had personal interests in his removal from office. However, the statements of so many historians coupled with the fact that his accomplices got off scot-free, show that, besides treason, there were other contributory causes that brought about his tragic end.

Let us now follow the whole story as told by Mahommedan historians. About 22 Dec. 1580, Shadman, the general of Hakim, had been defeated by Man Singh and in his portfolio three letters were discovered and sent to Akbar at Fatehpur. These were replies of Hakim to the favourable letters of Shah Mansur, Muhammad Qasim and Hakim-ul-Mulk. When the Emperor started against his brother he took the Vizier with him. On the way, either at Sonpat, 28 miles north-west of Delhi, or at Panipat, 25 miles further on, Malik Sani, formerly Diwan of Hakim, arrived and put up with Mausur and made him the channel of offering his services to Akbar. This heightened the suspicion of the Emperor. At Shahabad, in the Umballa District, the Kotwal of the camp, Malik Ali, produced letters which he had obtained from a courier of Sharaf Beg, Mansur's agent in his fief of Ferozepore. One of these letters contained a reference to the favourable disposition of Hakim towards the Beg. This sealed the fate of the Vizier and he was hanged next morning at Kot Kachwaha (28th February 1581). On reaching Kabul and making enquiries there (according to Nizamuddin and Badaoni) Akbar was convinced of the innocence of Shah Mansur.

conspiracy, and wrote to the brother of Zelaldinus, Mirsachimus[101] (who was the king of Kabul and a bigoted Musalman), a letter to the following effect: "Cease to be lazy and neglectful of your religion; for you have an opportunity of winning a great empire and of avenging upon the infidels the insults which are being heaped upon Muhammad. Know that there are many in my confidence here who will desert to you if you declare war upon your impious brother. I am their leader. When the battle is joined, your brother shall be slain, either by myself or by someone else who shall be able to do so more easily and safely. For many of his relations and friends have joined in my conspiracy. When he is dead, a bloodless victory will be assured." He made many copies of this letter, of which one was intercepted and brought to the King, who having discovered the conspiracy ordered its author to be kept in honourable confinement, and wrote to his brother advising him to keep the peace, unless he wished to be deprived of his kingdom. A month later, remembering all that the traitor had done for him, he ordered him to be released with a warning, and re-instated him in his old office; for he was a clever and useful minister, and Zelaldinus had such enormous resources that he entertained no fear of his brother. The rest of the conspirators,[102] whose names were found amongst Xaman-

---

101 Mirza Muhammad Hakim (1554-1585) was Akbar's half-brother. He was the nominal viceroy of Kabul, his mother being the real ruler. A bigot and a sot, he made two feeble and abortive attempts to displace Akbar at times when his brother was beset with difficulties at home owing to the rebellion of the Uzbegs in 1566 and the Bengal revolt in 1579-80. Hakim was supported in his attempts especially in 1581, by the orthodox or clerical party, who had been alienated by Akbar's religious vagaries.

102 We do not know the names of all the other conspirators. Three others were Muhammad Qasim the Engineer, Hakim-ul-Mulk and Sayyid Muzaffar. Of these the second had already gone off to Mecca in August, 1580. Probably, as Beveridge suggests, the reference is to Hakim-Ain-Al-Mulk, governor of Sambal, and not to Hakim-ul-Mulk.

surus' papers, were secretly warned and sent to distant parts of the empire, so that they might not be able to meet again.

Renewed Conspiracy of Shah Mansur.

The King, who was by nature simple and straightforward, imagined that by taking these steps he had carefully stamped out the conspiracy, though in the meantime he always went about armed. However the priests were in great danger. For Xamansurus, the ringleader of the conspirators, was no whit improved by the free pardon and all the benefits which had been conferred upon him. He began to revive the conspiracy with the same treacherous cunning as before. For he wrote again to Mirsachimus, in the same strain as his former letter. This the King soon found out.

Xamansurus pressed his plots with all diligence, and spent a great deal of pains in estranging the hearts of his subjects from the King. The strength of the Tartar armies lies in their cavalry, which is organized as follows,[103] in accordance with the system of Cinguiscanus,[104] the

---

103 This is generally known as the Mansabdari system, "beginning at Commanders of ten thousand and ending at those set over ten men." There were altogether 66 grades of Mansab mentioned by Abul Fazal, though, according to Blochmann, only 33 grades existed in actual practice. In Akbar's time the highest Mansab that could be attained by a subject was for long that of five thousand and it was only towards the end of the reign that a few were promoted to seven thousand, *e.g.* Man Singh, Mirza Shah Rukh, Mirza Aziz Kokah. But it may be mentioned that these men were connected with the royal family. Besides the usual Mansab, additional distinction used to be conferred on a man by tacking on an extra number of horsemen known as *Sawar*, whereas the original Mansab was called *Zat*. The *Sawar* rank was enjoyed only by commanders of five hundred and above. The system of Mansab was re-organised and introduced in India by Akbar though it was in use in Central Asia amongst the Moghals. For a detailed description of this system reference may be made to Irvine pp. 3-11 and Blochmann I pp. 236-47.

104 Chenghiz Khan (1155-1227). His original name was Temujin. For an account of his life, conquest, adventure and laws, see Pringle Kennedy's History of the Great Moghuls, Vol. I pp. 15-21, and Howorth s Articles in the Indian Antiquary, Vols. XI-XV, 1882-86.

ancestor of Zelaldinus. The lowest officers are leaders of ten; above them are the leaders of a hundred; above them the leaders of a thousand; and above these the leaders of ten thousand. When the total numbers were reckoned up, for the purpose of giving the cavalry their pay, complete confidence used to be put in the accounts submitted by the chief officers. However Xamansurus persuaded the King that these officers were cheating[105] him by drawing pay for more troops than they really had, and by counting infantrymen, or even their own servants, as cavalrymen. Hence, (he said), in order to prevent fraud, every man should be required to be present with his horse; the horses should be branded: and if a horse had died, its tail should be brought. No borrowing or substituting of horses should be permitted; and no horses should be sold without the King's sanction. Furthermore, the pay of the cavalry and its officers should be reduced. The King agreed to this scheme as likely to be advantageous; whereupon the unscrupulous villain, representing himself as the champion of the army, endeavoured to supplant and overthrow the King. For the Mongols so bitterly resented both reforms that a rebellion broke out in Gangaris, and the King's Viceroy was killed. The King himself became highly unpopular with all classes of people throughout the empire. He was accused of despotism. One thing[106] only was needed

105 In addition to branding, known as Dagh-o-Mahalli, the Descriptive Roll System was introduced, according to which the dwelling-places and race of the soldiers were registered. The system of branding horses to prevent borrowing or exchanging was revived in 1573, not however by Shah Mansur but by Shahbaz Khan, the then Mir Bakshi. The system was not new. It had been introduced by Allauddin Khalji. The causes of Shah Mansur's unpopularity were: (i) lowering the value of the Jagirs of the grandees in Bengal by one-fourth of their former value and those in Behar by one-fifth, (ii) reducing the allowances of Bengal Officers, (iii) interfering with the Sayurghal tenures, (iv) strictness in administrative matters. For branding and other cognate questions Blochmann I pp. 139, 140n, 232, 242, 244, 255-6 and 430 and Irvine Ch. V., will be found extremely useful.

(to promote a general revolt), namely that all should judge it to be their duty and interest to engage in a legitimate rebellion against the King, on behalf of their religion and their liberty. Rumours increasing apace, the priests approached the King to find out whether he wished, in consequence of the disturbances, to dismiss them; for it was said that he was repenting that he had ever invited them to the court. However, so little was this his desire, that he reproached them with being home-sick; but this was far from being their real trouble. They were only uneasy at appearing to be slothful in the work for which they had undertaken so long a journey. Shortly afterwards information was given to the King about Xamansurus' second conspiracy and attempted revolution; and hence the villain was again dismissed from his office, deprived of all his financial responsibilities, and handed over to custody.

Invasion of Mirza Hakim.

However Mirsachimus, having prepared an army of fifteen thousand Mongol cavalry, boldly and safely crossed the Indus, Bydaspes,[107] Sandabalis,[108] and Adris,[109] broad and rapid rivers, the last-named of which (a little smaller than the others) flows from the north past Lahorum[110] which is a very great and wealthy city. He was compelled to halt for a time near Lahorum. The fortress of

---

106 This was furnished by the Fatwa of Mullah Muhammad Yazdi the chief Kazi of Jaunpur, justifying rebellion against the Emperor for innovations in the matter of religion (Badaoni II P. 284).

107 The river Jhelum. The Sanskrit name of this river of the Punjab is Vitasta, which Alexander's historians grecised into Hydaspes, but Ptolemy put the name more correctly as Bidaspes (Ptolemy P. 89).

108 This seems to be a mistake for Sandabagus which may be said to be a latinised form of Chandrabhaga. The two mountain rivers Chandra and Bhaga unite and form the Chandrabhaga or Chenab (Ptolemy p. 89-90).

109 This is a corruption of Hydrastes which was the Greek name of the river Rabi, the classical Sanskrit name being Airavati. This was also called Rhonadis (Ptolemy p. 90).

110 Lahore.

Ruytasium[111] was held by Josephus,[112] who refused to surrender it: for he said it had been given into his charge by Zelaldinus, and that he could not give it up unless it were stormed and captured. However Mirsachimus did not consider it dangerous to leave enemies unsubdued behind him, and after a time marched forward. He had given strict orders to his troops that they should do no harm to anyone: no fields were to be devastated: and the citizens of Lahorum were to remain unmolested. He sent envoys to the governor[113] of that city, inviting him to surrender and to retire from the fort: but received the same reply from him as from Josephus. Whereupon he began to be sorry he had

111 This was the fort of Rohtas built in 1542 by Sher Shah and named after his other eyrie in Behar which had helped him so much in his rise to power. The Gakkhars were the friends of the Moghals and the inveterate enemies of the Afghans. Their then chief Rai Sairang (1530-42) had in consequence a harrassing war with Sher Shah. To keep the Gakkhars in check Sher Shah in 1540 laid the foudation of the fort of Rohtas in the neighbourhood of Jogi Tilla, on the banks of the Kahan (feeder of the Jhelum) and in 1542 the fort was completed. Todar Khettri was appointed to superintend the construction of the fort, though the name of one Shahu Sultani is also mentioned. "Todar Khettri," writes Niamatullah in his Tarikhi Khan Jehan Lodi, "represented (to Sher Shah) that the Gakkhars to whom the country belonged, would not allow any one to work for wages; and that they had agreed among themselves upon oath to banish every person that should contravene their intention." In reply Sher Shah is said to have scolded the Khettri for his stinginess and the result was that Todar Khettri first fixed a gold Ashrafi as the enormous remuneration for one stone, which induced the Gakkhars to flock to him in such numbers that afterwards a stone was paid with a rupee, and this pay gradually fell to five Tankas (20 Tankas=Re. 1) till the fortress was complete. The fort was of great strategic importance, as it commanded the road from Kabul to the Capital of Hindustan. It seems to have sunk into comparative insignificance from the time of Shah Jahan.

112 Mirza Yusuf Khan. Abul Fazl writes of him in connection with the event of 1580 as having defeated an advanced force of Mirze Hakim and as being in charge of the Punjab (?) (Blochmann I p. 346).

113 Man Singh (Blochmann I p. 339). Prince Mancin (Author's Note).

begun the war: for he perceived that none of the great nobles were prepared to desert his brother, and that even those traitors who had invited him into India would not stand by their promises, for he received no reinforcements. He began also to be afraid of his brother's far greater power and resources, and to regret that he had expended so much on an ill-conceived invasion, which was foredoomed to failure. His supplies were running low; and he began to think that he would have to retreat. He was encouraged however by the advice of Faridumcanus, his commander-in-chief, an energetic and experienced general, who bore a bitter grudge against Zelaldinus.

Soon afterwards he, Mirsachimus, learnt from spies that every thing was peaceful, and that there was no hostile movement. His brother knew of his invasion, but was undisturbed, had not taken the field, and thought as much of him as an eagle of a mosquito. For Zelaldinus pretended that he knew the reason of his brother's approach, and sent envoys to propose a friendly meeting—his real motive being to entice him further towards the capital[114] and there entrap him. Then Mirsachimus was informed that Zelaldinus had given orders for a hunting expedition, and had caused the royal pavilion to be erected. Thereupon Mirsachimus betook himself to flight by forced marches. He was obliged to swim the Sandabalis, for there were no bridges or boats available, and in so doing lost four hundred of his cavalry by drowning. Almost as many were said to have been lost at the crossings of the Bydaspes and the Indus. Such was the unhappy conclusion of an invasion inauspiciously undertaken out of express enmity to the religion of Christ.

Mirsachimus would have been well enough pleased if these disasters had marked the end of that fratricidal

---

114 Abul Fazl thus writes in this connection, "An order was given to the officers of the Indus that if the Mirza should proceed to cross the river, they were not to oppose him but to put off an engagement" (*A. N.* III 494).

warfare; but, unfortunately for himself, it was not yet finished. For Zelaldinus the Great, provoked by these injuries, cunningly ordered Xamansurus to be released, and excused this second treachery of his. He concealed from Xamansurus the fact that he had learnt all about the conspiracy, and pretended that he had imprisoned him on suspicion only. But in reality he was planning death for the traitor and war against his brother. His plans were well made; for first of all he sent a certain noble, a relation and foster-brother of his own, who, for this reason, was called Agiscocaa[115] with an army into Gangaris.[116] He carried those black standards, the sign of war to the death, which Timur the Lame—ancestor of the Mongol kings—had been wont to employ in his wars. He soon scattered the enemy, and the war concluded with their surrender, or rather execution. The King was unwilling it should appear that he had surrounded and ingloriously conquered his own brother on his own territory. He was moreover vastly superior to his brother in cavalry. So he resolved not to employ the mass of his infantry, whose numbers were almost infinite. He determined also to pay his brother Bachi in his own coin, and resolved that, since Mirsachimus had come as far as Lahorum, he himself would reach Kabul and there join battle, in his brother's own country, with him who had unprovokedly begun the war and aroused, as they say, the sleeping dog. He resolved also to pursue him if he fled.

---

115 Mirza Aziz Koka, Khan-i-Azam, son of Jiji Anagha, Akbar's nurse. He was learned and humourous and rose to a high post under Akbar and Jahangir. He fell into disgrace for some time because of his opposition to the Dagh-o-Mahilli law and to the emperor's religious innovations. But later on, after his return from Mecca where he was fleeced by the keepers of the mosque, he became an adherent of the Divine Faith. It was he who used to say that a man should have four wives—a Persian woman to have somebody to talk to; a Khurasani woman for house work; a Hindu woman for nursing children; a woman from Mawarannahr (Transoxiana) to have some one to whip as a warning to the other three. He died in 1624 (Blochmann I, p. 325).

116 Bengal.

Preparations for War against Mirza Hakim.

When all was in readiness for the campaign, the priests approached the King and declared themselves eager to share his journeys and his labours, if it so pleased him. He thanked them, and said that he had already seen ample proof of their good-will toward him, but that his opinion was that men of religion, devoted to peace and literary ease and divine meditations, should not be dragged away from their pleasant pursuits. Hence he had laid upon his mother[117] the charge of their kindly and hospitable treatment. He begged them to accept his decision without demur, and to pray for him. The priests replied that this was continually upon their hearts, and that they would gladly obey his orders, though they were greatly attached to him and desired to be with him. The next day he happened to meet the teacher of his son[118] in the school-room, and said to him, "Make your preparations, Father, for a journey; for you are going with me." Forthwith he ordered all necessary transport and provision to be immediately supplied.

The King, as was the way with him, declared that he was going hunting, and ordered his royal pavilion to be set up four miles away from the city. The following were the arrangements for the government of the empire in his absence :—His mother remained at Fathepurum with his youngest son Danialus. Agiscocanus was made the viceroy of Gangaris, and Cutubdicanus[119] of

---

[117] Hamida Banu Begum, otherwise known in history as Mariam Makani.

[118] Father Monserrate, tutor to Murad.

[119] Qutub-ud-din Khan. He was one of the Atgah Khail. After the conquest of Gujrat he was given the Sircar of Broach as Jagir. Subsequently he returned to court and was appointed ataliq to Prince Selim and received a dress of great distinction. In 1583, after the surrender of the fort of Baroda, he was killed by Mazaffar Shah III. He was one of the distinguished officers of Akbar and a commander of five thousand. He had two sons, Naurang Khan and Gujar Khan. Naurang served under Mirza Abdar Rahim in Gujrat (1584) and received Jagirs in Gujrat and Malwa. He was a commander of four thousand.

Gedrosia. The King's mother was to be superior to both of these, and was to have charge of the province of Indicum or Delinum. Ten thousand cavalry were left as a garrison in Gedrosia and twelve thousand with the King's mother. He gave Agiscocanus twenty thousand for conducting the war in Gangaris, and as auxiliaries four or five generals, with five or six thousand cavalry (or at the least four thousand) besides infantry and labourers. He left a suitable garrison in the principal cities. He took his eldest and second sons[120] with him and the priest who was the latter's tutor. He left his infant daughter[121] with her grandmother at Fattepurum. He took with him a few of his principal wives, and his older daughters. He gave instructions for a great quantity of gold and silver and of other stores to be carried along with him, by means of elephants and camels. On the day of his departure his mother set out with him, and spent two days in camp with her son, in his immense white pavilion. The priests likewise accompanied their companion to the camp, where they also spent two days with him.

The Moghal Camp.

The King ordered the camp to be made in the traditional Mongol style. The ancient custom is that the royal pavilion (which they call the Pexqhanaae,[122] or 'chief house') should be placed in a pleasant open space, if such can be found. On the right are the tents of the King's eldest son and his attendant nobles; these are placed next to the royal pavilion. On the left are those of the second son and his attendants. In ths second line are placed tents of the other royal princee

---

120 Selim (Jahangir) and Murad.

121 Father Monserrate gives her names as Ximini Beygum. Elsewhere he says that at the time of his stay at the court the Emperor had two daughters. But from this passage it appears that Akbar had more than two daughters. In fact the Emperor had three daughters: (i) Shahjada Khanum, (ii) Shahrunissa Begum, and (iii) Aram Banu Begum.

122 Peshkhana.

(if they are present) and of their attendants. If there are no princes in camp, the most important nobles (whether they owe their importance to high position or to the King's kindness and favour) have their quarters to the right and left in the second line, next to the King's pavilion. Behind these come the rest of the troops in tents clustered as closely as possible round their own officers. To avoid crowding and confusion they are divided into messes, each with its own location. A separate bazaar is established for the King and each of the princes and the great nobles, near the tent of the general who is in attendance on each. Those of the King and the princes are very large and very well-stocked, not only with stores of grain and other provisions, but also with all sorts of merchandise, so that these bazaars seem to belong to some wealthy city instead of to a camp. They are always made on one plan, so that anyone who has spent a few days in camp knows his way about the bazaars as well as he does about the streets of his own city. These bazaars are called Urdu.[123] During the advance for a campaign the artillery is grouped together in front of the camp, opposite the entrance to the royal quarters, in the broadest part of the open ground. The King had with him twenty-eight field guns, which would have been useless, however, for siege-purposes, as the largest of these guns was not as big as a hemisphere (to adopt the common military term). In this same spot a flaming torch[124] is each night erected on the top of a tall mast, to act as a guide to stragglers. If any

123 The Turki word Urdu properly means the camp of a Tartar Khan and is the original of the word *horde*. Though originally it meant a royal encampment it came to be applied to the mixed language which grew up in the court and the camp (Zaban-i-Urdu) The word is rarely used in the sense in which Monserrate uses it. Hanway (Hist Acct. I, 247) has the following interesting statement: "That part of the camp called in Turkish Urdu-Bazar or camp-market begins at the end of the square fronting the guardrooms."

124 This was known as Akasdiah (Blochmann I, p. 49-50).

tumult arises in the camp, everyone immediately rushes to this torch, as though it were the heart and head of the whole camp. During the return from a campaign the artillery is collected in the rear, behind the royal quarters. The King uses two pavilions, identical in size and appearance, which are employed for alternate marches, one being carried on ahead, while he occupies the other. These pavilions have curtains instead of walls, which divide the entrance-apartment from the rest of the tent. The area they cover is very great. The King has also a roofed building, like an ordinary house, with steps up to the roof. Such is the style and arrangement[125] of the Mongol camp.

Zelaldinus ordered Xamansurus to accompany him, in order that the latter might not increase the queen-mother's cares by attempting to destroy the empire with a revolution.

The army began to advance on February 8th, 1581.

The Advance against Mirza Hakim.

The next day the King devoted to hunting, as was his wont. Orders are always given that no one is to approach the line of march. The object of this is both to avoid crowds, to lessen the risk of treachery, and to prevent wild beasts being frightened away. These beasts are the same as those of Europe, with the exception of the blue cow, which is very similar to the red-deer, except as regards its size and the shape of its head. Zelaldinus spends enormous sums on keeping countless hunting panthers; for hounds such as those of the Gallic and Alan breeds are unknown in this country. These panthers are drown by horses, under the care of keepers;

125 Had the Emperor's mother and youngest son been present in this royal encampment, their tents would have been to the left behind of the royal pavilion. The *Ain* has it, "To the right, left and behind (the royal pavilion) is an open space of 360 yds., which no one but the guards are allowed to enter. Within it at a distance of 100 yds, to the left centre, are the tents of Maryam-Makani, Gulbadan Begum and other chaste ladies and the tents of Prince Danyal" (Blochmann I 47-48).

to the place where the game is feeding. They are blindfolded so that they may not attack anyone on the way. When they are freed, they dash ravenously upon the quarry; for they are kept in a state of starvation. The Mongols are not very fond of hawking. It is regarded, however, as a mark of royal dignity for the King to be accompanied on the march by fowlers carrying many birds on their wrists. These birds are fed on crows to save expense.

The distance of each day's march is measured with a ten-foot rod by special officers, who are instructed to follow the King closely and to measure the distance from the moment he leaves his pavilion. These measurements are afterwards found very useful in computing the area of provinces and the distances of places apart, for purposes of sending envoys and royal edicts, and in emergencies. Two hundred lengths of the ten-foot rod make what is called in Persian a 'Coroo,' but in the Indian tongue a 'Kos.' This is equal to two miles, and is the usual measure of distance.

After spending two days in camp near Fattepuram the King judged his army to be sufficiently well-equipped to advance with safety and dignity. The signal for advance was accordingly given on the afternoon of February 8th, 1581.

Order of March.

The march is conducted as follows, (I will omit ordinary details such as the signals for advancing and halting) :—Within the frontiers of the empire the army does not advance in order of battle, except for a few who are appointed to be on guard for that day. These guards, together with the rest of the royal attendants and the cavalry, follow the King at the distance of about a stone's throw, in a crescent-shaped formation. When the King halts, they await him in two bodies stretching in an unbroken line for two hundred paces on each side of the entrance to the royal head-quarters. On the one flank are the elephants, which are carefully protected by armour from being injured by missiles.

On the other flank are the mounted archers, the pikemen and the light-armed troops, for the Mongols have no heavy cavalry. As the King passes by, each man in the ranks salutes him. On the march he is followed first by the cavalry and then by the elephants. In front go drummers and trumpeters, mounted on elephants. All are silent except one, who sounds his drum at short intervals, perhaps at every tenth pace, with a slow and dignified rhythm. Mounted scouts go ahead, and drive off anyone they meet. The queens ride on female elephants, hidden from view in gaily decorated howdahs. They are guarded and escorted by five hundred old men of very dignified and venerable appearance. Great care is taken to drive away to a great distance all who are found in the line of the queens' march. The higher the rank and dignity of these old men, the more careful they are in fulfilling their functions. The ladies-in-waiting of the queens follow their mistresses on camels, under white sun-shades. There is a regular guard also in charge of the treasury, which is carried by elephants and camels. The rest of the baggage, ordinance, etc., is transported in two-wheeled carts: the King's furniture and effects being carried by mules.

For the first few days the army seemed remarkably small. However, it increased so rapidly that it soon seemed to hide the earth. It extended over the breadth of a mile and a half, covering the fields and filling the woods with a crowding multitude. No beast, if surprised on the way, could break through the ranks and escape. Even the birds, wearied by trying to fly out of danger, and terrified by the shouts of the soldiers, fall down exhausted to the earth.

The priest who was with the army was astonished by the cheapness of grain amongst so great a multitude, especially considering the number of elephants. This was achieved by the careful skill and foresight of the King himself. For he despatched agents chosen for their diligence, to the neighbouring cities and towns with instructions to bring in provisions from all sides:

and he announced to the merchants who brought grain, maize, pulse, and all manner of provisions and other merchandise into the camp, that if they would sell at cheap rates he would exempt them from imposts and taxes.

When he advanced beyond the frontiers of his empire, the King's foresight and carefulness was seen in the way in which he sent heralds to announce to the inhabitants of the country (in such a way that news of the announcement might be carried far and wide), that no one would be harmed or deported who did not take up arms: that, if they would bring supplies to the camp, they should be made to pay no imposts, but should be free to sell as they liked: that on his return after his victory they should receive his thanks and favour: but that if they disobeyed him they would be heavily punished. He bound to him the petty kings of the regions through which he passed by means of treaties, gifts and promises. All of them, terrified as they were by his huge army, could not doubt but that he would be victorious: and thus, even if at first unwilling, they obeyed him out of self-interest, especially when they saw how generous he was. Hence it was brought about that, in spite of the vastness of the army, there were no high prices and no lack of necessary provisions, even in a hostile country.

The King also saw to it, with careful diligence, that his army should not suffer for lack of water. For, since water is more plentiful near the foot of the mountains, and the hunting is better there, he ordered the army to be led towards those mountains. He overcame the difficulty of the roughness of the roads, which is due to the rocks and crags and deep torrent-beds, by sending sappers and labourers to level the way as far as possible. In charge of these was an officer who had formerly been governor of Agra fort,[126] having been

126 This was Muhammad Qasim Khan who under Akbar wa *Mir Barr-u-Bhar* (Head of the Admiralty and First Commissiones of Works). When Kamran had been besieged at Kabul in 1547r

raised to that exalted dignity from the humble position of a sapper, but who had lately fallen under suspicion of treason. He preferred the swampy glens of the mountains, as the scene of his labours, to the dry gravel of the plains, or perhaps of the amphitheatre.

In addition to this the King overcame the difficulty and danger of constructing bridges; for if these are built over a broad river-bed they are apt to be swept away by the force of the current, and hence to bring disaster upon an army crossing them. It is the custom in India to make temporary bridges of boats, which are tied together only by grass ropes. Over these boats is laid a roadway made of branches of trees, bushes and hay. The King, however, gave orders that care should be taken to see that only one type of troops or transport should approach the bridges at a time : and that the cavalry, the infantry, the camels, the other baggage-animals, the flocks and the herds, should pass over both separately and in single file, so that, if a bridge parted, the river should take no great toll of men or supplies. Wherefore on nearing a river, a small block-house was set up and occupied by the King's officers, who took care that a large number should not carelessly crowd the bridge at one and the same time, and so sink the boats. Moreover, elephants were not allowed to cross such bridges, lest they should sink them by their weight.

As soon as he entered strange territory, the King

Qasim Khan deserted to Humayun. He was the best military engineer of Akbar. The red sand-stone fort of Agra was his design and constructed under his supervision. The construction of Sabat for the siege of Chitor was under his inspection. In 1578 he was made Governor of Agra. He was implicated in the conspiracy against Akbar in 1580; but he was prudent enough to desist totally from it when the emperor detected it. In 1587 he was made Governor of Kashmir, which he conquered and kept in proper subjection and constructed some roads for military purposes. He was transferred to Kabul two years after. He was murdered in 1593. The amphitheatre mentioned just below is that in which criminals were crushed to death by elephants.

sent out three hundred scouts, in order to obviate the risk of being ambushed. These were stationed at a distance of eighteen miles from the camp in every direction, and watched for surprise-attacks or an open advance of the enemy. In narrow defiles he stationed outposts all around, thus saving the whole army from anxiety and danger by means of the service of a few men. In consequence of these precautions the army, when on the march, spread itself as freely abroad, in the search for shade and water, and slept as securely at night, as if it had been in its own country.

Discipline.

Zelaldinus rigorously enforced military discipline, and would allow no breaches of it. When the army was encamped on the bank of the Indus and, by the King's orders, a ford was being sought for, he gave instructions to a certain officer to proceed upstream, to a certain place, which he named, and try whether the river could be forded there by cavalry. The said officer went twenty-five miles up-stream, found no ford, and learnt from the inhabitants that none existed in the whole of that region. Hence, thinking it to be useless to go further, he returned to the King and told him that there was no place where the army could ford the river, but that a bridge must be built. The King asked if he had gone to the place which he had indicated to him. When he learnt that he had not gone so far, the King ordered him to be seized, dragged to the place which he had told him to go to, bound prostrate on an inflated bag of ox-hide, and launched upon the river. When the report of this was spread through the camp, almost the whole army flocked to the river-side to see this strange sight. The officer was being carried hither and thither in the middle of the river at the mercy of the current. He was weeping, imploring pardon with miserable cries, and trying to move the King to mercy. As he was carried past the royal pavilion, the King gave orders for him to be rescued from the river, entered in the inventories as royal property, exposed for sale in all the bazaars, and finally auctioned as a slave. He was bought by one of his friends for eighty pieces of gold, which were paid into the royal treasury. The King afterwards pardoned him; but he showed by this example how much store he set by military discipline and obedience. So great an army could indeed have been kept in control by no other method.

When the levy was held the King had summoned for this war fifty thousand cavalry, five hundred fighting elephants and camels, and an almost countless number of infantry. Some of the cavalry were Mongols, some Persians, others Turquimanni, Chacattæi,[127] Osbequii,[128] Arachosii,[129] Balochii, Patnanei, Indians and Gedrosii.[130] There were Musalmans and also Hindus, in whom he put a great deal of confidence. Many Parthians, Arii[131] and Paropanisadæ[132] also came to reinforce the royal army. And this was the reason why no one dared to raise a hand against Zelaldinus, or to contrive his death, even though he was reckoned an infamous outlaw by the Musalmans.

Fighting Elephants.

The methods of warfare employed by the Persians, Mongols, Chacattæi, Osbechii, and Turquimanni differ very greatly from those of the Gedrosii, or again from those of the Balochii

---

127 Chagatai. The Chagatais were that branch of the Mongols to which Akbar's ancestors belonged. They were so called because they dwelt in the regions beyond the Oxus which formed part of the territories or Chagatai or Jagatai, second son of Chenghiz Khan.

128 Uzbegs. They were a branch of the house of Juji, the eldest son of Chengiz Khan and were settled on the Chu river. Babar's struggle with the Uzbegs is a very exciting episode in Central Asian history.

129 Men from Arachosia which was the name given to the Kandahar country by the Greeks.

130 Soldiers from Gedrosia. This is the name applied loosely by Monserrate to Gujrat and probably a part of Rajputana. But Southern Baluchistan (Mekran) was called by this name by the Greeks; this is more probable here.

131 Men from Aria (Herat).

132 The Kabul Valley. Paropanisus is the Hindu Kush. (See note 227.)

or from those of the Indians. For the cavalry of the Gedrosii, who are called Rasputi,[133] and of the Indians, who are called Rati,[134] all ride on little ponies hardly as big as donkeys. Arriving in this manner at the place of battle, they dismount and await the attack of the enemy armed with short spears (or rather javelins) and light shields. The Musalmans say that these Rasputi and Rati know how to die, but not how to fight. The Balochii ride on camels and use bows and arrows. The Indians train elephants to fight. There are indeed extraordinary numbers of elephants in the royal camps and cities. They are taught to carry baggage as well as to fight, though the baggage is mainly carried by the females. Most of the males are trained for battle and are furnished with defensive armour, which they also use for offensive purposes, though indeed they are quite as dangerous without this armour. For they catch up the enemy's soldiers with their trunks, dash them down under their feet, and trample upon them. They do not cease from crushing their wretched victims till they are ground and smashed to pieces. Others they toss up into mid-air, so that they are killed by the fall; others they split in twain by placing a foot on one of their victim's legs, seizing the other leg with their trunk and tearing it forcibly upwards. The males go so violently mad for about three months of every year that sometimes they kill even their keepers; they are most useful for fighting during this period. When the time of madness is past, if they have to be enraged again on account of an impending battle, this is effected by giving them cat's flesh to eat mixed with their other food. They are kept quiet and harmless at home by the company of female elephants: for all their rage abates as soon as

---

133 Rajputs.

134 Probably Father Monserrate refers to the Marathas. In the inscriptions of Asoka the inhabitants of the Maratha country are called Rathikas (Sanskrit Rashtrikas). Possibly also he may be speaking of the Rathors.

they see a female. Some are trained to carry guns on their backs. When the black powder is ignited and the gun is discharged with a thunderous roar, the elephant does not become in the slightest terrified or unmanageable. The King directed that fifty elephants thus trained and armed should bring up the rear of the advancing army. They were under the control of Indians.

The Mongols, Persians, Parthians, Turks, Sogdians, Bachtræ and Scythians (or Tartars) all use the same fighting tactics. To pass over details, they are most dangerous when they seem to be flying in headlong riot. For, turning round on their horses, although they are going at full gollop, they fling their javelins with such deadly aim that they can transfix the eye of an enemy.

I must further remark in regard to elephants, that they become accustomed to the voice of their keepers and obey them implicitly. They can tie and untie knots, push anything, lift it, put it down again, turn it over. They can cast nooses, and unfasten them: gather up tiny straws and coins. They can even be taught to dance. In short they are ready to do anything that they are told by their keepers. They live in herds in the forests, having a sort of joint family life under the leadership of the father (as it were) of the herd and family, who is obeyed by his offspring and followed like a general in the wars which they carry on with the other elephants. When they are being hunted the herd retreats or attacks according to the command of this leader, who marches with a proud and insolent air, like a true general in the midst of his forces, and seems to threaten all who approach. He paces slowly to and fro, terrible to behold, and spares none but those who grant himself and his family feeding ground.

Zelaldinus takes as much pains to see that these herds of elephants in the forests are properly fed, as if they were droves of cattle. Every now and then he orders them to be brought before him, both that he may exhibit them as a spectacle, and that he may choose out the best of them. For the members of a herd who number about twenty, vary considerably, according to their age, in their size and the length of their tusks. Those are regarded as the best which have low hind quarters and strong legs and necks. Strabo writes that their period of pregnancy is normally eight months, but sometimes six or ten: that the mother suckles her young for six months: that the females reach maturity at ten years: that they live as long as a long-lived man: that some even reach two hundred years: that their health is delicate, and that they cannot be cured if once they become diseased. Pliny says that they choose for fighting those which excel in strength, size and vigour. Their keepers say that elephants live to two hundred years of age, reach full maturity at fifty, maintain their full strength for a hundred years, and grow old after they are over one hundred and fifty, dying at about two hundred. But they are very liable to diseases and especially to fever. If they are exposed to severe cold, or become ill of ague, they waste away and die in twenty-four hours. When they are sick they groan, toss themselves about like a sick man in his bed, weep, and allow themselves to be treated medicinally without resisting as do other animals. The females are extraordinarily timid. They are especially afraid of fire, and the noise of guns, muskets or thunder. They fly in such headlong panic as to endanger the life of anyone who is caught unawares. Their young are at one year old hardly as big as a pig. They are first submitted to training when they are ten. Those that are being trained to fight are fed by impious barbarians on human flesh, in order to make them more savage against man. Criminals are crushed to death beneath their feet. This, I think, must be the origin of the fable that elephants are incited to fight by showing them blood. For in reality they are no more moved by the sight of blood than by that of water. On account of this training they are apt to crush anyone who slips or falls down in mounting on to their backs; for they think that he has been thrown before them for that purpose. One of the priests ran a great risk of perishing in this way when compelled to cross the Narbada on an elephant. Through ignorance of their habits he was slow in mounting. For elephants bend down and allow one to mount on to their back by means of their feet and thighs, as though by a ladder. But one must mount as quickly as possible, for they try to get up as soon as they feel one's feet on them. Certain ancient writers, misled by falsehoods and absurd travellers' tales, have reported that elephants lack the joints in the legs which other quadrupeds have. But there is no truth in this.

Finally it is extraordinary and well nigh incredible what fierce enmity elephants are apt to entertain towards each other. For if two or more have conceived a mutual dislike, they attack each other on sight with great ferocity, dashing headlong together. They never look up towards, much less hurt, the keepers who ride upon them. It is hard to say what a dread elephants have of the rhinoceros, although it is a much smaller beast. Moreover the rhinoceros has an insolent contempt for the elephant. When an elephant sees a rhinoceros, he trembles, cringes, bends down, hides his trunk in his mouth, and humbly retreats until the rhinoceros has passed by. For the rhinoceros attacks from beneath, and buries the sharp horn on his nose in his opponent's belly. Meanwhile the elephant can do him no harm. The elephant sleeps with his trunk in his mouth. He is afraid of ants and still more of mice. He is as fond of water as a buffalo or a pig or any other such animal.

In order that this great animal might be tamed and trained, God—the Creator of all natural things, who made everything for the sake of man, and made man also that he might obey Himself—willed that the elephant should be weak and defenceless in two points. In the first place he cannot bear to have any of his legs tied. For if he is caught in anything, either through his own weight or through becoming entangled in a rope, he suffers the greatest pain, and kicks and struggles, most violently. Hence he is easily caught by means of a chain fastened in a pit-fall. In the second place his trunk and forehead are extremely tender. He cannot bear to be pricked on the forehead, as his skin there is very thin and weak. Hence he is easily guided and controlled by the blow of a hook. These hooks have long handles studded with nails, and are applied with great force to the elephant's forehead. If he becomes unmanageable and will not obey the hook, he is blindfolded, or his keeper fastens his foot by means of a long chain to a post buried in the ground. If he receives a blow on the trunk beneath his eyes he retires at once. If he is threatened with fire he seeks safety in a flight swifter than that of the south-east wind. For this reason, when the King is looking on at the Circus, he is protected from the elephants by a bodyguard of soldiers who carry sharp hooks fixed on long handles and bombs filled with powdered sulphur. These bombs are lighted and thrown into the arena, where they explode loudly. If an elephant attacks the King these men interpose themselves. Elephant-fights are also stopped by the same means. In order that the cavalry horses may not be terrified in battle by the huge size of the elephants, the grooms accustom them not only to the sight of the elephants but also to attacking them in a warlike fashion.

A Feudal Array.

To return to my subject—although the infantry, which has various types of arms, is entirely a fighting force,[135] yet the cavalry is regarded as in every way the flower of the army. Hence the King spares no expense in order permanently

---

[135] The Infantry were useless as a fighting force according to Irvine. "To keep night watches and to plunder defenceless people were their greatest services." True, Irvine's remarks refer to a subsequent period, but as applied to Akbar's time, they are substantially correct. Further, Irvine has it, "The high figures for Infantry as shewn in Ain-i-Akbari should commonly be accepted

to maintain an efficient, and, as far as possible, perfectly-equipped force of cavalry to guard the empire. There are forty-five thousand cavalry, five thousand elephants and many thousand infantry, paid directly from the royal treasury. In addition to these there are troops whose command is inherited by their chief officers from father to son, like an hereditary estate; these troops, consisting of cavalry, infantry, and elephant detachments, are paid by their commanding officers out of the revenues of the provinces which they hold from the King. For the ancient usage and custom still obtains that territories acquired by conquest can be granted by the King to anyone he likes, not on perpetual tenure, but to be held at his pleasure. Hence the government of such territories is vested in nobles on condition that they pay some stated tribute to the royal treasury. These nobles distribute in their turn cities, townships and villages to their companions-in-arms, and pay the royal tribute either by appropriating the revenues of certain districts to this purpose, or by direct taxation. The King takes great care, in the assignment of territories, to grant each noble a district large enough to enable him to maintain due state and dignity and to support properly his share of the military forces. Thus he, for instance, who has to maintain two brigades receives a richer province than he who has to maintain only one. The Mougols retain their ancestral system of dividing their troops into regiments, each under its own hereditary chief. In Persian these regiments are called 'Lascar.' Each regiment-commander has his own bazaar; these bazaars are called in the Tartar language 'Urdu,' or as the Portuguese pronounce it 'Ordae.' They are named after the regiment-commander, for example the "Urdu (Orda), *i.e.* regiment, of Mancinus."

---

under considerable reservation. These numbers can only represent the men called on to render strictly local duty, and they must have consisted almost entirely of villagers armed with long pikes or swords and shields, perhaps even with only an iron-bound bamboo staff" (Irvine 161-2).

Hence, although all the cities and lands in the empire belong to the King, and the whole army obeys him as commander-in-chief: yet most of the troops have their own generals and officers, to whom they are attached—as has already been pointed out—by an hereditary allegiance. This fact supplies constant cause and opportunity for conspiracy and treason. Wherefore, in order to prevent the great nobles becoming insolent through the unchallenged enjoyment of power; the King summons to court those whom he learns to have become enriched by the revenues of their provinces, and gives them many imperious commands, as though they were his slaves—commands, moreover, obedience to which ill suits their exalted rank and dignity. For he charges them with the maintenance of a certain number of elephants, horses, camels, panthers, fallow-deer and doves, which they have to produce before him on a stated day every year. When they are dismissed once more to take charge of their provinces, he does not allow them to reside for long in one place; and in order to prevent their abusing their power he himself appoints the judges and governors of the cities and towns, who have to report to him how the great nobles behave.

But let us now return to the advancing army.

Mathara.

Four days after leaving Fattepurum, Maturanum [136] was reached, a city dating from the first appearance in these regions of the superstitious religion of the Brachmanae. The city is believed to have been founded by Crustnu [137] who is also called Viznu [138]; at any rate there is no doubt that he was born in a small town near Maturanum. Temples dedicated to Viznu are to be found in many places in the neighbourhood, built in spots where the silly old-wives-fables (of the Hindus) declare that he performed some action. These fanes (or rather 'profanes') are elegantly built in the pyramidical style

136 Mathara.
137 Krishna.
138 Vishnu.

of India. Their doors face east, and the rising sun bathes the face of the idol with his light.

Krishna.

The Hindus throughout India worship Crustnu as a god. They say that he was the son of Parabrama[139] whom they call Para Maessuris[140], that is 'immortal God' and that he had two brothers, Maessuris[141] and Brama,[142] and a sister Sethis, who was born from the forehead of Paramaessur without a mother, and married Maessur, just as Juno married Jupiter. For the Evil One, in order to avoid inconsistency, implanted in the minds of the men of ancient India the same ideas about the birth of the gods as he implanted in the minds of our own foolish ancestors. For the ancients used to say that Saturn was the father of Jupiter, Neptune and Orcus, and that Minerva was born from his head. There is this difference, how ever, viz, that European poets used to give these names to the sky, to the elements and to things connected with the elements; whilst the Indians say that these are merely the ideas of vulgar people, and are due to faulty comprehension, (just as the Athenians thought that the Resurrection was some new goddess, and that Saint Paul was preaching new gods of this kind; or as the Manichaeans[143] declared that the gods were in reality the five elements mixing together by their own action; for they held that these elements were distilled one from the other, succeeding each other like the links of a chain; whence they were compelled to acknowledge that one was born from another; and this shows the folly of their notion that the elements are combined and united, as it were, in the bond of matrimony).

---

139 Parabrahma.

140 Parameshwar.

141 Maheshwar (Siva).

142 Brahma.

143 "Manichaeism is a gnostic creed named after Mani or Manes, born in Babylon in 216 A.D. During many generations it exercised very great influence both in the east and in the west" (*D.R.E.*, Vol. VIII., 394-402).

To pass on from Crustnu's parentage and the stories about his brothers—the religious preceptors of the Indians and of the Brachmanae[144] say that he was born nine times, first in the form of a sea-monster, in order that he might free his brother Brama from a sea-snail which was slaying him: secondly in the form of a tortoise, that he might support the world, which was being over-balanced by the weight of two giants: thirdly, in the form of a filthy hog, that he might purify the defiled world; fourthly in the form of a lion below his middle, and of a man above, that he might slay a giant by whom the world was being cruelly oppressed: fifthly in the form of a dwarf, who asked for alms as a beggar: sixthly in the form of a mighty warrior, who flew away to heaven as soon as he appeared on earth: seventhly he lay concealed in the belly of a shepherd who used to sell milk, and on being delivered from his belly he sold glass bangles and rings in order that he might secretly and wickedly assassinate his uncle, which he did: eighthly he became a king and reigned for 4673 years: ninthly he was born as a peasant, and slew unbelievers with the sword. He was a restless and unruly boy, a petty thief and a liar. He lived with a shepherd, and stole milk, ghi and cheese. He denied the theft when accused of it; and stole the clothes of some girls who were bathing in a river. He broke the pots and furniture of the neighbours, and let their calves out of the pens so that they might run away, thus giving trouble to the herdsmen. Beginning thus with childish mischief, he went on to steal eight wives from their husbands by force, and sixteen thousand by fraud and guile, as soon as he attained manhood (if indeed he be worthy of the name of man). The temples I have referred to preserve the memory of these wonderful deeds, lest they should be forgotten. Such is the shamelessness of the Brachmanaes, and the folly of the common people of India. How true was the saying

---

14 Brahmans.

of Cicero—the father of eloquence,—"What land is more savage than India: what land more barbarous?" True indeed; for the tales that old women tell over the fire in winter are more credible than such fables.

Since Viznu is the most famous of the Indian false gods, it follows that Maturanum has for long been the fountain-head of superstitions in India, just as Rome was in Europe. It used to be a great and well populated city, with splendid buildings and a great circuit of walls. The ruins plainly indicate how imposing its buildings were. For out of these forgotten ruins are dug up columns and very ancient statues, of skilful and cunning workmanship. Only one Hindu temple is left out of many; for the Musalmans have completely destroyed all except the pyramids. Huge crowds of pilgrims come from all over India to this temple, which is situated on the high bank of the Jomanis. The Brachmanae do not allow these pilgrims to enter the temple till they have been to the river-side and shaved off their hair and beards in the case of men and their hair and eye-brows in the case of women; then they must dip themselves several times into the river, that the water may wash away their sins: for the Brachmanae promise forgiveness of all sins to those who have bathed in this water. It is an extraordinary sight; for there are more than three hundred barbers, who very swiftly shave a huge multitude both of men and women standing up to their waists in the river, on steps which have been built there. The sexes are mixed together; but all is done with perfect modesty. For the cunning of the Evil One is such that he has put a false idea of religion into their minds: so that they regard it as a heinous offence to do anything foul or immodest in such a sacred place (as they regard it). They may not even think for a moment of any evil action whilst they are engaged in these impious ceremonies. Moreover, once they have bathed, they take the greatest care for the rest of their lives to avoid what they regard as sins. Surely it is greatly to be desired that real sins should be avoided with equal zeal and care by those who have been trained not in a false but in the true religion, and have gained true pardon by a genuinely pious ceremony—the Sacrament of repentance.

Hanuman.

About six miles from Maturanum is a shrine of Anumantus[645], near to which three hundred or more monkeys are kept in a grove, at the public expense. These monkeys, on the ringing of a bell, take up arms and, dividing into two companies, fight like gladiators, ceasing again and laying down their arms at the sound of the same bell. At the same signal they come to lunch or dine, and return to their grove after their meal, greatly to the wonder of the poor folk, who imagine this to be achieved by a divine miracle; for they are miserably deceived by the Brachmanae, so that in their folly they not only believe in but are entranced by such tricks. For the monkeys are carefully and laboriously trained to perform these actions, following the example of the older monkeys who have already been trained. But the Brachmanae declare that the monkeys do all this of their own accord, paying honour and worship to their patron Anumantus.

The following is the story of this Anumantus. He is said to have been the brother of Maessur, Crustnu and Brama, and the son of Paramaessur, who had visited his mother by means of the wind, when she was praying alone on a mountain. She afterwards gave birth to Anumantus in the form of a monkey. When he asked his mother who his father had been, they say she replied 'The wind.' But the wind was unwilling that such a miracle should remain unknown: or perhaps was afraid that it would be compelled to support the child. It was also continually busy with causing storms and sending rain, and had no settled abiding place, except when it was shut up in the cave of Aeolus. Hence it was afraid that the child would be in danger, or else it was

---

145 Hanuman.

displeased by his monkey form. At any rate it suddenly declared that Maessur and not itself was the father of the monkey. Maessur then caused it to be proclaimed to all mankind that no evil spirit should enter the house of or do any harm to him or the sons of him who should worship that monkey. They say that monkeys dart from tree to tree because Anumanthus was begotten by the help of the wind; and there is also a story that this Anumantus gave assistance to the gods when they were warring against the giants. Even Zelaldinus has a credulous belief in these fables. For, by the advice of a certain sorcerer, he inscribed the name of Anumantus amongst the titles of God.

These tales which I have been writing down are indeed unworthy of the ears of wise and pious and clean-minded men. But I have recorded them in order that my readers may feel pity for the ignorance of these poor people, and pray to God that His light may illumine their minds. I purposely pass over the stories about Ganessus,[146] who is called the door-keeper of the gods, has an elephant's face and trunk, and a protruding belly, and is said to have been born from the sweat of a goddess (if such expressions may be allowed). I also pass over Madaeus,[147] and the huge hodgepodge of other deities who are worshipped by these miserable people, and whose statues and idols are placed in their temples. I return to my main subject.

Delhi.

Delinum was reached in six days after leaving Maturanum. It is a very great and very rich city, built near the Jomanis, and has been the capital of India from the time of the Christian kings. After their fall it was the seat of the Patan kings. Emaumus,[148] the father of Zelaldinus, was very fond of it, residing here during his lifetime and meeting here his tragic death. He is buried in a tomb built by his son Zelaldinus.

146 Ganesh.
147 Probably Mahadeo.
148 Humayun.

This tomb is of great size, and is surrounded by beautiful gardens. One of his wives,[149] the mother of Mirsachimus, king of Chabulum, who was then fighting against Zelaldinus, had loved Emaumus so faithfully that she had had a small house built close by the tomb and had watched there till the day of her death. Throughout her widowhood she devoted herself to prayer and to alms-giving. Indeed she maintained five hundred poor people by her alms. Had she only been a Christian, hers would have been the life of a heroine. For, as some writer has wisely said, the Musalmans are the apes of the Christians. In many ways they imitate the piety of the Christians, though without gaining the reward of that piety; for they have wandered away from the true faith and the true charity.

Delinum is noteworthy for its public buildings, its remarkable fort (built by Emaumus), its walls, and a number of mosques, especially the one said to have been built by king Peruzius.[150] This mosque is constructed of wonderfully polished white marble, the exterior is covered with brilliant whitewash, made by mixing lime with milk, instead of water. It shines like a mirror; for this mixture of lime and milk is not only of such remarkable consistency that no cracks appear in it anywhere, but also when polished it shines most magnificently. Peruzius, who was by race a Patan, was much devoted to piety; for he gave orders that throughout his dominions, at intervals of every two miles, resting-places should be built, in which a shady tree should be planted, a well dug whence man and beast might get water, and a mosque built, where travellers might pray. He also planted trees in a long avenue on both sides of the roads, wherever there was room, in order that tired wayfarers might find shelter. He

---

149 This refers to Haji Begum and not to Mah Jujak, mother of Hakim. Haji Begum was put in charge of Humayun's tomb in Delhi (Blochmann, I 465).

150 Feroz Shah Tuglak—a king noted for his many works of public utility.

built bridges over torrents, rivers and ditches. He reduced the gradients on the roads, and paved them in soft and marshy places. In short he omitted nothing which might contribute to the public convenience and to his own magnificence. In a valley three miles from Delinum he built a wonderfully beautiful and very costly palace. On the terrace in front of it he set a solid marble column[151] all in one piece, thirty feet high and about five feet thick. He also had a subterranean passage[152] made to Old Delinum, where the Christian Kings are believed to have lived, (a distance of nearly forty stadia)[153] in order that he might withdraw unattended from the Court and from state business, as often as he had leisure, and refresh himself in the solitude of his country-seat there. Many stories are told of his kindly actions, which—if they are true—would have exalted him to heaven, if only he had been a Christian.

Delinum is inhabited by substantial and wealthy Brachmanae, and of course by a Mongol garrison. Hence its many fine private mansions add considerably to the magnificence of the city. For the neighbourhood is rich in stone and lime, and the rich men construct for themselves well-built, lofty and handsomely decorated residences. Thanks to Emaumus, who was devoted to architecture and loved fine buildings and broad roads, the streets of the city are more imposing and impressive than in other Musalman towns. They are planted down the middle with beautiful green trees which cast a grateful shade. Time fails me to describe

---

151 The reference is to the Asoka Lat.

152 "Sultan Firuz (1351-88) gave his name to a large town which he founded and by a cutting from the Jumna brought its water to flow by. He likewise built another palace at a distance of 3 kos from Firuzabad, named Jahannuma (the world-view). Three subterranean passages were made wide enough to admit of his passing along in mounted procession with the ladies of the harem; that towards the river 5 Jaribs in length, the second towards the Jahannuma, 2 kos, and the third, to old Delhi, 3 kos." (Jarret, II 279.)

153 One stadium—606 ft 9 in. English.

the lovely parks and the many residential districts on both sides of the Jomanis, which passes close by the city on the east. The parks and gardens are filled with a rich profusion of fruit and flowers; for the climate is mild, and the land around Delinum is very rich and fertile. The ruined towers and half-fallen walls of old Delinum may still be seen. They show it to have been a populous city. It is situated at a distance of about thirty-two stades from the new city, to the westward.

Two days later Sonipatum[154] was reached—a small town, but more famous than many a city on account of the swords, scimitars, daggers, poniards, and steel points for spears, pikes and javelins, which are skilfully manufactured here and exported to all parts of the empire. For there is in that region great store of iron and steel, the ore for which is mined in the neighbouring spurs of the Himalayas, and very many manufacturers of this kind of weapon live here.

Death of Shah Mansur.

On the next day the King for the third time intercepted letters written by Mirsachimus to Xamansurus; he therefore ordered Xamansurus to be thrown into prison.

The camp was next moved to Panipatum, where the inhabitants, especially the women, filled the balconies and the roofs in their eagerness to see the King. Leaving Panipatum and passing by the town of Camaris,[155] we came to a tributary of the Jomanis. The infantry crossed this by a stone bridge, without any of the crowding or tumult which sometimes occurs in narrow places. The elephants, camels and cavalry, in accordance with the orders which had been given to them, crossed by a ford.

Three days later Tanissaris[156] was reached—a town of Brachmanae and merchants—and then Baadum,[157] where Xamansurus was hanged, thus reaping the fitting reward of his faithlessness and treason. The execution was

---

154 Sonepat, 28 miles N. W. of Delhi (See *Note* 100.)

155 Karnal.

156 Thaneshwar.

157 Shahabad (See *Note* 100)

carried out as follows: The King ordered the officers of his bodyguard and those of the corps of executioners, and a few prominent generals, together with Xamansurus, to halt at Baadum. He then told Abdulfasilius to recite in the presence of these witnesses all the benefits which the King had conferred on Xamansurus from his boyhood. After this he was confronted with the proofs of his ingratitude and treason. The criminal was convicted and condemned to be hanged on the evidence of specimens of his autograph-correspondence with Mirsachimus, which were produced and shown to him. Abdulfasilius then exhorted him to bear manfully the punishment he had so richly deserved. This was all carried out in such a way that those who were present were convinced of the justice of the measures taken by the King against Xamansurus, and were incited to do their duty better in future. Abdulfasilius, who acted in this matter for the King, sustained his part to perfection. After the execution they all returned to the camp, which was not far distant. The King's mournful countenance plainly showed how much pained he had been by the wretched man's fate. However, the whole conspiracy was at once stopped by the execution. The news was received by the King's followers with loud acclamations and the whole camp showed by its joy how much it approved of the villain's punishment. There being no longer any fear of internal sedition, the result of the war became a foregone conclusion, as was soon proved by the success which—through the grace of God—followed the King's arms. As soon as he heard of the execution, Mirsachimus, repenting of what he had done, began to think about asking for peace.

About this time the army was compelled to halt for some time owing to a violent tempest, which rendered the roads impassable by reason of mud and sudden torrents. As soon as the weather cleared, the advance was resumed; and to the east the snow-covered Himalaya mountains were seen gleaming white. The inhabitants of that region call this range Cumaum.[158] From the

158 Kumaun Range.

mountains blew a cold wind. The Hindus who inhabit Cumaum do not own allegiance to Zelaldinus, and are protected by exceedingly thick forests. The source of the Jomanis is said by the inhabitants to be situated in this district on the side of the mountains which looks westward towards the district of Delinum. The source of the Ganges is however on the opposite, *i.e.*, eastward, slope of the mountains. To adopt the language of geographers, it is in the same latitude (as the source of the Jomanis) but is 280½ miles eastward in longitude.

Next, Ambala was reached. On a large plain near to this city Emaumus, the father of Zelaldinus, caught the Patanaei, who had been repulsed[159] from before the town of Sarindum (or Ceynandum). Having been entrapped in a deep and precipitous ravine they were put to the sword.

Religious discussions.

The priest who was with the army endeavoured to do his duty by becoming acquainted with, and being of some service to, those, whether Musalmans or Hindus, with whom his lot was now cast: for such was the rule of his life and the practice of the Society. His arguments led a certain old man, who was said to be an astrologer and was known and favoured by the King for this reason, to confess that the law of Christ excels that of Muhammad (which seems an absurdity to the Musalmans). For this old man declared in the course of controversy that in Hell many devils obey the law of Muhammad, but some disbelieve. The priest asked whether there are any Christian devils? The old man replied, 'No indeed: for they all bear eternal enmity towards Christ; whereas, though some hate Muhammad because he destroyed the worship of idols, others are his followers because he sanctions unbridled lust and other crimes. All the devils hate Christ because he forbade both idolatry and lust.'

Inspired by curiosity many Hindus also came to

159 This alludes to the events of 1555, when Sikandar Shah was defeated by Humayun before Sirhind.

see the priest. He set before these a parable to admonish them of their folly in not accepting the messages of God (*e.g.* the teaching of the Christian Priests) regarding Salvation and Life, and in holding absurd and incredible the doctrine of the Trinity, although they themselves believe in many silly old-wives' fables. For instance, they hold that men can be created out of flowers, which flowers are not only beautiful, and pure white in colour, but also have red cheeks, great wisdom and many virtues, and are produced in Europe without father, mother, birth or any means of origin.

Moreover, a certain Musalman, who came with religious inquiries, was convinced by an illustration that the nature of God may be believed to be that of one nature and substance but three persons. For, just as no one can deny that a single human personality consists both of body and soul, which are diverse, so no one should refuse to believe that three persons may form one nature and substance.

By the express order of the King himself no fatigues of travel were allowed for one single day to interrupt the education of the prince.

Sirhind.

Ceynandum is two days' journey distant from Ambala. Camp was pitched in the eastern outskirts of the city, which is said to owe its name to the following circumstance. It is recounted that in this place a certain king fought with and vanquished a lion. The town is also called Sarindum,[160] because it is situated on

---

160 Major-General Cunningham in 'The Ancient Geography of India,' pp. 145-6, remarks: "The name of Sirhind or Frontier of Hind is popularly said to have been given to the city when it was the boundary town between the Hindus and the Mahomedan kingdom of Ghazni and Lahor. But the name is probably much older, as the astronomer Baraha Mihir mentions the Sairindhas (people of Sirindh) immediately after the Kullutas (people of Kulu) and just before Brahmapura which, as we learn from Hiouen Thsang, was the capital of the hilly country to the north of Hardwar."

the frontier of the provinces of India and of Lahorum.[161] For Sarahat means frontier; and thus the name of the city signifies the frontier of India. The city is of great size and is divided into separate quarters, in which respect it resembles Memphis in Egypt, which is commonly called Cayrum. At Sarindum is a very famous school of medicine, from which doctors are sent out all over the empire. Bows, quivers, shoes, greaves and sandals are also made here and exported by traders to all the cities of the empire. Sarindum is situated in a very broad plain, beautified by many groves of trees and pleasant gardens. This plain is dry; but the inhabitants have met the difficulty of lack of water by the making of a deep artificial lake on the southern side of the city. Care is taken to fill this lake during the rainy season by means of irrigation channels. In the middle of the lake stands a tower, which is open to the public for their enjoyment. From this tower there is a pleasant prospect over the lake and the surrounding parks and gardens. Setting out from Ceynandum the army encamped at Paelum,[162] where the King was informed that Mirsachimus had fled. The King was so pleased by this good news that he ordered it be told to the priest who was in camp. On the following day the priest congratulated the King with the greatest delight, and the King showed that he was pleased by his congratulations. Up till then the King had seemed to be constantly frowning with deep anxiety; but after receiving this good news his cheerful expression showed that he had laid aside all his care. Moreover he went on several pleasure excursions in his two-horse chariot.

Passing by Machivara,[163] that is, 'the village of

---

161 This country was formerly callad Arachosia) *Author's Note*).

162 Pæl, a mahal of Sirhind (Ain, Vol. II, 295; III, 69).

163 Machiwara. 30'55° N 76° 12' E. It is in the Ludhiana district. It was the scene of Humayun's defeat of the Afghans in 1555.

The Sutlej

fishes' the army encamped on the bank of the Satanulga[164], which was called by the ancients the Zaradrus. A halt was necessary while a wooden bridge was being built. The source of this river is not far distant from that place. The King next ordered the army to be led towards the Himalayas, from which the Zaradrus flows towards the west, joining the Indus. This river contains crocodiles, or water-lizards, of the girth of a barrel. They are called '*cissares*,' that is 'three-headed'. They have six feet, on which they crawl: and they swallow men unawares from below when they are swimming in the water. They seize by the foot, and drag down under the water, oxen and buffaloes and sheep and other animals whilst drinking at the side of the river, The ignorant people call this same river 'Machivara' from the neighbouring village, or 'Ludiana' from the town of Ludianum. The latter place is about 26 miles downstream from Machivara along the direct road to Basilipolis [165] (by which flows a stream whose water is a deadly person), Govindivicus and Lahurum. However, the army left this road on the left-hand; and after reaching the Zaradrus at Machivara followed the river up towards the mountains. Here the camp was pitched in a rough and very cold country.

On the fifth day after leaving the Zaradrus a certain stronghold of the Patanaei was reached, which is called Dungarii, that is 'two hours'. Here the King ordered fifty pieces of gold, to be given to the Priest, in order that he might distribute them to the Christians. This was to signify the joy of Zelaldinus at having on the previous day received express despatches from Mirsachimus, in which he besought pardon for his treachery, prayed that the horrors of war might be

---

164 Sutlej. Monserrate was of course seriously misled in declaring its source to be near at hand.

165 Sultanpur Lahori (*Author's Note*). Sultanpur (31° 13' N and 75° 12' E) was founded in the 11th century, by Sultan Khan Lodi, a general of Mahmud Ghaznavi.

averted, and begged that the King who enriched others with the grant of provinces would allow himself to remain in possession of his kingdom. He seemed, however, not so much to pray for forgiveness as to demand a gift; and therefore Zelaldinus continued the advance. Fording a small river,[166] the army marched for two days along the Bibasis,[167] which is now called the Beas, searching for a ford which the elephants could cross and for a narrow place in the river, where a wooden bridge could be erected. When the scouts found a suitable place for their purposes, the camp was pitched there.

The Beas

The King hastened with a few chosen cavalry to Nagarcottum[168] in order to help a certain petty king, who had been driven out by his son and had begged for assistance. When the usurper heard of the arrival of Zelaldinus he hid himself, with his band of soldiers, in a fastness situated amongst precipitous and inaccessible mountains, and hence the King had to return to camp without fulfilling his errand. This district produces in abundance those fruits and crops which are characteristic of Spain and Italy, but which are not found elsewhere in India.

Nagarkot

On the next day the army crossed the Bibasis by a wooden bridge, and advanced nearly ten miles, to the neighbourhood of the town of Pachangarum in the district of Peytanum. The chief of this district is Biliballus,[169] the King's Lord Chamberlain, who enter-

---

166 Not far from this river a terrified bull suddenly made a fierce attack upon a poor woman and dashed her to the ground. (*Author's Note*).

167 Beas or Hyphasis

168 Nagarkot or Kangra.

169 Birbal or Bir Bar. His real and original name was Mahesh Das, a Brahman by caste. He became a convert to Akbar's Divine Faith. He was well known for his jokes and *bon mots* which secured him the royal favour; and the Emperor conferred on him the title of *Kabi Rai* or Poet Laureate. He was

tained Zelaldinus to a rich banquet on his return from the expedition to Nagarcottum or so it was reported. This district, which is an open one, lies about forty-five miles from the Himalaya range.

Kalanaur

The next day's march brought the army to Calanurum.[170] Near this town Zelaldinus had routed the Patanaei,[171] vanquished Beyramcanus,[172] and been hailed king of Lahorum. He had received the sceptre and other marks of royalty in a very large and beautiful park, which is near the city. In this park the former kings of Lahorum had been wont to receive their title in the same way. Calanurum stands on a small river which flows into the Bibasis. It is the stream which Strabo, as has been noted above, calls the Hypanis: and on its further bank he says that Alexander the Great stopped his march, not daring to advance beyond this point. The Roman authors say that Calanurum is a large city: and indeed the ruins and fallen walls show clearly that it once was so; but in our time it seems absurd to call this paltry place Calanurum.

Nagarcottum is 18 miles from Calanurum. The

---

killed in the Yusufzai expedition in the 34th year of the reign. Badaoni shows unseemly rancour toward the Raja for he, as all pious Musalmans, thought that Akbar's deviation from orthodoxy was to a great extent due to the influence of the Brahman courtier. Badaoni calls him Brahmadas, probably because when he was in the Jaipur service he used to sign his compositions as *Brahm Kabi*.

Above, 'Peytanum' will be Pathankot

170 Kalanaur in the Gurdaspur District of the Punjab. Here Akbar was planning operations against Sikandar Shah when Humayun died. The formal enthronement of Akbar took place there in a garden (Feb. 1556). Kalanaur seems to be corruption of the Hindu name Kalyanpur.

171 Pathans. The author seems to refer to the campaign against Sikandar Sur.

172 Bairam Khan. The reference here may be to the rebellion of Bairam Khan (1560); but he was not defeated by Akbar himself, but by Atgah Khan. Akbar no doubt was on his way to the Punjab. Father Monserrate's ideas about Bairam Khan are confused.

former name signifies the citadel or fortress of Nagaris. Its chief, against whom Zelaldinus had just led an expedition (in answer to the petition of his father, whom he had driven out), harried, burnt and devastated the district of Calanurum, in order to show his contempt for the King.

Tibetans.

Eastward of this fortress the valleys of the inner Himalayas are inhabited by a savage and barbarous people, called the Bothi or Bothentes.[173] They have no king, but dwell in villages by clans. They clothe themselves as far as possible in a fabric of felt such as is used for hats. This is sewn tightly on to their bodies, and is never taken off again till it is worn out or has been so rotted away by sweat that it falls to pieces of itself. On their heads they wear a conical cap, made of the same kind of felt. They never wash their hands, faces or feet. They give as their reason for this the pretext that it is sacrilege to befoul with dirt so clear and beautiful an element as water, and one which when drunk quenches thirst. They have only one wife; and as soon as they have had two or three sons by her they return to bachelor life. If either husband or wife dies, the other remains unmarried until death. They are greatly opposed to idolatry, and are governed by astrologers, or rather magicians. When one of them dies, these magicians are summoned and after consulting their books of magic decree what must be done. If the magicians tell them to devour the corpse, to throw it into a stream, to burn it, to expose it that it may be devoured by birds or beasts, to hang it up in a tree, or to retain it for future disposal in some other way, their directions are at once obeyed. They use human bones for domestic utensils, the skull for a cup, the shoulder-

---

173 Tibetans. Monserrate gives a similar account of the Tibetans in the *Account of Akbar* (*J.A.S.B.*, Vol. VIII, 1912, Pp. 218-20). According to Peruschi the Tibetans used to come to Kalanaur to sell their products. Father Hosten identifies Monserrate's name 'Bothentes' with the Bhotias,

blades for plates, the thigh and arm-bones for sheaths of daggers or other weapons. They tip their arrows with the harder portions of the joints and ribs. Their colour is white, their stature medium, their hair brown, their faces ruddy. Many of them have fine eyes, round in shape. They are armed with short swords, bows and arrows. They wear blankets made out of camel's wool, of which they have an abundance. For purposes of sale they also make shawls of the finest wool. Such articles of trade they bring to Nagarkottum, and sell them. The snows on the slopes of the Himalayas towards India lie unmelted throughout the year, except in the months of June, July, August and September, in which they are melted by the extreme heat of the sun in that region. These Bothi are very pious and merciful. They give alms generously, and entertain travellers (so the Joges say) very kindly and hospitably. They are peaceful and hate war. Their country is fertile in wine, wheat and many European fruits. There are also abundant herds of cattle, sheep, camels and wild asses. There is also said to be a kind of wild sheep, as large as a goat, which lacks joints in its legs and thighs, and thus progresses by leaps only. Hence it is easily captured, and yields in captivity a very fine quality of wool, finer indeed than silk. From this wool the shawls mentioned above are woven. The things reported of these people sound incredible, especially those relating to their bachelor habits. The Fathers, however, made very careful enquiries regarding the reliability of the information given in that neighbourhood to the Priest who went thither with the army, and it was proved by the testimony of many witnesses that everything that is reported about this people is true. Hence the Priests were much inclined to run the risk of endeavouring to penetrate those regions in the guise of traders. The sequence of events and the return of the mission compelled them, however, to give up this idea. These people are said to inhabit the Himalayan heights from Nagarkottum northwards as far as the country of the

Caspirii.[174] They are said also to have a language of their own. They seem to be the people whom Pliny calls the Casiri[175] when he says 'The Indian tribe of the Casiri, who dwell in the interior towards the land of the Scythians, still eat human flesh.'

The Ravi.

Advancing from Calanurum, the army crossed the river Baohi[176] which is also called the Adris, by means of a bridge which was built for the purpose. The river Cingarous[177] was next crossed, close to the foot-hills of the Himalayas. Thence, along a rough and dangerous road, with constant steep rises and descents amongst marshy glens and overhanging crags, the town of Samba[178] was at length reached. This town is situated in a strong position on the slope of the Himalaya, and belongs to a tribal chief, who owns allegiance to Zelaldinus. In its fertile soil and its abundant population it resembles Nagaracottum. The inhabitants, with the exception of the Moghul garrison, are of the heathen religion of the Brachmanae. The climate is European in type, for this region stretches northward from the thirtieth to the thirty-second degree of latitude. The majority of the inhabitants are tall and thin; they are light-brown in colour, and wear their hair and beards long.

The Chenab.

Advancing from Samba, the army encamped on a green and pleasant plain beside the river Nanis, which flows into the Sandabalis four miles from Samba. The region from the Adris to the Sandabalis, lying as it does between two rivers, excels all others in the north for beauty

---

174 Obviously Kashmir is meant. Kasyapapur, the city of Kasyapa, is the original Sanskrit designation of Kashmir. (Ptolemy pp. 108-9).

175 For the cannibalistic habits of the Casiri, see M'Crindle's *Ancient India as described in Classical Literature*, p. 113.

176 Ravi.

177 Arrian mentions the Saranges as one of the tributaries of the Ravi.

178 Chamba.

and fertility, for the variety of its gardens, and for the number of its hamlets and villages. On the next day the Sandabalis was crossed, but with a good deal of difficulty. For the river would brook no bridge, and a number of those who tried to ford it were drowned. The King and many others crossed in a boat. The whole army was delayed for three days during the crossing. For there were extraordinarily few boats to be had, although the King ordered any available to be brought from the neighbouring villages and towns. The reason for this lack of boats was (we were told) the fact that Mirsachimus, in order to delay the King's pursuit, had after crossing the river ordered all the boats in which his army had crossed to be broken to pieces and burnt: for he knew that he would be much delayed by the two remaining rivers, and he was afraid lest he should be attacked by his brother's advance-guards before he could make good his flight. He resolved therefore to counterbalance these future delays by this means. There were lost in the crossing of this river about four hundred men of all ranks, who could not swim. It is wonderful how large a body of water there is in this river considering that its source is not far distant from that place. It is moreover divided into three branches by obstacles in its course. Two of these branches there surround an island, which lies in the broad bed of the river. This stream, whose current is not rapid, flows after many meanderings into the Bydaspes.

The King ordered the army to be led along the bank of the Sandabalis to Qhunia (that is, the place of blood,) and Saddaris,[179] in order to obtain good water. These two towns are three miles apart. Half way between them he altered the direction of his march towards the Bydaspes; for this is the shortest and best route. Praise should be given to Zelaldinus' carefulness and foresight in giving such earnest attention to the safety of his army that he consulted its interests not only in

179 Sodhra (?)

the matter of water supply and of cheap corn, but also in the passage of rivers.

In spite of all his care, however, the army suffered severly from thirst on the first day's march away from the Sandabalis. This march was seven miles in length ; but on the next day, in order that the same trouble might not recur, the King extended the march to fifteen miles, (although a shorter route was taken than had been originally intended) : and encamped by the Bydaspes, where he granted the army eight days' rest. Each day he took his sons out hunting. Meanwhile a bridge was being built over the river, which has a broad and deep bed, and is unfordable even to elephants. It cannot even be crossed by swimming in the case of cavalry and infantry. Hence it was essential to build a strong bridge. This river flows into the Indus, and forms the frontier of the kingdom of Lahorum. The original inhabitants of this kingdom were the Getae,[180] whom the ancients called Geretae. They regard it as a sin to cut the hair or the beard, since these are the chief and distinctive signs of manhood.

Having crossed the Bydaspes, the army encamped at the foot of mount Balnatinus,[181] an outlying portion of the Himalaya mountains. These mountains run in an unbroken line from Delinum as far as this, and are everywhere called the Himalaya by the inhabitants. But from this point the range bends gradually westwards, and becomes more accessible and open. Its

---

180 Jats. Payne in his *History of the Sikhs* writes, "The origin of the Jats is uncertain. Some writers affirm their Scythian extraction, and hold that they were the descendants of the Getae, one of the many Scythian tribes who swarmed into India before the Christian era. Beyond the fact that many of the Punjab tribes are of undoubted Scythic origin there seems little to support this view. The Jats themselves claim to be derived from the same stock as the Rajputs, and point to Central Asia as the cradle of their race."

181 *Balnat qua thile* (*Author's Note*). *i.e.*, the Tila (hill) of Balnath (see note 186).

name also is altered; and it is called by the inhabitants of that region 'Casp' or 'Cas.' The mountaineers themselves are called Caspirii by European geographers; but by the natives of that and the neighbouring lands they are named Casmirini—a title formed by combining two words, viz., 'Cas' (the name of the mountains) and 'Mir,' which means a governor. Hence is derived the name 'Casmir.' The inhabitants of the plains are called Gaccares.

The Kashmiris and Gakkars

The Casmirini or Caspirii were conquered by the Musalmans[182] one hundred years ago, and were compelled to adopt their laws and system of government. But all the inhabitants of that region say that long ago they were, by race and custom, Jews. If questioned on this point they acknowledge that this was their origin. Their type of countenance, general physique, style of dress and manner of conducting trade are all similar to those of European Jews. For those that live in Lahorum deal in rubbish, cast-off clothes, ironmongery, shoes, armlets, bolts and bars, and all manner of second-hand goods. Others must judge whether there can be any truth in the following story, which has reached my ears in a round about manner. All classical scholars agree that Alexander the Great transported Jews to the Caspian mountains where he left them in captivity.[183] According to Strabo he also invaded India as far as the Bibasis. At any rate he reached the Caspus, or Caspian, range. Now the nature of that region is such that it can be aptly described as having gates, since there is only one entrance to it. For the mountains fall back and leave a gap which, seen from afar, has a distinct resemblance to a gate. Now the priests made very careful investigations as to whether or not the Caspirii were Jews. They discovered that by race they clearly

---

182 It was early in the 14th century that the Mahomedans became rulers of Kashmir. The first Muslim king was Shah Mirza, formerly minister of the Hindu Raja.

183 Lit. shut up (in prison)—Tr.

were Jews, but had become Musalmans by religion one hundred years ago. With regard to their mountainous country, although the ascent is rough and difficult and provides the inhabitants with a useful means of defence especially against cavalry: yet at the top there is a level and fertile plain. I am well aware that, in the opinion of some, Alexander is held to have transported the Jews to that district of the Caspian mountains which is near the Caspian Sea. I do not question their opinion. On such an evenly-balanced point I will adopt Terence's saying, 'If they say so, I say so: If they say no, I say no.'

Now the Gaccares,[184] who inhabit the plains hereabouts, are Musalmans. They are warlike, of medium stature, sturdy, and much inclined to theft and brigandage on account of the character of their country. They are hated by all; being notorious for the crime of man-stealing. They lie in wait for, and intercept, free travellers, shave their heads, ham-string them, take them to Persia, and there sell them as slaves. If any other member of their tribe arrive whilst they are in the act of capturing or shaving their wretched victim, the new-comer is made a sharer in the price obtained for him. Their capital[185] city is called Ruytasium. It has an exceedingly strong citadel, fortified after the European fashion; by the side of this flows a stream which runs into the Bydaspes. The town is situated on the crest of a ridge which descends westwards, to a

---

184 According to the author of the *Census Report of the Punjab for 1881*, the Ghakkars were emigrants from Khorasan who settled in the Punjab about 300 A.D. and were Shiahs by religion. Delmerick writes, "Whether the Ghakkhars have sprung from the Grekoi whom Alexander the Great located in Pothwar or are Hindus converted to Mahomedanism or are, as they themselves assert, the descendants of Persian Kings, it is impossible now to speak with certainty." (*J.A.S.B.* Vol. XL, Part I, 1871, p. 67).

185 The Gakkhars often changed their capital, it appears. At first they had their capital at China Ponir in the Jammu district, whence it was shifted to Dangali on the right bank of the Jhelum. (*Ibid* Pp. 71 and 73).

distance of about nine miles, from the Balnataeus range. The ridge is barren and rocky, but well-suited to defence.

This Balnat Thile,[186] that is crag of Balnath, is very high and steep. Ascent is difficult, and cannot be accomplished on horse-back. On the crest itself is a level space; on this are built several small dwellings, in which it is said that a certain Balnat used to live, with his sister. He was the founder of a sect of which the following are the customs. For the space of two years before novices are admitted to full membership and allowed to wear the peculiar dress of the sect, they have to act as servants to others who live in that place, helping the cook, cutting the wood, bringing it to the kitchen, pasturing the flocks and herds, fetching water (a very arduous task, especially in summer), and acting as table-servants to the full members, of whom about three hundred are always to be found living here. If the novices perform these duties diligently and carefully for two whole years, they are then invested with

---

186 Hill of Balnath, the word Tila (Thile) meaning in Gakkhar dialect, a hill. It is said that Guru Goraknath settled at the Tila in the Tretayuga, after Ramchandra, and adopted Balnath as his disciple. Balnath underwent penance on the hill; hence it was called Balnath Tila. Cunningham in his *Ancient Geography of India* writes, "The name of Balnath is most probably even older than the time of Alexander, as Plutarch relates that when Porus was assembling his troops to oppose Alexander, the royal elephant rushed up a hill sacred to the sun." The sun was worshipped under the form of Balnath. The ancient temples on the hill were all destroyed by the Mahomedans. The existing temples were built in the reign of Raja Man. Sir E. D. Maclagan (See *Census Report of the Punjab 1891*, p. 117) is of opinion that the Jogis of the Tila are not a very estimable body, though they enjoy a considerable reputation. At any rate in the time of Akbar the devotees of Hindustan regarded the Tila with great veneration, and Jogis especially used to make pilgrimage to it. Some interesting details will be found in the *Glossary of the Tribes and Castes of the Punjab*, Vol. I, p. 289. (See also Jarret II, 315; Cunningham's *Ancient Geography of India* 164-5; Oman's *Mystics, Ascetics and Saints of India*, pp. 264-9; *A.N.* III, 513-4).

the garments of the sect. But first they must promise to keep themselves for ever pure and chaste, and to do nothing contrary to the dignity and rules of their order. The garments mentioned above are a cloak, a turban and a long dress coming down to the feet (similar to that which was vulgarly called by the ancients the 'toga harmiclausa,' and which some in our time call the 'scapulare'). These are all dyed with a species of red chalk, so that they look as though painted red. Those who have been invested with these garments may go where they will and live by begging. If they do anything unworthy, they are dismissed from the sect. They have one leader, who, once he has been raised to that dignity, may never leave the hill. He has also with him a number of old men to help him by their advice and authority. When the leader dies, these old men elect his successor. The mark of this leader's rank is a fillet; round this are loosely wrapped bands of silk, which hang down and move to and fro. There are three or four of these bands. It is absurd enough that they should adopt this sign for their high priests. By this alone he whose heart has been enlightened by the least gleam of the true faith, can clearly recognize the vanity of their superstition. For although they are not enslaved to the superstitious beliefs either of the Musalmans or of the Hindus, they have others of their own not less full of absurdity and ignorance. For they honour a certain Balnat as though he were a prophet and servant of God. He lived as a hermit on this mountain with his sister three hundred years ago, or so they say. Since then he has been no more seen: but he is still an object of universal reverence, since it is said that he still lives and shows himself in various places and under various forms, like Prometheus, and hangs strips of cloth on the tops of trees or in high and precipitous places, which are signs of his having been there. They say that he taught the right way of worshipping God, namely that at dawn all should turn towards the east, and greet the rising sun with the concerted sound of flutes and conches. They do the same in the evening, facing westwards. When they eat, they give thanks, as it were, to God. Balnath laid upon his followers no restrictions with regard to food or human society. Their mode of living, when at home, is exceedingly frugal: for they eat only cooked lentils and ghi. There are two orders amongst them, one of married people and the other of celibates. The former wear a shorter dress. The latter only differ from the former in their view of chastity and in their duty of teaching. They give oracles ostensibly from Balnat, and are devoted to divination, so that they may more properly be called magicians than religious teachers. Our Priests considered Balnat himself to be a devil, since he deceived the ancestors of these people by false miracles, and still shows himself to them from time to time. For the Evil One has beguiled these foolish Hindus into calling and worshipping himself by many names which end in 'nat': such as Manquinat, Septenat, Jagarnat, etc. In honour of Balnath travellers hang strips of cloth on trees along the road-side.

At the time that Zelaldinus visited this place the high priest was an old man who was said to be 200 years of age. In reality he can hardly have been 80. For this type of man is accustomed to claim that he is of very great age, in order to impress the common people, as though virtue and sanctity could be measured by the number of years a man has lived. When they heard of the King's approaching visit, a huge number of the members of that sect gathered at this place, many of whom, in order to show off their sanctity, betook themselves stark naked to certain caves which either nature or the art of man has made there. Many people did reverence to these naked ascetics and proclaimed their sanctity abroad. They are however extremely greedy of money. All their trickery and pretended sanctity is aimed at the acquisition of gain. The King, who has a leaning towards superstition in all its forms, was conducted by the Balnataei to the place where Balnat is said to have lived. Thereupon he did reverence to the place and to the prophet with bare feet and loosened hair.

Rohtas.

While the King was dallying with Balnat, the army was halted for four days on the plain below. Thence it marched, in two days, to Ruytasium, and encamped on the bank of the stream which almost surrounds that fortress. Josephus, governor of the fortress, who had defended it so stoutly against the attacks of Mirsachimus that the latter had not dared regularly to besiege it, entertained Zelaldinus at an exceedingly sumptuous banquet. After Ruytasium the line of march led along the bank of the stream. Here the rashness of some of the cavalry and of those who rode upon camels and elephants and who did not know the right path, led them into considerable danger. For the sand of the river bed absorbs the water, so that all appears flat, solid and dry. However, if any one goes into such a place, he sinks down and sticks fast, and the more he strives to get out the more deadly is his danger of being swallowed up. Thus the troops aforesaid, thinking there could be nothing to be feared in a level plain, rushed into the gravest danger.

An Obelisk.

On the sixth day a large plain was reached over rough roads, through narrow defiles and across numerous rivers. The sky was heavily overcast, and the air sultry. There were thunder-storms, swift whirl-winds, and extraordinary floods of rain. In the middle of the plain was an obelisk[187] (or rather a mound) of great size. It is in ruins, on account of its great age; but some parts of it are perfect and show elegant and artistic workmanship. Ramxandus,[188] a Hindu king of a thousand years ago, is said to have set it up, as the boundary-pillar of his kingdom. This obelisk stand on

187 The reference is to the Manikyala Tope.

188 Ramchandra. This statement has no basis in historical fact.

a square base seven feet high and ten feet broad from the edge to the foot of the obelisk itself. This base can be ascended by means of steps at the sides: and these steps are set into the base, so as to be enclosed on each side by walls. The height of the obelisk is twenty feet and its diametre ten. It is perpendicular for about seven feet, this portion being distinguished from that above by its massive circular shape. At the top it slopes to a blunt point, which is rounded and very cleverly executed. The whole is built of large hewn stones, without cement or bitumen to unite them.

Next the army halted at the town of Rhavadum,[189] whose inhabitants, like those of the rest of this district, are Gaccares. The nearer one gets to Indoscythia the fiercer do these people become. They exchange men for horses, and have a proverb 'Slaves from India, horses from Parthia.' The country from Ruytasium to the river Indus is dry and barren, the climate being as harsh and dangerous as the character of the inhabitants. These latter, though born on this side of the Indus, differ markedly, both in colour and speech, from the true Indians. For their complexion is light and their stature short. They have broad shoulders and sturdy legs. From chin to forehead the shape of their heads is low, but they have broad cheek-bones and foreheads. Their faces are covered with wrinkles; and their appearance clearly indicates that they are hostile rather than hospitable to strangers.

Hazara.

From this place, after crossing a small river, the army reached Gagaris,[190] which is situated on a steep and narrow ridge, with three peaks. Beyond Gagaris a branch of the Indus was crossed, which rejoins the Indus a little lower down, thus forming a broad island, which was called by the ancients Prasiane[191] on account of its

---

189 Riwat.

190 Gagar.

191 In the time of the Macedonians the Indus bifurcated above Aror, to run for about a distance of 2 degrees in two beds

greenness, I suppose. Camp was pitched on the bank of the Indus in a valley of the district of Hazara.[192] The island mentioned above belongs to a clan of Patanaei who are called Delazacquii.[193] This region is milder and more fertile than the one just traversed. For though it has no fine trees or gardens, the soil is rich and deep, bearing abundance of corn, pulse and grass for grazing. Hence it has many flocks and herds, and abundance of ghi and milk. The character of the inhabitants is gentle and friendly. They are employed in tilling the ground, in pasturing their herds and flocks, and in breeding cattle. Unlike the Gaccares they live in villages. Their language is that of other Patanaei, namely Pastoum.[194] Its sound is like that of Spanish, and—what is more to be wondered at—it has some of the same words.

Religious Discussions.

The priest who was with the army, anxious lest the King should forget what he had learnt about Christianity, wrote a brief summary of the events of Christ's passion, and handed it to the King whilst he was in a state of delight owing to the enemy's flight. Zelaldinus, as though in a fit of absent-mindedness, ordered Abdulfasilius to read it carefully to him. While the reading was going on, he asked many questions, especially the following :—"Why did not the Lord Jesus, who was so anxious that the Jews should believe in him and be saved, accept the challenge of these same Jews, when he was on the cross, 'If thou art the Son of God, descend now from the cross and we will believe in thee?'" The priest gave the following brief reply,

---

which enclosed between them the large island called by Pliny Prasiane, the Prarjuna of the inscription of the Allahabad column. It now runs at that point in a single stream. (Ptolemy p. 83).

192 Hazara, now included in the North-West Frontier Province.

193 The Delzacs settled in the Peshawar valley in the 14th century A.D., and seem to have been, like the Ghakkars, friendly to the house of Babar.

194 Pashtu.

though there was of course much more that might have been said on the subject:—"By the decree of God men can only be justified by faith. Abraham believed in God against hope, when he was ordered to offer up Isaac, although he had received a divine promise that from Isaac should his posterity be descended. For he laid his son on the pyre, nothing doubting that God would fulfil what he had promised: and by this action he pleased God, and was justified. If Christ had come down from the cross, this proof would have removed the possibility of faith, by which alone must men be guided to the gaining of salvation and eternal life. Nor could the will of God and His everlasting law be broken at the request of a few men, and those men unbelievers. For if Christ had come down from the cross, they would not have been made better, but would probably have put down the miracle to magic, as has frequently happened; for many miracles which could only be performed by God are attributed to the Prince of the devils."

The King heartily approved of this reply. He understood the Priest's meaning, although the latter's Persian was both clumsy and scanty, and explained it to the others who were present. These were all so much pleased by the reply that they declared their doubts to be removed and no further explanation to be needed. Then the King asked why Christ allowed St. Thomas to put his fingers and his hand into the wounds: at a time moreover when St. Thomas still doubted. The Priest replied to this—"Because it was of advantage to men, who were to be redeemed by the death of Christ through faith in him, that patience should be shown to the doubts of Thomas. But if Christ had acceded to the request of the Jews that he should come down from the cross, men would not have been redeemed in accordance with the eternal law of God, who had willed that redemption should only be achieved by the death of Christ. Moreover, Christ met Thomas' doubts, like a father pitying his son, of his own kindness and grace, showing him his hands and his side, lest Thomas should fall and be lost. Thomas himself made no conditions or demands."

The King also asked what we mean when we say that God the Father has no mortal body, yet that Christ sat down at the right hand of his Father. The Priest answered that we do not mean by this a bodily sitting-down: but we say that Christ sits at the right hand of his Father because, since Christ is God, he has the same glory, honour and power as his Father, to whom he is equal: but since he is also man, and thus less than his Father, he has received from this same Father greater glory and honour than has been given by the Father to the angels and all the saints, who are enjoying the delights of heaven, or to the kings and princes who rule on earth. The honour and glory which has been conferred upon Christ is superior to that which others have received: and this is typified by the name of the right hand, which is superior to the left.

The King and nearly every one else, was satisfied by this reply; but one shrewd fellow present made objections, and impiously, impudently and stubbornly denied that it was by miraculous means that Christ restored the ear of the servant Malchus. He was severely reprimanded by the King, and silenced by the rest. For, although the Musalmans deny that Christ was the Son of God, they confess in other respects his superlative greatness. Indeed they would be saved, if only they would abandon the superstition of Muhammad and confess this one point which they deny. The man who refused to acknowledge the miracle was the King's chief physician.[195] He was learned in natural

---

[195] Hakim Ali was the chief physician, and was learned in natural science. But he was a docile courtier; thus the refusal to acknowledge the miracle might have suggested the name of Hakim-ul-Mulk—a man 'Not to be trusted in matters of religion and faith,' had not Hakim-ul-Mulk already been sent off to Mecca (Aug. 1580).

science. The King retained the summary of the events of Christ's passion, and ordered it to be carefully preserved.

The Indus.

The army was allowed a rest on reaching the bank of the Indus. The camp was situated on a large open plain, rich in flocks, and well-stocked with wood and all needful supplies. Moreover the neighbouring woods and forests afforded a powerful incentive to induce the King to rest there and to engage in hunting. Hence the army was halted for fifty days in this place, near Azaarana, which is a town about nine miles from Nilabhum. Nilabhum is a fort situated on a hill near a narrow place in the river,[196] where it can be crossed out of India into Paropanisas, which is now called the kingdom of Chabulum. This is the reason why the King ordered the place to be fortified.

The Indus is the greatest of all the Indian rivers: for it receives from its very source a great body of water gathered from the melting snows of the Himalaya, or Caspian mountains. Moreover it receives, and bears to the sea, the waters of five great rivers, which have been named above. On its banks near its source the neighbouring peoples find great quantities of the best and finest gold. It winds about in various meanderings, amongst mountain-defiles and Himalayan. valleys, to the north of Caspiria and Casiria and of the country of the Bothi or Bothantes. Thence it turns westward to reach the plains. It is divided into eight branches, which enclose seven islands in addition to that on which the army was encamped. The force and quantity of water in the river is such that even elephants can only ford it with difficulty. Afterwards it turns south-

196 Atac Balanaz—Author's Note. The author refers to Attock, then regarded as the western limit of Hindustan. This place is said to have been called Atak (the bar) Benares because the name rhymed so well with Katak Benares, the eastern limit. It was also said to be called Atak (the bar) because the Hindus would not go beyond the Indus.

wards in a great bend near to the narrows between Nilabhum and the hills of Arachosia. In the same neighbourhood it receives the waters of the rivers Coas[197] and Suastus,[198] which unite just before joining the Indus. Finally it flows into the sea through seven mouths. The Suastus is now called the Axtnagaris[199] by the natives of that part, and the Coas the river of Chabulum. After the Suastus joins the Coas, the combined rivers are called the Coas by geographers, but the river of Chabulum by the natives. From the middle of June to the middle of August the Indus is so much swollen, not by rain-water but by the melting snows, that its mighty body of water divides the sea (or so it is said) and sweet water may be drawn up out of the ocean to a distance of forty miles from the shore. The common people of this region generally call the Indus the Nilabhus, which means in Persian 'blue water.' The name is appropriately given, since at the narrow place where the crossing into Parpanisas is effected the river is so deep that its water is of a blue colour, running with great force and rapidity.

Whilst the army was encamped by the Indus, Zelaldinus regarded it as very important to conciliate the Delazacques, in order that they might supply him with ferry-boats and light craft suited to the carrying over of the army, and also with timber for building a bridge. It happened—fortunately for the King's designs—that two chiefs of the Delazacques, who had become involved in a bitter feud, came to visit him from the other side of the Indus, in order to advance their respective interests. He effected a reconciliation between these chiefs, and quickly secured by their diligence a great amount of timber, with which he built more than forty small boats. He obtained as many more by the friendly help of the Delazacques.

---

197 The Kabul river.

198 The Swat river. The Sanskrit name is Suvastu and the Greek form of it is Souastos or Souastene.

199 Hastanagar. (*I.G*, Vol. XIII, pp. 60-61; *A.G*, p. 50)

While this was going on the King's nights were spent in prolonged councils of war, and his days in hunting, in holding games and shows, and in exhibiting his vast resources. With these amusements he seasoned, as it were, his great cares and responsibilities. Had he not introduced magicians and diviners into the council, in order that they might decide by auguries and astrology when the advance might auspiciously be resumed, and had he not paid great respect to their decisions, one might have given generous praise to the prudence which he showed, on approaching the enemy's territory, in all his preparations and arrangements even though his foe was so vastly inferior to himself. Such prudence is the more to be wondered at and admired in a general rendered arrogant by countless victories. He knew well, indeed, that the issues of battle are uncertain, that Mars is impartial, and that the enemy, though his inferior in numbers, was yet superior in courage. Moreover, he shrank from the coming conflict when he remembered that the enemy was his own brother, whom, though he had been deceived by the lies of traitors and renegades, he still loved. When he heard that Mirsachimus had fled, he announced the fact to the Priest, and asked if he should pursue him. The Priest replied, 'Stay where you are, and do not pursue: for he is your Highness' brother. That relationship is strong enough to cool your anger, though it has been so justly aroused, and to make you refrain from overtaking and destroying the offender. For the glory of mercy is greater than the glory of vengeance, since vengeance cannot be achieved except by the hurt and destruction of many who are innocent.' The King applauded this reply, and said to his courtiers, 'See how heartily disposed to peace and gentleness these Priests are: for he is of the opinion that we should spare the fugitive.' However, fearing lest his brother should abuse his patience, if he went unpunished, and should thus begin the war anew, Zelaldinus resolved to fight the matter out in such a way that his brother should be compelled to recognize his own inferiority. At the same time he determined that he himself would show all kindness and mercy towards the vanquished fugitive.

Murad sent ahead

Hence a great number of boats were prepared, in which the army was to be ferried over; for the river—swollen with water from the snows which had been melted by the great heat—prevented the erection of a bridge. The King made his son whom the Priest was educating leader of the vanguard, since the soothsayers and sorcerers had declared that the stars foretold a great future for the boy (what nonsense). He associated with him Calichumcanus,[200] governor of Surat, an experienced and stalwart old man, and Nourancanus[201] (whose father was the prince's tutor), governor of Champanelium[202] in Gedrosia, and Mancinus,[203] an active and energetic chieftain, by race an Indian and a worshipper of idols. Calichumcanus had a corps of Mongols, Nourancanus four thousand Xacattaean cavalry, and Mancinus his own troops. Associated with these were other subordinate leaders with their forces, which, though in small detachments, amounted in all to at least a thousand cavalry. The King added 500 elephants to this force of cavalry. He paid great attention, with undue superstition, to the army's setting out at exactly the right time. He accompanied his son to the door of the royal headquarters, and embraced him, after he had bidden him God-speed after the Musalman fashion. He then dismissed him with his

---

200 Qulij Khan. Subsequently he was made governor of Lahore, then of Agra. He was one of the most faithful servants of Akbar, but an inveterate enemy of the Portuguese and their religion. As Viceroy of Lahore he showed great hostility to the Christians (Blochmann 1. 34, 354-55). He died in 1613.

201 Naurang Khan, son of Qutubuddin Khan, tutor to Selim (see note 119). Akbar is said to have honoured Qutub once at a feast by placing Selim on his shoulder.

202 Champanir, 25 miles N. E. of Baroda. It had a very strong fortress.

203 Man Singh. His career is well known.

attendant nobles, who followed him to his boat. The prince embarked, crossed the Indus, and set out on his march on the day after the feast of St. John the Baptist, 1581.

An Embassy from Mirza Hakim.

After despatching his son in advance with his forces, the King began actively to arrange his army for the march and to establish garrisons. The Mongols never fight a pitched battle with the whole of their forces. If they invite battle with six thousand troops, they are sure to have twenty thousand hiding in ambush; and in the rear of these again several thousands more are held in reserve, that they may support the advance-guard in case of a reverse, or rally them, if routed. Such reserves often turn defeat into sudden victory by checking the pursuit, by restoring the fight through their freshness and unimpaired vigour, and by compelling the weary enemy to retire. When Mirsachimus learnt from his scouts that the prince had crossed the Indus and was marching upon him with a great army, he resolved to ask pardon, and to surrender unconditionally to his brother, with the promise that he would take no further share in wars, seditions and revolutions. Hence he sent envoys to arrange peace. They brought gifts of horses and mules (in which that region abounds), and also considerable sums of money and supplies. These were designed to show Mirsachimus' respect and good-will towards the King. The bearers of these gifts were two old men[204] with long beards. The King, surrounded by a great company of his nobles, received these envoys with dignity and regal authority. He himself stood apart from the rest, leaning on a lance. He was attended only by his eldest son and a few sons of the chief nobles. Whilst he was listening to the embassy, gladiators were fighting with sword and shield, and bison were being pitted against each other. All this had been

204 One of them was Khwaja Abul Fazl and the name of the other is not given. (E. D. V. 424).

arranged beforehand in order to create the impression that the King was not engaged in warfare, but was amusing himself as he was wont to do in the circus—the object being to show the envoys how little respect he paid to his brother's power, and how great was the superiority of his own court and army. He ordered Abdulfasilius, his confidential adviser, to read the despatches, which he said satisfied him. However, he immediately sent the envoys back again.

Zelaldinus was daily informed of all that his son Pahari did. He had arranged beforehand not to break camp till he should hear that his son had arrived near to his brother's army. Those who were with the King were very restless at this delay, and set fire to the forest which supplied the camp with firewood in order to compel him to advance (or so it was said). Many however believed that the forest was fired by seditious supporters of Mirsachimus. The conflagration so enraged the King that he threatened its originators with death, should they be caught. But desiring to mitigate his anger, some of the courtiers persuaded him that the forest had been accidently fired through the carelessness of herdsmen, whereupon he gave instructions that the investigation of the crime should cease.

Monserrate has a discussion with the King.

Two days after his son's departure Zelaldinus had the Priest conducted to him by night in order to ask him certain questions, both religious and secular. First of all he had an atlas brought and asked where Portugal was, and where his own kingdom. He wondered how we knew the names of the provinces and cities of India. Then he asked why the Priest was a celibate: for was it not a divine command, as it were, that all men should have wives: and he (the Priest) appeared either to condemn matrimony or to contradict himself when he said that celibacy was good and matrimony also good. The Priest replied, 'Does not your Highness know that, of two good things, one often happens to be better than the other? Thus silver is good, but gold is better: whilst wisdom is better than gold, and virtue than anything else. The moon is beautiful: but the sun is more beautiful, and superior to her.' The King agreed to this; whereupon the Priest added, 'Therefore priests remain celibate and unmarried, that they may follow better things: that they may imitate Christ: and that, free from the cares of a wife, children and family, they may spend their time apart from all desire. For by the sixth commandment of God all luxury is forbidden to Christians, and indeed to all mankind.' The King here interjected, 'You declare, do you not, that Christ is God. Do you not then act rashly and insolently in wishing to be like him?' The Priest replied, 'We do indeed believe and asseverate that Christ is God, but we declare at the same time that he is man. And, being man, he practised chastity as an example to us, and also praised it highly very many times in the Gospel. As regards his being God, it would indeed be the mark of a proud and insolent mind to wish to be like Christ. It is indeed an impossible ambition; and hence to entertain it shows the height of folly and madness. But on the other hand it shows piety and devotion to follow his footsteps in practising the virtues which he himself practised. For one of the many causes which led him to wish to become man was his desire that (since we cannot imitate his work of creating and ruling the universe, and the other functions of his Deity) we might imitate him in the attributes and activities of his true manhood, such as his humility, self-sacrifice, chastity, poverty, obedience and other allied virtues. No painter or sculptor, however accurately and carefully he may paint his picture or carve his statue, endeavours actually to imitate nature: he would say rather that he desired to appropriate for himself the strength and virtue of nature. It has been found that, though we all struggle with our hearts to imitate Christ in those virtues which can be reproduced in a man, yet we are left far behind by him. Wherefore Christ greatly commends our endeavour to imitate himself, and is far from imputing it to pride or insolence or rashness.'

The King then added, 'The descent from Adam thus perishes in you.' The Priest replied, 'What if I had died when I was a boy eight years old, or (as frequently happens) just at the time of my marriage? What if my wife had been barren, or I myself, as many are? What if I had been born, or made, a eunuch, like the many that are in your palace? Let not your Highness mistakenly imagine that marriage is enjoined. God indeed allowed much stress to be laid on the value of matrimony under the law of nature, in order that the human race might be increased: and also, amongst the Jews, under the law of Moses, in order that the religion and worship of the true God might be extended. But under the law of the Gospel, which excels all other laws as the substance excels the shadow, the human race having been sufficiently increased, Christ laid down the principle in regard to marriage that each man may freely follow what course he chooses, and stop where he wishes.' Here the King interrupted (and not at all to the point), 'If God ordered anyone to cross a river, he would be a sinner if he disobeyed.' The Priest replied, 'That is true; but I declared a few moments since that marriage is not enjoined. Nor must you imagine that celibates, though they have no wives, lack offspring. For there is a spiritual begetting; and those whom a man instructs in the faith and virtues of Christianity are in a manner called his sons; for those whom he baptizes and whose confessions he hears are not less his spiritual sons than if he had begotten them by his body. Permit me to declare to you, O King, that if you listen to the advice of Rudolf and myself, and believe in what we say, and are baptized by him, you will be more truly and spiritually the son of Rudolf than the son of King Emaumus. For those who are only parents by nature, merely beget a body: but he who baptizes you will beget a soul. It may of course happen that some are compelled and commanded to marry.' 'Who?' asked the King. The Priest replied, 'A king who must have an heir for the sake of the peace and tranquility of the state. For this reason learned men urged Henry, King of Portugal, though he was a priest, to marry, and (in order that he might do so) to obtain a dispensation from the Pope, who has been constituted interpreter and high judge and moderator in such matters by Christ himself, whose representative he is. Yet King Henry was old and weak, and devoted to chastity, as he had ever been, and thus he died of old age still unmarried, as he desired.' This example was quoted because Zelaldinus was wont to respect and praise King Henry's sanctity, fortitude and constancy, as though he had been a second St. Sebastian.

When the question of celibacy and marriage had been so thoroughly dealt with that the King had no objections left to bring forward, he made detailed enquiries about the Last Judgment, whether Christ would be the Judge, and when it would occur. Having dealt with the other points the Priest said, 'God alone knows the time when the judgment will take place: and in his unsearchable wisdom he has desired this to be hidden from us. Christ himself refused to make it known to his disciples. He did not wish either that we should become negligent through knowing it to be far distant, or that we should be saddened by knowing that it is near at hand. But he wished us so to prepare ourselves for that day that we may make good use of the gifts which he has given us, and abstain from sin and from all that he has forbidden, being in fear of the Judgment, though we know not when it will come. Yet signs shall precede that day which will enable men to conclude with confidence that it is at hand.' The King asked what these signs should be. The Priest replied, 'Christ mentioned especially wars and rebellions, the fall of kingdoms and nations, the invasion, devastation and conquest of nation by nation and kingdom by kingdom: and these things we see happening very frequently in our time.'

The King listened most attentively to all this. He then asked some foolish and absurd questions about the Gospel, showing lack of faith therein. Gradually he turned the subject to Muhammad and the differences between the Bible and Alcoranus. This most wicked impostor wrote that he was mentioned in the Gospel, and his coming foretold: for the impious villain and rascally babbler wished to persuade men that Christ had spoken of him under the name of the Holy Spirit. Nor did he hesitate to attribute to himself the name 'Mustafaa,' *i.e.*, paraclete and advocate, asserting that God had entrusted to him the defence of believers. Hence the Musalmans are convinced that Muhammad is mentioned in the Gospel. When Christians deny this, they assert that the text of the Gospel has been corrupted by the Christians themselves, and reproach the latter with this corruption. They are entirely ignorant of Greek, and thus declare that Muhammad was promised in the Gospel under the name of 'Pharaglitaa'—a distortion of 'Paracletus.' This idea was derived from Greek renegades and apostates, or perhaps from Sergius, emperor of Constantinople, and a follower of Nestorius, who knew Greek and attached himself to Muhammad, and was his assistant in fabricating the Quran, or perhaps even its sole author. The idea derives some colour of truth from the etymology of the corrupted form of the name, which was perhaps purposely so derived. For 'Pharag' means in Hebrew, Arabic and Persian, a division, difference or section. 'Litaa' indeed has no meaning either in Arabic or Persian, though the Persian learned men absurdly declare that it denotes agency, and hence 'one who makes.' Thus the impostor is termed 'he who makes a division.' This interpretation indeed clearly demonstrates the folly of the Musalmans: for Alfurcanus, the name of their book, may be derived from 'Pharag': and in the chapter entitled Albacaraa, or The Cow, Muhammad wrote that his book was a divider. To cut their throats with their own swords, let us acknowledge (if it be lawful to make use of a forged name) that it is very fitting that Muhammad should be called 'Pharaglitaa'—the Causer of Division,—since his teaching differs from that of Christ, even though he falsely and impudently boasts that he was sent by Christ. On the other hand the fact that he was not the Holy Spirit is proved, in spite of what they say, by the authority of the Gospel itself, which they twist against us. For Christ foretold in regard to the Holy Spirit that 'the Paraclete, the Holy Spirit which the Father shall send in my name, will teach you all things and will bring to your minds whatever I shall have said to you.' And again, 'But when the Paraclete shall have come, whom I will send to you from the Father, even the Spirit of truth, which comes from the Father, he shall give testimony about me.' And again, 'When the Spirit of truth shall have come he shall teach you all truth. For he shall not speak of himself, but he shall speak whatever he hears, and he shall foretell to you the things that shall happen. He shall glorify me: for he shall receive of what is mine, and shall announce it to you.'

To pass over other points, it would be clear and evident, even to a man born blind, how inconsistent, contradictory and irreconcilable are the statements and teachings of this interpreter of devils to those of Christ the Creator and Preserver of mankind. Hence the King asked the Priest, 'Is it true that Christ does not mention Muhammad in the Gospel, and that his name is nowhere found there?' The Priest replied that Christ made no definite mention of Muhammad by name in the Gospel, but that he spoke in general terms of many false prophets who were to come. The King then said, 'Surely Muhammad cannot be he who is to appear at the end of the world as the adversary of all mankind,' (that is, he whom the Musalmans call Dijal) [205]? The Priest replied, 'No; but many European

205 Anti-Christ—*Author's note.*

scholars apply to Muhammad the words 'His hand shall be against all men and all men's hands against him, and he shall pitch his tent far from all his brethren.' For Muhammad was of the race of Ishmael, and he gainsays the Law and the Gospel, and he declared warfare against all nations that did not accept his teaching.' The King asked, 'In what respects does Muhammad gainsay the Law and the Gospel?' 'From beginning to end of his book, all his words conflict with the Law of Moses and the Gospel, except a few sentences which he repeats in order to gain a reputaton for sanctity. Indeed the Law and the Gospel have no points of agreement at all with Muhammad.' 'What then,' said the King, 'do you consider Alcoranus to be?' As the Priest smiled and hesitated, the King urged him again to express plainly the opinion of his companions and himself regarding Alcoranus. The Priest then replied, 'Muhammad indeed declared that God had given him that book; but we deny that this was true. For God is not wont to gainsay through one messenger what He has said through another, nor to contradict himself, nor to be inconsistent. The Law and the Gospel, the books of God, say one and the same thing. Alcoranus says things very different indeed to what the Law and the Gospel say. Wherefore we must either say that the Law, the Psalms and the Gospel are not sacred books, in order that we may regard Alcoranus as sacred, or we must say that Alcoranus is profane, forged and lying, in order that we may regard the other three as sacred.'

The King listened attentively to this reply and remained silent; but Abdulfasilius broke in with—'Are the Law and the Gospel different books?' The Priest replied, 'They are indeed different books and written at different times; but they contain no statements mutually inconsistent or contradictory. But Alcoranus contains much that is contradictory both to these two books and to itself. The teaching of all really sacred books is the same. God sent the Law to the children of Israel by Moses, in order they might be led by it till the coming of Christ: at his coming God brought the Law to an end.' 'Why then,' said Abdulfasilius, 'was the earlier book superseded and the latter granted to man, if both contain one and the same teaching?' The Priest replied, 'God, the Most High, accommodates Himself to the understanding of men, as though he were the Father of all mankind. For a father gives one kind of food to his son when an infant, another to him when a boy, another to him when a youth. He gives him also one kind of teaching in boyhood and another in youth. Thus God apportioned and accommodated His food to the Jews as though to children, when He wished to draw them to the worship of Himself, away from the heathen superstitions and corruptions of the Egyptians. Hence he attracted them by ordaining many ceremonies, attractively similar, as it were, to the sacrifices to which they had been accustomed, in order that they might make offerings to Himself as well as to the demons of Egypt. But afterwards, the human race being further advanced towards maturity, He prepared and seasoned solid food in the Gospel, not for the Jews, alone, but for all mankind: so that the whole mass of humanity, having left behind ceremonies, which are as it were the husk or shadow of true virtue, should serve God Himself. It is manifest that the Law and the Gospel give food to the souls of men. The Law is suited to infancy and the Gospel to maturity. The only difference lies in the manner of preparing and seasoning the food.' 'But,' said Abdulfasilius, 'Alcoranus also supplies spiritual food.' 'No indeed,' replied the Priest, 'not food, but poison. For teachings so contrary to the Gospel and to the Law can give no more sustenance to the souls of men than can poison to their bodies.'

The Priest asked for pardon, in case the Musalmans present should blame the King for having allowed him to speak so freely and plainly against Muhammad. The King answered with some heat, 'By God, I am not the man to have my feelings outraged by these things. I am only seeking for the truth, and by Rhohalcuduz (the Holy Spirit) I conjure you to expound the truth to me, and not to be afraid of exposing the crimes of Muḥammad.' The Priest bowed at the word Rhohalcuduz, and the King said to those who were near him, 'It is Jesus Christ.'. The Priest forebore to explain the distinction between the persons of Jesus Christ and the Holy Spirit; for it was already late at night, and it was neither the time nor the place for discussing so important a question. He merely added that he had in good faith set forth what he believed and knew. The King then rose to retire to rest, and thus the discussion came to an end.

Akbar advances across the Indus

When Mirsachimus perceived the serious nature of the invasion, he desired to avoid battle, and to make peace before he should have to fight matters out with his brother. Accordingly he resolved to surrender, and would indeed have done so, had not Faridumcanus,[206] whom he greatly respected alike for his warlike courage and his skill in statesmanship, opposed this resolution with all his might on account of his ancient enmity towards Zelaldinus whom he had basely deserted. In thus consulting his own safety (for he was afraid of falling into the hands of Zelaldinus) Faridumcanus ruined the miserable Mirsachimus, and led him on to his death. For he declared that the forces of Zelaldinus mainly consisted of a scanty herd of swarthy Indian infidels and idolaters: that he was convinced Mirsachimus' picked cavalry would have the best of it: and that battle should neither be feared nor avoided. When Zelaldinus learnt from his scouts and

---

206 Faridun Khan was maternal uncle of Mirza Muhammad Hakim. In 1566 Akbar despatched him against Hakim when he had invaded the Punjab, and he went over to his nephew's side. In the beginning of 1586 he surrendered to Akbar after the death of his master in July 1585. For some time he was kept under surveillance and then sent to Mecca.

from the messengers who came very frequently from his son Pahari that Mirsachimus, belying his intentions as expressed through his embassy, was preparing for resistance, he dismissed the envoys from his brother and sister[207] in order to have everything settled before crossing the Indus. He gave a large sum of money to his sister's envoy, and a few cast-off clothes to those of Mirsachimus. Having dismissed the embassy, he twice began to cross the river, but desisted again in consequence of the absurdly superstitious prohibition of the magicians and sooth-sayers. When at length the auspices were found favourable, he crossed the Indus and encamped on the bank of the Coas, at about two miles' distance from the point where it joins the Indus. The King was so affectionately disposed towards the Christian Priest, that far from forgetting him in the midst of such urgent cares, he ordered a certain general to be responsible for his crossing in safety, for the passage of the Indus was rendered so hard by the lack of boats that even chiefs and nobles only succeeded in getting across with the greatest difficulty.

This region is called after its capital city, as is the custom amongst these tribes, Chabulum. It is divided into three natural areas, that on this side of the Coas, that beyond the Coas and below the junction of the Coas with the Suastus, and that between the Coas and the Suastus. The tract of country which lies on this side of the Coas towards the west is part of the region called by the ancients Paropanisas, and by later ages Indoscythia. The tract beyond the Coas and below the junction of the rivers, lying to the east between the Indus and the Suastus, was called by the ancients Gandara[208]: that

207 Bakhtunnisa. She was also called by two other names Najibunnisa and Fakhrunnisa. She was half sister of Akbar and full sister of Hakim and was married to Khwaja Hasan of Badakshan.

208 Gandhara. For the extent, history and importance of Gandhara, see Rapson's *Ancient India* Pp. 81-85. It comprised the modern districts of Peshawar and Rawalpindi, but in the old Persian inscriptions it seems to have included also the district of Kabul.

above the junction and northwards beyond the Suastus was called Suastene[209]: and that between the Coas and the Suastus Gorica.[210] It is now inhabited by Patanæi under the rule of Xacattæi or Mongols. There is not a vestige remaining of the ancient names, districts, cities and towns. The Patanæi originated in Gandara and Suastene. They invaded and occupied a great part of India, having defeated the Christians. Their country, lying as it does between the Indus, and the Coas or the Suastus, is level and of the same climate as its neighbour India.

Religious Discussions

The King stayed at the halting-place until the whole army had crossed the Indus. In order not to remain inactive he spent his time partly in artisan-work, partly in discussions. His learned men initiated a debate regarding holy books, whereupon he ordered the sacred volumes to be brought and the Priest to be called. First he learnt from the priest what each volume contained: and then he gave him an opportunity to say what he liked. The Priest thereupon addressed the King as follows:—"In the past some of Your Majesty's learned men have asserted, as the Musalmans are wont to do, that the Torah is the book of the Jews, the Gospel the book of the Christians, Alcoranus the book of the Musalmans, and the Zabur (*i.e.* Psalter) the book of the Georgians (these are commonly called Gorgi, and are Hircanians living in the mountains near the Caspian Sea; they are very hostile to the Persians). But this is an ignorant mistake; for the Georgians are Christians: and all Christians recognise the Law, the Psalms and the Gospel, attributing equal trustworthiness and authority to all three, as being given by God.

---

209 Swat, to the north of the river of the same name.

210 This is Gorya of Strabo. "Gouryaia designates the territory traversed by the Gourais or river of Ghor which is the affluent of the Kabul river now called the Landai, formed by the junction of the rivers of Panjkora and Swat. Alexander on his march to India passed through Gouryaia." (Ptolemy).

They devoutly reverence and worship one undivided Trinity of Father, Son and Holy Ghost—One God. They recognise Jesus Christ alone, the Son of God made man through the Virgin Mary, as the giver of the Gospel law, to whom all other law-givers, though sent by God, even Moses and David and the other prophets, yield place in humble submission. Wherefore the Georgians, who are counted Christians, do not—any more than other Christians—regard any one as a law-giver in the strict sense except Christ, neither Moses nor David. In declaring, in spite of what I have said, that the Armenians deny that Christ is the Son of God, this man is utterly mistaken. He is deceived by the common but erroneous supposition that all the Christians of Asia are Armenians, whereas in reality there are many Greeks, Chaldæans and Syrians and a few Nestorians. In the same way Portuguese, Spaniards, Italians, Germans are erroneously all called Franks. It is true that the Nestorians, who are only nominal Christians, agree with the Musalmans in denying that Christ is the Son of God. But Armenians, Greeks, Egyptians, Syrians, Chaldæans, Latins, and indeed all Christians, disavow these Nestorians no less than they do Jews and Musalmans. For this is the difference between Christians and Musalmans, Jews or Nestorians:—the Christians with one accord most resolutely assert that Christ is the Son of God: but the Musalmans, Jews and Nestorians with equal unanimity shamelessly deny the same. I have explained this, O King, lest Your Majesty should wrongly suppose that there are any disagreements or controversies amongst Christians on this question. The Christian religion is supported by the authority of sacred books, which in many passages plainly teach this doctrine. Hence no doubt of its truth can creep into the hearts of true Christians. I am not surprised that he had been easily deceived on this point: for he is ignorant of Christianity. But he is renowned for his prudence and insight. Hence I cannot but blame him for his carelessness in making rash assertions before Your Majesty, when he might have learnt from me the true state of affairs."

Then the Priest, at the King's command, unrolled the books; and, seizing his opportunity, explained the pictures. He told the meaning of the Ark of the Covenant and of what was kept in it. He explained the golden candlestick and the golden table of unleavened bread. All this he did in a simple manner suited to the understanding of his hearers. The Musalmans hate idolatry; and hence he discoursed at some length on the images of angels on the ark and in the shrine. He pointed out that God had only prohibited the making and worship of images of false gods—not the making of statues of saints. For He who said "Thou shalt make thyself no graven image," also commanded that the figures of angels should be painted and carved in His tabernacle and temple. And, since He is God and cannot change or forget, it is blasphemous to believe that He gives inconsistent and contradictory commands. Religious men, inspired by the divine will, explain by the right interpretation passages of Scripture which appear to conflict. These men declare that the words 'graven image' and 'idol' denote only the images of demons and false gods; and God, the Creator of the universe, forbids both in Law and Gospel the worship of such images. Wherefore it is wrong to accuse of idolatry Christians who do reverence to the painted or carven images of God and divine beings.

A discussion was also held on the subject of Noah's Ark, which the Priest clearly explained to have been a type of the Saviour Christ. The King appeared to be no little impressed, and received the teaching quite attentively. But he sometimes pretended to be thinking of other matters, lest his courtiers should imagine him to be attracted towards Christianity. However, he did not hesitate publicly to reverence and kiss a picture of Christ.

Meanwhile the advance guard, consisting of four thousand cavalry under Nourancanus the son of Cutubdicanus, received a severe check near Chabulum. It was attacked by the whole army of Mirsachimus, consisting of fifteen thousand Mongol horse. Nourancanus was compelled to apply to Mancinus, who was in support, for instant help, but his corps delayed its arrival. Thus there was something approaching a panic in the advance guard under Pahari, and a few had already even begun to fly. When he perceived this, the prince dismounted, seized a spear, and declared that he would not retreat an inch from that spot, though the whole hostile army should attack him alone, and overwhelm him with its missiles: but if he survived the danger, he would right well remember who had deserted him. Seeing the prince's boyish courage (for he was only twelve years old), and hearing his brave words, the troops were overcome with shame, and rallied round him. Mancinus at last came up, bringing much-needed relief to the prince, who was hard beset and all but overcome. Some elephant-detachments also arrived, the sight of which generally terrifies horses which are unaccustomed to them, and thus throws cavalry into confusion. Thus the prince was able to rally his forces on the open plain.

A Check to Murad

Meanwhile Mirsachimus accused Faridumcanus of having deceived him by his previous assertion that the forces of Zelaldinus were but scanty: and of having shown gross carelessness in allowing so large an army to enter his kingdom without his knowledge. He then ordered the retreat to be sounded even before Mancinus' corps came up; and thus the battle was broken off.

Pahari, who had arranged his line of battle in accordance with the traditional Mongol tactics, bivouacked upon the field: and remained there some time awaiting his father's orders. The Mongol armies are arrayed for battle as follows:— The squadrons of cavalry are drawn up in the form of a

Moghal Tactics.

half moon and are arranged in three divisions, one on the left wing, one in the centre, and one on the right. Behind the cavalry is the infantry, and behind the infantry the elephants, which are never allowed in advance of the other troops, both in order to prevent their catching sight of the enemy, and to obviate the danger of their being wounded and flying in panic: for in this case they madly attack their own troops, throwing them into confusion, and crushing many to death. On advancing to the attack Mongol generals extend one or both wings in the endeavour to outflank and encircle the enemy. The elephants terrify rather than harm the enemy: and are more useful as a spectacle than as a real agency of victory. When hurt they attack any one who comes in their path, without distinction between friend and enemy. They are easily driven off by means of fire-arms, and retreat headlong if stabbed in the trunk. If horses have been accustomed to elephants they pay no attention to them. There is a camel-corps of Balochii among the King's cavalry. If there are enough of them to form a compact body, they are grouped closely together in some special part of the battle-line. Camels are as nimble and skilful in a battle, if I may say so, as horses. Nor are they less fierce. They fight with teeth and feet. If they catch hold of any one, they kneel upon him so hard and long, pounding and crushing him, that their wretched victim is destroyed.

Peshawar.

The King advanced to Pirxaurum,[211] where he learnt of what had happened to the army of Pahari. Thereupon he hastened by forced marches to Chabulum, taking with him some picked cavalry and some squadrons of Delazacques. Before leaving, he arranged military affairs in the following skilful and statesmanlike manner. He left a brigade on the east of the Indus in his own territory, and about half a brigade west of the Indus near the Coas, in

211 Peshawar.

order strongly to guard the passage of the Indus. He directed his eldest son, whom he loved best of all, and who was then fourteen years old, to follow him with the rear-guard, consisting of the remainder of the army, the whole train of the baggage and supply, the treasury, the artillery, and the rest of the military stores and equipment. He was to halt at Gelalabadum,[212] three days' march from Chabulum on the bank of the Coas, where he was to encamp. With him were left the queens and princesses and all the women, together with the whole of the royal furniture and domestic appurtenances. Bagoandas,[213] father of Mancinus, was appointed governor of the prince's household, and commander of the troops.

Besides the two Delazacquian chiefs mentioned above, each of whom brought with him a contingent of 14,000 cavalry, another young chief joined the King with a company of about three hundred men. He was an inhabitant of Paropanisas, *i.e.* Indoscythia, by race. His father had been the originator of a sect of fanatics,[214] which practised forcible conversion to its views. Had not the neighbouring princes taken care to bring about the destruction of the first leader of his sect, he might have given a great deal of trouble to the people of Paropanisas (Indoscythia), Gondara, Gorias and Suastene, and indeed to the Mongols themselves. For he had a band of four hundred desperadoes and fugitive debtors, who had been attracted to him by hope of plunder and revolution, as is the way with Musalmans, (so long, that is, as they reverence the name of Muhammad). They were so devoted to their leader and his beliefs

[212] Jalalabad.

[213] Bhagwan Das. He was a commander of 5000 and had the title of Amir-ul-Umara. In the 23rd year of the reign (1578) he was made governor of the Punjab and in the 30th year (1585) governor of Kabul. His daughter was married to Selim; but he protested strongly against Akbar's new religion. He died at Lahore in 1589. Man Singh was his adopted son. His own sons were Madhu Singh and Pratap Singh.

[214] The Roshaniyya sect.

(and after his death to his son, who succeeded him in the leadership of the sect), that none of their own lawful rulers could ever move their allegiance to him and his teachings either by threats or by violence. Many were destroyed, but the survivors remained obdurate. When they heard of Zelaldinus' approach they threw themselves upon his mercy. The King received them graciously and promised them freedom to follow their religion and customs, and to obey and reverence the son of their prophet (as they call him). He held that if he granted them this religious freedom they would remain contentedly in their own district. He cared little that in allowing every one to follow his own religion he was in reality violating all religions.

On the line of advance lay Pirxaurum, a town with a citadel on a hill, but unfortified. Mirsachimus had held this place for some time, but had evacuated it and retired to the mountain when he heard of the approach of his brother's forces under Mancinus. It is said that in time of peace the town has a population of two thousand ordinary citizens in addition to the garrison. But at that time there was nothing to be seen except ashes, as all the houses had been burnt. On the eastern outskrits of the town is a colony of Jogues similar in belief, manner of life and dress to those who live on the peak of Balnatus. This colony is called by the local people Gorcathiri,[215] which means 'Cell of Gorus.' They say that this Gorus, who lived here, was the preceptor of Balnatus, and that the place is so holy that

---

215 Gorkhatri or Korkhatri. It is mentioned by Babur in his Memoirs as one of the holy places of Hindu Jogis, who came from great distances to cut off their hair and shave their beards. It was originally a monastery built by Kanishka. In the 9th and 10th centuries it was a place of Buddhist education. It was rebuilt as a Hindu shrine and is now used as a Sarai (Jarret II 404 n. 6). Jarret says that the word means a Grain Merchant's House (See also *I.G.* XX, 125; A.G. pp. 80-81. Murray's *Handbook of the Punjab* p. 277, *Glossary of the Tribes and Castes of the Punjab* Vol. I, p. 679). But see A. R. 1908, p. 39 n.

God, the Creator of the Universe, modelled the rest of the universe upon it. The King was reported to have visited this cell of Gorus, and to have done reverence to Gorus himself with loosened hair, and hands and eyes uplifted to heaven.

The Khaibar

On the day after the King's departure the prince began to advance and in two days' time came to a difficult, steep and narrow pass over a very high range, which is called by the natives Caybar.[216] The ancients called it the Capissenian Pass. The army crossed this pass, but with the greatest difficulty. Care had been taken to pave the road, though in a hasty manner. Even this had taxed to the utmost the skill of gangs of sappers and workmen. In spite of what they had done, the elephants (of whom there were a great number), the laden camels, and the flocks and herds, found the pass most difficult and dangerous. If they had slipped, they and their riders would have been in imminent danger of death. Amongst these riders were the queens, the princesses, the other noble ladies, and the chief queen of David,[217] king of the Patanæi, by whom he had had several sons. Zelaldinus was taking her with him in honourable custody, both as a reminder and proof of his own victorious glory, and as a hostage in order to prevent any insurrection amongst the Patanæi, who were being kept in subjection by fear only. This queen had with her several of her daughters. The horses were not so hard put to it during the ascent as the elephants and camels. For horses of this breed are strong and nimble, accustomed to speedily negotiating rough roads and difficult passes.

The prince ordered heralds to make proclamation that no one should precede the royal elephants and camels; and when these had passed on ahead the horses

216 Khaibar Pass. For an interesting discussion about the surrounding district of Capisene and its ancient capital of Capisa which was destroyed by Cyrus, see *A.G.* pp. 18-26.

217 Daud of Bengal.

accomplished the ascent with little risk. The prince regarded it as an honour to be able to show this polite service to his mother and sisters and the other ladies. He himself halted on a high crag until they had reached the crest of the pass. Camp was pitched in a narrow plain near a spring, from which flows a considerable stream of sweet water. This stream, which is large enough to water an army, later joins a brackish torrent, and thus loses its sweetness.

The royal pavilion was set up at Ahalimexit,[218] which means the Mosque of Ahalis. Near by a rock is shown, on which it is falsely reported that the prints of Ahalis' fingers may be seen. The story is as follows, (for it is well that such stories should be told in order that Christians may discern the folly of Musalman superstitions, not only on obscure general questions, but also in particular instances):—Ahalis, the son-in-law of Muhammad, was wandering over the earth in order to induce infidels, whom they call Cafares, to accept the falsehoods and superstitions of his father-in-law. He reached this place and seduced the daughter of the local chieftain, who, on learning what had happened, determined in revenge to destroy Ahalis by means of a trick, since he could not do so by open warfare. Above the mosque rises a steep cliff, from the top of which the chieftain flung a great rock down upon Ahalis whilst he was praying with his eyes upon the ground, as is the custom of the Musalmans. Ahalis was undisturbed, and without interrupting his prayer caught the rock in his hands, so as to save his head, as if the hands indeed were more suited than any other part of the body to be the means of a miraculous escape from danger. As a proof of what had happened his finger-prints remain (if God please) on the stone. Oh, the madness of men who think it possible that a seducer and adulterer should have performed miracles! Hence this tale is no more worthy of belief than that of a

218 Ali Masjid.

certain Qhojamundus[219] who is reverenced as a saint at Azimirus[220] not from Fattepurum, because, being the companion of Muhammad, he killed all who refused to accept the superstitious beliefs which he was preaching. Yet it is not to be wondered at that men are deceived who have no knowledge of history, and who are wont by means of falsehoods to curry favour for themselves, their country, their sect and their Prophet.

The style in which this mosque is built and the appearance of the place correspond to its patron-saint. For you would say that it was a stable rather than a mosque. Its walls are in ruins, its court-yard small, and it has no roof even of thatch.

Advancing yet further, the army came to the narrowest part of the pass, where two high crags overhang it from either side, so that a hundred stout warriors could forbid passage to many thousands; for a laden elephant can hardly get through the defile. Further on a slope was reached, so precipitous that the beasts scarcely found foot-hold, whilst the infantry were compelled to run down the hill. The cavalry and baggage trains had to make a long détour. At the bottom was a plain large enough to camp upon. In it was a spring flowing from a crag, near which a camp was measured out. The place is called Caybar. In ancient days it was named the city of Capissa. On the plain stood an obelisk, very similar in size, age and workmanship to the one of which I have already given some account. They say it is the other boundary of the kingdom of Rhamxandus. This is the only route through the Paharvetus mountains from the Paharo-

219 Khwaja Muinuddin, the celebrated saint buried at Ajmir. He had many disciples. Akbar used to make pilgrimage to the tomb for the realisation of his cherished wishes (Smith pp. 96 and 102).

220 Ajmir. It was a holy place, to the Emperor, as to all Moslems of the time, as containing the tombs of Shaikh Muinuddin Chisti Sigizi (mentioned above) and other holy men, and also as being the residence of Selim Chisti.

panisus to India for those who would avoid a very long détour. The pass is about sixteen miles long. Its middle point lies approximately in Latitude 34 north and Longitude 110 east. Its direction is roughly east and west.

The plain is overhung from the west by a crag, on which the ruins of a town can be seen. It is locally called Landighana,[221] *i.e.* the house of women; and stories are told about its ancient inhabitants, resembling those which are told about the Amazons. It is said that the stronghold used to be occupied by women, who waged war on the surrounding tribes. In order to keep up their numbers they attacked and carried off travellers. Boy-babies were killed or exposed: girls were brought up and trained to arms. They were finally conquered and driven out, but they have left their name in these ruins. In reality, fables apart, a band of wicked women must have lived there and given their name to the place: as sometimes happens with fugitive slaves.

Near to Landighana are the ruins of a town named Xaregolamum,[222] *i.e.* the city of slaves. It was founded by run-away slaves, as a means of preserving their liberty. They lived by brigandage and were driven from their stronghold, it is said, with great difficulty. For the whole region is rough and mountainous, with forests in which the slaves hid when chased by the neighbouring chiefs. They were wont to make raids out of these forests against the near-by settled districts, and to waylay travellers. Having obtained their booty they would retreat to their stronghold. In order to prevent drought in summer they dug for themselves four tanks of remarkable size and depth, in which all the rain-water from the surrounding hills used to be collected.

Emerging from this pass, the prince encamped on

---

221 Landikhana. The word *landi* however does not mean a woman but a stream.

222 Shahr-ghulam.

the bank of the Coas near the town of Bissaurum in the neighbourbood of Mount Beedaulatus. This hill is 2000 feet high, 4000 feet long, and about 8000 feet in circumference. It is composed of a single enormous rock, whole and without cracks or interstices. It projects towards the east from the neighbouring range, from which it is divided by deep gullies, to a distance of about two miles. On this mountain, as is commonly reported, the most careful examination has never discovered any tree, grass, or other vegetation, not even moss. For this reason Emaumus, father of Zelaldinus, having halted here and observed the mountain's barrenness, gave it the name of Beedaulat, *i.e.* 'graceless.' On its western side may be seen the openings of many triangular stone cells, which are entered from the top, and in which, they say, hermits used to live. The place is indeed bleak and rough, well-suited to a life of austerity, hardship and mourning. I do not believe that Hindu ascetics, who only desire to attract popular notice by a show of piety, ever committed themselves to a life of such severity, especially as the cells are now deserted though there are in our times great numbers of these worthless ascetics. I should rather say that they were built and inhabited by Christian solitaries, or hermits, especially since the Fathers of the Church have recorded that St. Bartholomew preached the Gospel in these regions, which were reckoned by the ancients to belong to India, as also were Aria, Aracosia and Gedrosia. These provinces made up indeed what was then called Hither India. We read in the ecclesiastical histories that St. Bartholomew travelled to Hither India, which had been allotted to him in the distribution of the world (into areas of evangelization). It is generally agreed that Christians once inhabited this region. The ancient Fathers were also greatly devoted to this sort of asceticism, and preferred to live near streams and rivers. When the Christians were driven out, the cells, which are excavated in the flinty rock and seem exceedingly well-fitted to a life of piety, were deserted by the hermits who had inhabited them, and thus became material for the tales and speculations of travellers.

Three miles further on is the fort of Beoxpalangum[223] ('mad lynx'), from which Mirsachimus had withdrawn his garrison. It had also been deserted by the rest of its inhabitants, in fear of Zelaldinus.

Jalalabad.

Two days later Gelalabada ('fervour in worship') was reached. Camp was pitched on the bank of the Coas a mile from the town, where the prince awaited his father's return in accordance with orders. The Priest also stopped there. For the King was unwilling that a man unused to war, devoted to religious and literary studies, and above all of a delicate constitution, should undertake an arduous and rapid march. He had instructed the prince to treat the Priest with as much solicitude and kindness as he himself was wont to do; and the prince, who was exceedingly affectionate and obedient towards his father, behaved towards the Priest with the greatest kindness and love, as indeed he had always been wont to do. The prince, whilst at Gelalabadum, appeared publicly at certain hours each day, armed with a sword and surrounded by a company of those guards whose turn it was to be on duty. In this fashion he attended to public business, in consultation with the chieftain Bagoandas. All this he did in imitation of his father. He showed also no small presence of mind in quelling a riot, which had spread panic through the army in the fear that it might be due to treachery. For he sent Meacanuus,[224] who was in command of the couriers, with a band of soldiers to order the rioters, on pain of instant death, immediately to cease the disturbance.

This district of the Paropanisus, lying between Caybaris (or rather the pass of that name) and the city of Chabulum, is very mountainous and covered with forest. The peaks are snow-capped all the year round.

223 Behosh-palang
224 Miyan Khan.

Even in July the Baalanum range, twelve miles south of the city, cools with its snows the surrounding air. This range is prolonged to within a mile of the city by another snowy height, which bends round so as to enclose within its numerous folds the plain on which the army was encamped. Hence the position of the camp was well-chosen; for even in the hottest part of summer the climate of Gelalabadum is cool. God the Creator has vouchsafed that the inhabitants of this region should not suffer from want of the necessities of life; for He has granted that certain plots of ground in the recesses of the snowy mountains shall receive enough heat from the sun to enable them to produce fruits as abundantly as other regions which are far distant from the snows. For the country round Gelalabadum has many vineyards and gardens, in which grow the pear, the vine, the pomegranate, the peach, the mulberry, the fig, and other fruit-trees. The inhabitants of the Province are the Patanaei, who are controlled by a Mongol garrison. These Patanaei, whom the Mongols call 'Aufgan,' live by agriculture. They are miserably off for draught animals and ferry-boats. On land they carry their goods themselves, slung on their backs by means of loops of rope through which they put their arms, just as a breast-plate is worn. They walk upright in this fashion even under heavy burdens. On the rivers the loads are carried by means of ox-skins daubed with liquid pitch. Corn or vegetables are enclosed in these skins, and the steersman binds himself on the top. They launch themselves thus downstream on the rapid current of the river: and endeavour to keep a fairly good course. They wear a short garment coming down to the knee. They are devoted to music and sing sweetly to the pipe or lyre, with free high tones in the European manner, not with low quavering notes in the Asiatic manner.

The citadel of Gelalabadum has been fortified by nature rather than by the art of man. For on the east the high and precipitous crag on which it stands overhangs the Coas. It was held by Faridumcanus, who cravenly evacuated it, against the orders of Mirsachimus, before the coming of Zelaldinus. Gelalabadum stands on a hill surrounded by a plain, from the borders of which rise mountains extending all the way to Chabulum.

Chabulum itself is built in a lofty position, and is so cold in winter that the King is always compelled to descend to Gelalabadum, together with his guards and attendants and the whole court. But in summer the climate is so cool that even midsummer—the worst part of the year—is passed without feeling the heat of the sun; and for that season the King removes from Gelalabadum to Chabulnm. The latter city is remarkable chiefly for two things; firstly it is the capital, secondly it is crowded with merchants, who resort thither out of India, Persia and Tartary. For it is situated in the very heart of the mountains, which stretch out their arms, as it were, to touch the surrounding countries—India, Sogdiana,[225] Bactriana,[226] and Tartary.

These mountains form the Caucasian Imaus,[227] which is the same as the Caspian Paharopanisus and the Paharvetus. The Caucasius lies in the middle of these. On a spur of these mountains stands Chabulum, which

---

225 Bokhara.

226 Bactria, *i.e.*, Balkh.

227 A quotation from Arrian's *Anabasis of Alexander and Indika* will explain this: "In Bactria the Taurus unites with Mount Paropanisus which the Macedonians who served in Alexander's army called Caucasus, in order, it is said, to enhance their king's glory, asserting that he went even beyond the Caucasus with his victorious arms. Perhaps it is a fact that this mountain range (Paropanisus) is a continuation of the other Caucasus in Scythia,' (p. 253). And again, on page 400, he writes; "It is known by various names in different districts: in one part it is called Paropanisus (Hindu Kush) in another Emodus (Himalaya) in a third Emaus (Pamirs), and probably it has several other names." But there is much difference of opinion about the exact identifications of Emodus and Emaus or Imaus. We read in M'Crindle's *Megasthenes and Arrian* that Emodus was the name given to that part of the Himalaya range which extends

was anciently called Carura[228] (or so it is said). The Paharvetus, in which is the pass mentioned above, continues the Caucasius to the south, whilst to the north it is defended by the Paharopanisus. Eastward lies the Imaus, and westward an extension of the Paharvetus, of equal dimensions, which bends to the north to join the Paharopanisus; it is separated from this, however, by great ravines. All these mountains are now called after Chabulum, but by the ancients they were all called the Paharopanisus. They used to be infested by the descendants of Temur the Lame, who dwelt amongst the forests in a state of chronic warfare and disturbance. Later they broke forth, conquered and held almost the whole of inland India. In order to prevent confusion in the names of these mountains two points must be borne in mind. First, that all this far spread mass of mountains belongs to one main chain, but has various and ill-defined names; for instance geographers sometimes give the name Imaus to what is still really the Caspius, and the name 'Caucasius' to what is still really the Paharopanisus, and vice versa. Secondly, that in our time the names are entirely different from what they were in antiquity. I have however taken great pains to determine the exact localities, or those that are approximately exact, corresponding to the names. In many cases I have the best of all authority—the testimony of my own eyes. I have written Paharopanisus and Paharvetus because in the vernacular 'pahar'

---

along Nepal and Bhutan and onwards towards the ocean. In any case the Greeks by these words meant the Himalayan range, the Vedic name for which was Himavant. Imaus and Emodus reproduce in Greek form the Sanskrit words Himavant and Hemadri. The word Paropanisus is said to have been derived from *Paru Nishadha*, *Paru* being the word for a mountain, while Nishadha was the name of the range north of Kabul. But whence, asks Cunningham, comes the insertion of *Pa ?*

228 Karoura or Kaboura was the name given by Ptolemy to modern Kabul. The whole of Afghanistan was called *Kaofu* by Chinese writers. Kaofu was the name of one of the five tribes of the Yuechi.

means 'mountain.' The latter part of each word is the actual name of the mountain. Thus Paharopanisus means 'Mount Panisus' and Paharvetus 'Mount Vetus.'

Akbar enters Kabul

Whilst the prince was at Gelalabadum various rumours were current prophesying the downfall and death of Mirsachimus. It was however found to be true that, on learning of his brother's approach, he had taken to flight, and lost the younger of his two sons, who fell from his horse and was accidentally trampled to death by the horsemen, who were following their leader in headlong flight. The prince's body was not found—it was not even sought for. Mirsachimus took refuge on a very lofty and precipitous mountain, where he could successfully offer resistance to his brother if he pursued him. This stronghold had only one approach.

On hearing of his brother's flight Zelaldinus ordered his herald to announce to the people of Chabulum that they need have no fear for their safety: for he fought not with merchants, workmen and common people, but with his brother's army which had now fled. When he heard that the city was quiet he entered it in triumph, after first traversing the surrounding region, and took up his quarters in the palace. He was greatly delighted at being permitted by the mercy of God to take his seat upon the ancestral throne once occupied by his father and grandfather, especially since his triumph had not been achieved without a double loss. For whilst Pahari was in command of the advance-guard, a sum of 15,000 pieces of gold, sent by the King as pay for the prince's troops, had been seized by an ambush of Mirsachimus. The paymaster himself had been captured and ill-treated, though some time later he was ransomed for a large sum. The King upbraided him soundly for his carelessness and cowardice. For it was said that, though he had enough men with him to have enabled him to put up a resistance, he fled in panic and was captured without receiving, much less inflicting, a single wound. In the second place Faridumcanus' scouts had fallen upon Xecus Gemalus,[229] the King's brother-in-law, from an ambush, and had put him to flight, though he had a hundred troopers with him. In shame and fear of Zelaldinus, Xecus Gemalus adopted the scanty clothing, bare head and unshod feet of a Darvexius[230] and began to live a religious life after the Musalman pattern. For he knew that the disaster was due to his own fault in not keeping to the direct line of march; and Zelaldinus is generally severe to breaches of military discipline. However, since the offender was his own brother-in-law, the King gave careful directions that he should be recalled, and when he came, remarked to him that the chances of war are various and uncertain, comforted him in his dejection, and far from sternly reprimanding him merely told him to be careful on the return journey.

The King stayed at Chabulum for 7 days in order to give public indication of his victory after the fashion of his ancestors. His sister came to him, asked for pardon, and begged him to have mercy on his conquered brother and to give him back his kingdom, for he was sorry for what he had done. However the result of her interceding was this only that the King, in reliance on her virtue, faithfulness and tact, handed over the kingdom to her charge.[231] He declared that he would have no dealings with Mirsachimus, whose very name he had forgotten, and whom he could not bear to hear mentioned. He would choose his own time for asking her to hand over charge of the kingdom again. He cared not a straw whether Mirsachimus, lived at Châbulum or anywhere else in the kingdom. He himself would soon leave the city in compliance

229 Shaik Jemal. His sister Goharunnisa was one of Akbar's favourite wives. Blochmann says that Jemal was excluded from court (and hence turned a Fakir) because of his offensive drunken habits. He died in 1585.

230 Darvesh.

231 She however tacitly allowed her brother to resume the government and Akbar connived at it.

with her wishes, for he loved her dearly, and he trusted her so completely that he would leave no forces or garrisons in the kingdom. He advised her to tell Mirsachimus never to return to his intrigues. He was old enough, and experienced enough, to know what was to his genuine advantage. If he kept quiet, he himself would be a true brother to him; but if he persisted in his mad schemes, he would be even less inclined than at present to be generous to him and pardon him. If he liked, he could occupy the approach to the crag on which Mirsachimus had taken refuge, and soon starve him into abject surrender; but he did not intend to do so, since she had come to intercede for the offender.

Return to India.

Having thus addressed his sister, and written out the edict by which the kingdom was given into her charge, the King prepared to depart. The army was ordered to move on a certain date, and he himself preceded it by forced marches to the camp at Gelalabadum, attended only by a small staff. The whole army, and the Priest amongst the rest, went out to meet him and congratulate him. He received the Priest's congratulations with a pleased expression, probably because, being very greedy of glory, he hoped that through him his fame would reach Spain. When the whole army was re-united at Gelalabadum, a start was made for Fattepurum. Remarking, in the midst of a number of his generals, that the war had been concluded without bloodshed, he asked the priest for details of the disaster in Africa, in which four Kings had been destroyed in as many hours. What had induced Sebastian[232] to trust to, and ally himself with a Musalman? When the Priest had explained the whole affair to him, the King exclaimed, 'I can never sufficiently praise the heroism of those who fight hand to hand and in deadly

---

232 King of Portugal, who fell at Alcazar Kibir in August 1578, while fighting against the Moors in North Africa (Danvers II 12-22).

earnest. But I shall never cease to condemn the cowardice of those who prefer the safety of their bodies to the eternal glory of war. O hardy and courageous youth, who for the joy of battle crossed the sea and accepted the call to invade a foreign land, at the risk of all he had!' Being of the same nature and character as Sebastian in his intrepidity and carelessness of danger, Zelaldinus very frequently extolled his brave deeds.

The King granted the Priest leave to precede the army by two days in order to avoid the dangers of the Caybarene pass. However whilst ascending the steep approach to the pass, the Priest ran a great risk of being stoned to death, (for the ground is here covered with stones which have been brought down by floods). A certain Musalman approached and asked him if he believed in the Prophet. The Priest replied, 'No indeed.' The Musalman asked 'Why not?' 'Because he was not a prophet.' 'Do you believe in Alcoranus?' 'No.' 'Why not?' 'Because it is not God's book.' 'By the living God,' said the Musalman to a large crowd of people who happened to be passing, 'Look at this unbelieving villain. He denies that Muhammad is prophet, or Alcoranus the book of God.' He repeated this several times in a tone of fierce eagerness, and doubtless the Priest would have been stoned, had the crowd not been afraid that the King would be so enraged, if they killed him, that he would delight and revel in their own execution. This alone kept them from the murder.

When the King reached the Mosque of Ahalis, which has already been mentioned as being situated at the entrance to the Caybar, he ordered a piece of gold to be given in alms to each of a huge crowd of beggars (or rather worthless good-for-nothings) who polluted the army with their presence to the number of 3000. He himself performed his prayers there after the Musalman fashion.[233]

---

233 This was politic hypocrisy. Akbar had ceased to entertain any respect for Islam.

It may be of interest to students of the classics if I tell them that I am convinced that the Caybar, and the mountains named after it, are so called from the city of Capissa (or Capissenae) which was destroyed by Cyrus.[234] The passage of ages had caused the change in the name given to the neighbourhood. Before I pass on, I must mention that not far from the road are the ruins of a very ancient city, whose name has perished together with its buildings. Moreover these mountains border upon the region of the Indus, as was the case also with the district of Capissa.

During the march to Chabulum Zelaldinus had had a white tent erected within the enclosure of the royal head-quarters, and in this he had performed his prayers, but on the return journey he pretended not to notice that it was no longer erected. On emerging from the Caybar pass and reaching the plain, the King had several villages near the Coas burnt, because their inhabitants had refused him grain and supplies on the way up, and could not be persuaded to sell him any food either by entreaties or by large offers of money. The wretched people of these villages fled across the river, as soon as they heard that the King was returning, and helplessly watched the burning of their property from a height on the other side. They suffered for their loyalty to Mirsachimus, illustrating the words of the poet : "The people must suffer for the sins of their rulers." Camp was pitched on the bank of the Coas, near its junction with the Indus: and the army waited whilst a bridge of boats was thrown across the latter river at a narrow point near Nilabhum. For the climate of that region begins to get cold in September, and the snows cease to melt; thus the size of the river decreases so markedly that it can be bridged with safety.

When the bridge was ready the King, in accordance with his promise to his sister, ordered the whole army to cross, together with the garrison which had

---

234 Gandhara was the eastern limit of the vast empire of the Persian Emperor Cyrus (558-30 B.C.).

been left on the bank of the Coas. He then marched for three days in the direction of Casmiria. He intended to annex that province as a punishment to its king for his ingratitude. For this king had received marked benefits from Zelaldinus not long before, but had shown no tokens of gratitude for these benefits whilst Zelaldinus was marching through his territory. It was his duty to come to greet the King, either in person or at least through ambassadors, to send presents and supplies, and to offer reinforcements in token of his allegiance. For he had been driven out of his kingdom shortly before by his uncle, and Zelaldinus had re-instated him. However the King was dissuaded from carrying out his intention of invading Casmiria by the advice of his ministers, who plainly pointed out to him that the whole army was exhausted by the eight months' arduous campaign just ended so successfully, and that it must be given an opportunity for rest and refreshment. Moreover the enterprise would be impossible for elephants, since the mountains are steeper, higher and more impassable even than those of Chabulum. Nay more, a large part of the way must be traversed on foot, since horses can hardly struggle along even without a rider. Again, winter was at hand, when the passes are blocked by very deep snow, so that the right path cannot be seen, and hence there would be great danger of numbers of men slipping and falling over the cliffs. In accordance with this advice the King turned back towards Fattepurum, putting off to another occasion his revenge (as he himself called it), or more properly the gratifying of his craving for adding to his dominions.

Illness of Rudolf

On reaching Ruytasium the King informed the Priest that Rodolfus was ill at Ceynandum. He asked also the significance of the name Rodolfus, and whether it had belonged to any of the Apostles. He told the Priest to repeat the names of the Apostles and to tell him what their number had been. Having satisfied him on these points the

Priest added that 'Apostle' means the same as 'rassul:' and that, whilst the Musalmans recognize only one Apostle, the Christians recognize twelve, who lived long before Muhammad and were mightier and wiser than he. These Apostles taught moreover that Christ is the Son of God, which Muhammad denies. The Priest begged earnestly to be allowed to go and visit Rodolfus, in order to fulfil the latter's desire to make his confession. The King first put a few questions regarding the nature of this sacrament, which the Priest answered. The King then asked, 'What sins can you priests have committed, who for the love of God live this kind of life, and wear black clothes?' For amongst the Mongols black is the sign of mourning and the symbol of death. The Priest replied 'I should indeed believe that the sins of Rodolfus are few and small. For he excels all others in his character and in the purity of his life. But we are commanded by Christ and by the Church to disclose to priests at certain stated times our actions, our words and the thoughts of our hearts. Wherefore, if you enable me to visit him, you will confer an unimaginable benefit upon both of us: for we most earnestly desire to see each other.' Then the King observed to some of the bystanders 'See how they love each other.' He also told Xecus Faridius[235] to find out how much money the Priest stood in need of for his daily expenses and for any debts he might have incurred: and to enquire whether Rodolfus had undergone any expenditure for medicine and treatment during his illness. After making these enquiries Xecus Faridius[235] made a report to the King, who ordered the Priest to be given

---

235 Shaikh Farid. He served in the Orissa campaign against Kutlu (1584). In 1585 he was made commander of 700 and gradually rose to be that of 1500. It was he who saved Selim from the trap laid for the Prince by Mirza Aziz Kokah and Man Singh in order to ensure the succession for Khusru, son-in-law of the former and nephew of the latter. Under Jahangir he filled responsible positions and held a command of 5000. He never built a palace for himself and always lived as if on the march.

more than twice as much as he had asked for. Having obtained leave from Zelaldinus the Priest hastened at full speed to his friend, crossing the Bydaspes, Sandabalus and Adris, which last-named river flows from the north past Lahurum. He reached this city in four days; but it was the will of God that the Priest should only leave the army to fall very dangerously ill and be nursed by Rodolfus. Before his departure the Priest had gone to bid farewell to the King. On that occasion the King was accompanied by some nobles[236] who had transferred their allegiance from Mirsachimus to himself that very day. These nobles appeared to be astonished at the sight of the Priest, and to be wondering who he could be. The King went up to them and remarked (as a description of the character of the foreigner whom they were gazing at) 'This man is regarded by the Franks as a saint.'

When Zelaldinus reached Lahurum, Rodolfus hastened to the camp in order to congratulate him. The King received him with much joy and many signs of affection. Having received his congratulations and good wishes, the King disclosed to him his intention of sending an embassy to the king of Spain,[237] and one of the priests with it. On Rodolfus telling him that the Mongols had raided the district of Daman, he expressed himself as exceedingly sorry to hear the news.

Lahore.

I must now give some account of Lahurum. This city is second to none, either in Asia or in Europe, with regard to size, population, and wealth. It is crowded with merchants, who foregather there from all over Asia. In all these respects it excels other cities, as also in the huge quantity of every kind of merchandise which is imported. Moreover there is no art or craft useful to

---

236 One of these was Khwaja Muhammad Husein, brother of Qasim Khan, *Mir-Bahr*.

237 The object of the Embassy was to invite Philip II of Spain to join Akbar in a league against the Turks. The letter however was addressed to the Scholars of Europe (see *Introduction*).

human life which is not practised there. The population is so large that men jostle each other in the streets. The citadel alone, which is built of brickwork laid in cement, has a circumference of nearly three miles. Within this citadel is a bazaar which is protected against the sun in summer and the rain in winter by a high-pitched wooden roof—a design whose clever execution and practical utility should call for imitation. Perfumes are sold in this bazaar and the scent in the early morning is most delicious. The remainder of the city (out side the citadel) is widely spread. Its buildings are of brick. Most of the citizens are wealthy Brachmanae and Hindus of every caste, especially Casmirini. These Casmirini are bakers, eating-house-keepers, and sellers of second-hand rubbish, a type of trade which well suits their Jewish descent. The surrounding district is fairly fertile.

Mirsachimus reached this city in his invasion, and established his camp on its eastern side, near some very large gardens. He ordered the commander of the citadel—Mancinus son of Bagoandas—to surrender; but he replied, 'I shall not break my promise to your brother Zelaldinus, who gave this fortress into my charge. If you wish to make trial of your fortune, advance to the storm; for I am ready to resist you. If you trust in your superior forces, I on the other hand am confident on account of the valour of my men, who will a thousand times sooner die than surrender. If you storm and capture the citadel, I care not for my life. I only desire to be faithful to my emperor, Zelaldinus.'

However Mirsachimus, hoping that this great town would fall into his hands, and thus desiring to conciliate the citizens, allowed no thefts or plunderings in the city, which has no walls: and assured all the merchants and citizens that they need have no fear for their safety, saying that he was waging war only against the commander of the citadel. He was eventually compelled to abandon the siege, as I have recorded above, by the approach of his brother.

At Lahurum the King dismissed almost all his forces into winter quarters, and proceeded by a rapid march to Fattepurum, attended only by the guard, which he is accustomed to employ, for the sake of dignity, in the capital city. He was welcomed there by his mother with the greatest joy; and, as is the custom, public games were held in honour of his arrival.

Akbar's return to Fatehpur.

Every one must be amazed at the triumphs of this emperor. For there was not one among his ancestors, from the time of Temur the Lame, who equalled him either in the greatness of his empire or in the multitude of his victories. He obtained control of the kingdom of Delinum, which had been bequeathed to him by his father, through defeating the rebellion of Beyramcanus the Persian.[238] After this he conquered, first the province of Malvana, then Gedrosia, then Gangaris and the Gangetic coast both on this side of and beyond Mount Uxentus,[239] *i.e.* between the Tindus[240] and Ganges rivers—the region whose inhabitants used to be called the Coccanagae,[241] Sabarae,[242] Gangaridae,[243] and Dryllo-

Akbar's conquests.

238 This refers to Bairam Khan's rebellion in 1560, its suppression and the assumption by Akbar of direct charge of the government. But Akbar fell under feminine influence; and Maham Anaga (his foster mother) and Hamida Bano Begum (his mother) conducted the government. Father Monserrate's information about Bairam Khan is confused.

239 "Ouxentos designates the eastern continuation of the Vindhyas. All the authorities are at one in referring it to the mountainous regions south of the Son, included in Chhota Nagpur Ramgarh, Sirguja, etc. Ptolemy places its western extremity at the distance of one degree from the eastern extremity of the Vindhyas" (Ptolemy p. 80).

240 Lassen has identified this river (Tyndis or Tindus) with the Brahmani. Yule differing from Lassen, makes it one of the branches of the Mahanadi.

241 Lassen locates this tribe in Chhota Nagpur between the upper courses of the Vaitarani and Suvarnarekha. He explains their name to mean the people of the mountains where the *koka* grows—koka being the name of a kind of palm tree. Yule suggests that the name may represent the Sanskrit *Kakamukha*,

philittae,[244] but are now known by other Indian names. To these provinces he had just added the kingdom of Chabulum. He shortly after also conquered Casmiria,[245] as he had intended, and the kingdom of Syndus[246] and Jambus.[247] At the present time he is threatening the kingdom of the Deccan,[248] which adjoins the possessions of the Portuguese, and the districts south of Gangaris, which he is weakening by a desultory and protracted form of warfare. David, king of the Patanaei, was killed in one of these wars. In another perished Rampartaosinguis,[249] the suzerain of twelve chieftains, who was pierced by a musket ball shot by the Emperor himself. Meytarsingues,[250] who

---

which means 'crow-faced' and was the name of a mythical race. He places them on the upper Mahanadi and further west than Lassen, (Ptolemy p. 172). Knowledge of the geography of India was not a strong point with Father Monserrate. He probably simply put down the names of the tribes which he had read in Ptolemy.

242 Cunningham identifies these with the aboriginal Suvaras or Suars, a wild race who lived in the woods and jungles without any fixed habitations and whose country extended as far southward as the Pennar river. These Suvaras or Suars are only a single branch of a widely spread race found in large numbers to the south-west of Gwalior and Narwar and S. Rajputana, where they are known as Surrius. Yule places them further north in Dosarene, towards the territory of Sambalpur, which produced the finest diamonds in the world. (Ptolemy p. 173).

243 They occupied all the country about the mouths of the Ganges. (Ptolemy Pp. 173-5).

244 These are placed by Ptolemy at the foot of the Ouxentos, and probably had their seats to the south-west of that range. Their name indicates them to have been a branch of the Phyllitai, the Bhils or perhaps the Pulindas. Lassen would explain the first part of their name from the Sanskrit *dridha* (strong) by the change of the *dh* into the liquid. Ozoona, one of their three towns is, perhaps, Seoni, a place about 60 miles N. E. of Nagpur, (Ptolemy p. 171).

245 Kashmir was not subjugated before 1586.

246 Sind was annexed in 1591.

247 Jammu.

248 Berar was obtained in 1596; and Ahmednagar fell in 1600.

249 Ram Partap Singh (?) Whom does he mean?

250 Mahtar Singh (?)

was also the overlord of several feudatories, was killed by Zelaldinus in a similar way. He drove into exile Mussapharcanus,[251] king of Gedrosia. The ruler of Arachosia[252] was expelled and part of his kingdom occupied. Mirsachimus, the King's own brother, was forced to take refuge in a mountain fortress. The prince of Caspiria was captured. Zelaldinus also either destroyed or took prisoner about forty chieftains and minor rulers, feudatories of the kings named above; but I purposely omit the names of these, as they are outlandish, very hard to transliterate and similar to those just recorded. In terror of his power, which they despaired of resisting, the neighbouring petty kings of their own accord paid him tribute and acknowledged him as their suzerain. His empire stretched from the false mouth of the Ganges to Chabulum (a distance of nearly 18 degrees in latitude), and from the coast of Gedrosia to the Uxentus range, east of the Ganges (or 19 degrees of longitude). Yet, in spite of his conquest of so many provinces and districts, and his capture of so many towns, it is not to be wondered at that he scarcely passed beyond the basins of the Ganges and the Indus. For India is the greatest, broadest and longest of all the countries of Asia. If God be willing, I propose to write a further account of India in a future book.

An embassy to go to Spain.

After reaching Fattepurum the King reopened the subject of sending an embassy to Philip, king of Spain; and talked it over with Rodolfus. He recommended that the same Priest who had been with him in camp should accompany his ambassadors, of whom he chose two, one to sail to Spain—a noble of very high birth,—and the other to stay at Goa—the same man who had conducted the Priests from that place. This latter was one of the sect called Xaaei,[253] being a

251 Muzaffar Shah, King of Gujarat.

252 Muzaffar Hussain Mirza, the Persian governor of Kandahar, quietly handed over the Province to Akbar in 1595.

253 Shia.

Persian, and was as good a man as his treacherous heart permitted him to be. The sect of the Xaaei was originated by Xa Ismail,[254] the king of Persia, about 80 years ago (*i.e.*, about 1500 A.D.). Its adherents are marked by the following novel superstition—they invoke Ahalis as the representative of God and call him Vahallah, *i.e.* the representative of the divine lordship and law, or the holy saint of God. For they say that Muhammad met Gabriel whilst he was taking the book Alcoranus to Ahalis (what an old wives' tale !). Gabriel asked him if he were Ahalis; whereupon Muhammad asked in his turn what boon the angel was bearing to Ahalis, for he had espied the book. The angel replied, 'I am taking him this true book from God, whereby men are to be directed and ruled. For Ahalis is himself the messenger of God.' Then Muhammad, who was greedy both for fame and for an honourable position to fill, said that he was Ahalis. Believing what he said, Gabriel gave him the book—an angel befooled by the lies of a man, forsooth! The folly and impiety of these people is seen best of all in their alleging that God permitted what had happened to remain unchanged because Muhammed was a good man and a prophet. He was thus allowed to keep the book and to be the messenger. Therefore, in the opinion of God, Ahalis is greater than Muhammad, and only failed to attain the dignity of a divine messenger through the falseness of Muhammad and the credulity of Gabriel (if God permit me to write such things). They say moreover that it is better to deserve a boon than to obtain it: and, being unable to call Ahalis the messenger of God they call him the representative of the Deity on earth. These ideas are the seed-bed and fuel of all

---

254 Shah Ismail, founder of the Safawi dynasty, died in 1523. Shiaism (upholding the rights of Ali and his children) owes its establishment as a national religion in Persia to Shah Ismail; and he is styled in Persian history 'Shah Shian' or King of the Shias. For his reign and achievements see Malcolm's *History of Persia*, Vol. I, pp. 500-505.

the wars between the Persians and the Turks. Other Musalmans call these Xaaei by the insulting name of Rafficini *i.e.*, heretics, and they are supposed to some extent to have returned to idolatry. For they pay reverence to the lion, as the symbol of Ahalis, on the precarious authority of a certain fable into which they drag the name of Gabriel, and which declares that when Muhammad had ascended to heaven he was met by a terrible lion. He was retiring in fear, when Gabriel said to him, 'Fear not. Throw the signet ring which you wear on your finger into the lion's mouth.' When Muhammad did this the lion departed. But when Muhammad again descended to earth, Ahalis came to welcome him, bearing the ring which Muhammad had thrown into his mouth under the disguise of a lion. Consider, I pray you what silly tales the Musalmans believe, what unworthy leaders they follow (endeavouring to tread in their very footsteps), what messengers of God and interpreters of religion they reverence! The most detestable feature in this fable is that they impudently and impiously drag Gabriel upon the scene as the communicator of their nonsense, although this Gabriel is by the authority of the sacred books, by the writings of the saintly Fathers, and by the common consent of the Holy Church and of all Christians, regarded as one of the chief princes of Heaven and ministers of God. But indeed in this matter the Persians may justly be held to have returned to the ancient superstition under which in former times they worshipped the sun by the title of Mithras, whose symbol was a lion with widely-opened jaws bearing a crown on its head and holding a bull by its horns. For a certain poet sings as follows:—'Be present, O thou who favourest all hospitable scenes; be present and bless most graciously the fields of Juno, whether it pleaseth thee best to be named the glorious Titan, as is the wont of the Persian race, or fruit-bestowing Osiris, or Mithras dragging by the horns the bull that was so loath to follow him, beneath the craggy roof of the Persian cave.' (Status Theb. I 716-20.)

In our own times the Persians display on their flag, which is white, the figure of a roaring lion with widely opened jaws, which seems to be attacking an enemy. When this flag is unfurled they salute Ahalis under the guise of this lion with wild shouts of Vahallah.

Outrage committed on Portuguese sailors.

But we must pass on. Whilst arrangements were being made at Fattepurum for the embassy, news was brought to the priests that war was being carried on between the Portuguese and the Mongols at Damanum over the question of Butzaris, which had been given to the Portuguese by the aunt of Zelaldinus[255] when she was staying at Surat and preparing for a journey to Mecca. Her object in making the gift was to ensure friendly treatment in case she fell in with the Portuguese fleet on the voyage. However after her return from Mecca the old lady, no longer requiring to be on good terms with the Portuguese, told the people of Surat to demand that Butzaris should be given back again, together with its land. They sent a body of cavalry to occupy the town, but these were routed by the Portuguese with considerable loss. Now the King and indeed all the Mongols, who are a proud and arrogant people (being trained from tender age to arms and hence to insolence), take it exceedingly ill that they are compelled, if they wish for safety on their sea-voyages, to come to Diu and ask for a safe-conduct, which they can only obtain on certain conditions. If they refuse to do this, and their ships afterwards fall into the hands of the Portuguese, they are treated as prizes of war. However, the governors of Baroccium and Surat obstinately persist

---

255 Gul Badan Begum (in 1575). The quarrel about Butsar or Bulsar and the consequent war with the Portuguese, due in no small measure to the hostile attitude of Qutubuddin towards the Europeans, have been well narrated and discussed in *J. A. S. B.* 1915, (July and August number) and in Smith's *Akbar* Pp. 203-204. It may be noted here that the order to organise an army to capture the European ports had been given as early as February 1580. (*A. N.* III 409). The war did not begin till 1582.

in sending off ships without a safe-conduct, and hence suffer great losses, for which cause they bear the greatest ill will towards the Portuguese. In addition to this quarrel about Butzaris there was another regarding a ship captured by the Portuguese; and as a result of this the concealed jealousy of the Mongols, due to the King's kindness towards the Christians, flamed up into open hostility. The Mongols basely sent spies into the district of Damanum under a pretence of friendship: and when a Portuguese fleet under Jacobus Lopezius Coutignus was lying at the mouth of the Taphtus river, which falls into the sea at Surat, they suddenly attacked (out of an ambush, which had been laid at night) a party of young soldiers who had landed, relying on the King's friendship towards us, with the object of catching birds and of enjoying themselves on shore. Being thus attacked, the sailors fled, and most of them reached the ships, though with great difficulty and danger. However nine were captured, dragged in triumph to Surat, cruelly treated, and on the next day executed. For they had refused to become Musalmans, even though they were promised not only present safety from the terrible danger in which they stood, but also riches, honours and beautiful and noble wives. The Mongols regarded this as a very generous offer. However, the sailors resolutely refused to accept it, declaring with hatred and contempt that it was an impious and hateful suggestion, and that Muhammad himself was an ill guide to follow. Hence they bravely bore their punishment. Their leader to martyrdom was a noble and high-born youth, Edvardus Pereyra of Lacerda, to whose faithfulness and constancy his companions owed it that, being almost persuaded by the cruelty of the Musalmans to forswear their faith, they delivered themselves from the wicked impudence of their persecutors by declaring that they would follow Edvardus whatever he should decide to do. Thereupon Edvardus, boldly drove away the wretches who were endeavouring to convert himself and his companions to Islam; and all offered their necks to the stroke. For the rest followed his example, and with wonderful courage gave their lives for the Christian faith, passing to the shores where dwell those who have lived nobly and gloriously, and are at last set free. The lives of these sailors were brief indeed, but the duration of their glory everlasting. I have not been able to ascertain their names, with the exception of that of their leader. Their heads were brought to the king at Fattepurum, though the priests pretended to be ignorant of this fact. The King also pretended that he had never heard of what had been done:—not only so, but when it became so well known that the governor of the citadel of Surat himself reported it to the priests, and the King could no longer pretend to be ignorant of it, he denied, when asked by the Priests, that he had seen the heads of the victims, and declared that he had heard with the greatest regret of the fighting which had been going on at Damanum and Surat.

Qutub-ud-Din of Broach makes war on Daman.

This war was not yet finished. For Cutubdicanus, the ruler of Barocium, gathered an army of fifteen thousand horse, partly from his own tributaries and partly from those of his son Nourancanus, governor of the district of Campanerum, who was then at the court of Zelaldinus. This army was joined by the forces of the district of Surat. Cutubdicanus then marched upon Damanum, intending to storm the citadel. He overran and devasted the whole district, as far as the river Agassainus, compelling the miserable countrymen and fishermen, and the rest of the common people, to fly to some cliffs on the coast as a place of refuge where the Mongols could not reach them. However a sudden rise of the tide drowned a countless multitude of women and children. Not long afterwards Cutubdicanus suffered a fit penalty for this crime, being defeated by the army of Mussafarus as king of Gedrosia, who had been driven out of that kingdom. Cutubdicanus was discovered by a soldier shamefully hiding in a cotton-factory,[256] and was summarily put to death. For Mussafarus had suddenly attacked the Mongol garrisons in the hope of recovering his father's kingdom, of which Zelaldinus had forcibly and cruelly deprived him.

On the occasion of Cutubdicanus' attack on Damanum, Martinus Alfonsus of Melium, Governor of Damanum, Fernandus of Castrium, Governor of Xeulum, Emanuelis of Saldanha, Governor of Bassainum, and Fernandus of Miranda, Admiral of the royal fleet, showed such valour and military skill, and were so well supported by the courage of their veteran soldiery that they succeeded in driving off the Mongols with loss. For when report was received of their approach, reinforcements were rapidly gathered from the neighbouring garrisons, and the governors aforementioned themselves hastened to Damanum. The Mongols besieged Danuhum, a village held by a small guard of Portuguese. But Joannis of Athaidium, who was in command of this guard, met the attack with such a shower of spears, bullets and other missiles that the enemy were driven off with the loss of an elephant and a number of men.

When all this was reported to the priests, they handed on the information to the King, saying that they were grieved at the unprovoked attack on the Portuguese. Whereupon he swore that the war had been started without his orders or knowledge. He said that Cutubdicanus and Xaebcanus[257] were men of age, experi-

---

256 Rather Muzaffar Shah III of Gujarat was (during Akbar's first campaign against him in 1572) found in a corn field. Qutubuddin was treacherously slain by Muzaffar after the capture of Broach in Nov. 1583. Father Monserrate always speaks derogatorily of him, for obvious reasons.

257 Shihab Khan. In the beginning of the reign we find him commander of Delhi. He was one of the arch-plotters against Bairam Khan. In 1567 he was appointed governor of Malwa to expel the Mirzas from that province, and next year was placed in charge of the administration of imperial domain lands. He was for some time governor of Gujarat; and after the death of Qutubuddin he distinguished himself in the conquest of Broach (1584) He was again appointed governor of Malwa in 1589. Died in 1591.

ence, and authority (factors which, as they knew, count for much in India), and that they took upon themselves with the self-confidence of old age to initiate many enterprises of which he himself knew nothing. Moreover he declared that he dare not reprimand them, because these enterprises always seemed to be undertaken in his own cause and for the public benefit; for the Christians were held to be the enemies of the Musalmans. This reply of the King's appeared to the priests to represent what was probably the true state of the case, for these nobles hated the King on account of his fickleness (in religious matters). Moreover the Mongols are endowed with such natural sagacity that under unsettled conditions of government they seize every opportunity for fulfilling their own ambitious schemes, and never cease from consulting their own interests until compelled to do so by some actual crisis. At the request of the priests the King ordered the two generals to withdraw their forces from the district of Damanum; and they obeyed his orders with immediate promptness. This led the priests strongly to suspect that the King had connived at the commission of the above-mentioned horrible crimes, and that he was fomenting war in a clandestine manner. This was afterwards found to be true; for Zelaldinus ordered a great quantity of arms to be conveyed into Diu hidden in bales of cotton, and instructed the Mongols to approach the town under the pretence of friendship to ask for supplies from the Portuguese as though they were allies, and then to seize the fortress as soon as opportunity offered. These orders were carefully obeyed. The Governor of Diu, Petrus Menesius allowed the Mongols to purchase corn as though they were allies, and to wander about unarmed in the fortress. He had however stationed Portuguese soldiers in ambushes and special places, with orders to put the Mongols to the sword if they made any disturbance. For Petrus preferred to pretend that he was ignorant of any treacherous attack being intended, rather than to begin a war with a King whose resources were so immense and so near at hand, without the knowledge of the Portuguese Viceroy of India. Thus the Mongols were disappointed in their intentions, and on the following day moved their army away from Diu. While all this was going on the King very frequently asked the Priests who was the governor of Diu, though at the time they had no idea why he was asking them this.

The Fathers recalled.

About the same time the priests received letters from the Provincial in which he recalled them to Goa, but left them at liberty to do whatever seemed to them to be for the greater glory of God. They had concrete proof that all Zelaldinus' professions of friendship for our master the King of Spain were a hypocritical and malicious pretence; but nevertheless they asked him with humility and submission for leave to depart. The King supposed that they made this request because they were aggrieved by the wanton attacks mentioned above, and affirmed with an oath that he was not responsible for the massacres. They knew that he was swearing falsely for no reliance must be put on the oath of a Musalman, since Muhammad himself teaches that it is lawful to swear falsely to an enemy. Still they thought it well to arrange that one of them should set forth with the ambassadors and should inform the Provincial in detail of everything that had happened, whilst the other should stay behind. They were unwilling to seem to desert the King, so long as a glimmer of hope yet remained of their performing any spiritual service. For though all the hopeful signs recorded above might be delusive and fraudulent, yet there were others which were still giving us very definite encouragement; and these I will now briefly recount.

Discussion with Akbar.

In the first place the King seemed to have conceived fresh zeal for learning the truths of religion since his return to Fattepurum after the war. For on the very day of his return he said to Rodolfus, 'God well knows how favourable my mind is to the Christian Law, and how earnestly I desire thoroughly to learn it. But I cannot follow your teaching about there being three Gods.' Rodolfus replied at once, 'We never say, O King, that there are three Gods; for this is blasphemy and contrary to the Christian faith. But we worship one God and three persons in one God, Father, Son and Holy Spirit.' After repeating this to his courtiers, the King again said to Rodolfus, 'Write to your superiors and ask them to search diligently for a man who knows well both Persian and Portuguese—one, if possible, who has once been a Musalman, and is well-versed in both Laws.' In a private conversation he afterwards told Rodolfus that he wished to make a treaty with the king of Portugal against the king of the Turks; and that he would supply money to the former. He also wished to send Rodolfus' companion, if Rodolfus himself would consent to remain behind, to bear his greetings to the Pope. He showed quite clearly that he was unwilling to allow both the priests to depart, and was greatly delighted when he heard that one would remain. He was indeed so delighted by this, that in the presence of a great number of his courtiers he congratulated and praised the priests in such extravagant terms that they were put to the blush. To Rodolfus, who was to remain behind, he said, "I think it is undoubtedly more pleasing to God that you should remain here than that you should desert me. For amongst your own countrymen there are many who can fill your post there. But if you depart from here, there is no one at all to take your place here." Moreover, when the three of them were talking over the projected embassy in a private conversation, he asked them about the Pope's dignity and greatness, and what was the meaning of the term Pope, (and not without grief do I recollect that the pontifical dignity, which this Musalman King so much respected, merely because he had heard from two foreigners that the Pope is the representative of Christ, is despised by those who boast themselves, though wrongfully, to be

Christians and the restorers of the ancient Gospel). On this occasion the King said, "You must tell the Pope that I have learnt how great and august is his dignity, as being in the place of Christ on earth: and that I have heard that all kings fall at his feet. Say then that you are sent by me to kiss his feet in my place, since I cannot be present publicly to kiss them myself. Ask him to order something to be written to me from which I may learn the way of God (for I desire greatly to know the truth) and the right manner of governing my dominions in fear and reverence towards God: so that, when heaven and earth are consumed and I am brought to that fearful judgment before God, I may be able to render a good account of the brief career of my life." He went on in the same strain, saying things which might have been uttered by some pious Christian King. He even declared that he was no Musalman, and attributed no value to the creed of Muhammad, saying that he was a follower of the sect which calls upon one God alone without a rival (these were his actual words), and searches earnestly for Him, and regards wives, children, riches and dominions as of no value in comparison with the knowledge of the truth, (the King referred to the sect of the Sauphii[258]). Nothing, he said, should prevent his accepting the (Christian) Law if he should learn anything which touched his heart and mind, either from the Pope, or from the General of the Society, or from the two priests then before him, or from any other man, however poor and humble. With regard to his sons, he was a descendant of Cinguiscanus, who was said to have had ten sons, and to have allowed each of them freely to choose his own religion: so that one of them, it is said, became a Christian. He would in like manner leave his sons at liberty to follow whatever religion they chose.

The priests regarded as no small proof of his sincerity the fact that he was so warmly attached to

---

258 Talabqhoda, *i.e.*, seekers for God—Author's note.

them, although they were foreigners, and followers of an entirely different religion. For he allowed them freely to rebuke him, when this was called for: and was as careful for their welfare as if they had been his own sons. He showed his regard plainly to both of them when they were ill, for he enquired very affectionately after their health, spent money very freely for them, and ordered the chieftain Bagoandas, when he was starting for Lahorum, to pay generously for anything they might need. When one of the priests remained behind ill at Ceynandum and was being threatened by the local Musalmans, the king directed Jadondas,[259] a Brachmana of Delinum, to make arrangements for his being conducted by his own servants to Fattepuram, and for all necessary and even many superfluous expenses on the way to be met from the royal purse.

Hence the priests concluded that they should be influenced by all these facts, and that it would be better to be deceived than to be too cautious. They therefore committed the future to God, and resolved to entertain no more doubts concerning the King's good will. Rodolfus, who was to stay behind, undertook to continue the Prince's education, whilst the other Priest began to prepare for his journey.

The Nauroz (March 1582).

In March the King arranged for a festival to be held in commemoration of his recent victory. This was called Naorus,[260] *i.e.* 'the nine days,' or perhaps 'the new days.' For the Mongols begin the year from the month of March (as also do the Jews), having learnt

---

259 Jadu Das (?)

260 Nauroz. New Year's Day festival, lasting for 6 days. It is an Iranian festival. Iranian Zoroastrianism had great influence on Akbar. The general scheme of the celebration as given by Al-Biruni is that "the King opened the festival and proclaimed to all that he would hold a session for them and bestow benefits on them. On the second day the session was for men of high rank and families; the third day was for warriors and priests; the fourth day for his family, relations and domestics; and the fifth for his children and clients. When the sixth day came and he had done

this, not from Muhammad, but from the Hindus; and they are accustomed, in accordance with ancient tradition, to regard these days as a holiday. For in Sogdiana, Bactria, Scythia and other countries lying north of the 36th parallel, the fruits of the earth first appear in March, which is the beginning of spring as in Europe. The trees are then clothed with all manner of flowers, sweet scents are wafted from the blossoms, and everything on the verdant and beautiful plains and hills appears to smile and laugh. Hence during the first nine days of this month the people cease their labours, resort to the fields and gardens, eat splendid banquets, and wear richer and finer clothing than usual.

On the present occasion this nine days' festival was celebrated by Zelaldinus with such lavish expenditure of money, with such magnificence of clothing, ornament and all manner of appurtenances, and with such gorgeous games, that the like, as we were told, had not been seen for thirty years. For the walls and colonnades of the palace courtyard were decorated with hangings of cloth of gold and silk. Games were held and pageants conducted each day. The King himself was enthroned on a high golden throne approached by steps. He wore his crown and insignia of royalty. He distributed gifts to many generals who had accompanied him on the campaign; and he gave instructions that all classes of the citizens should be bidden to show their joy either by leaping, singing or dancing. He welcomed all who came to see the festival with largess, free supply of wine, and free banquets. Hence whole communities of Jogues arrived, with their chiefs. These men were evidently devoted to religion in appearance rather than in fact; for they profanely and frivolously laid aside all pretence of piety, danced impudently and shamelessly, and fulsomely flattered the King in the songs they sang. Women were allowed to visit the

---

justice to all of them, he celebrated Nauroz for himself and conversed only with his special friends and those who were admitted into his privacy." The festival at one period was spread over thirty days.

palace and see its magnificent appointments. It was so widely reported amongst the Musalmans that the King had become a worshipper of the Virgin Mary, the Mother of God, that a certain noble,[261] a relation of the King, secretly asked the officer in charge of the royal furniture for the beautiful picture of the Virgin which belonged to the King, and placed it (unknown to the King himself) on a bracket in the wall of the royal balcony at the side of the audience-chamber, where the King was wont to sit and show himself to the people[262] and to give audience to those who desired it. The aforementioned noble surrounded and draped the picture with the most beautiful hangings of cloth of gold and embroidered linen. For he thought this would please the King. Nor was he mistaken; for the King warmly praised the idea, which also gave great pleasure to the priests, who perceived that non-Christians were worshipping and reverencing the picture, and—as if compelled by the unaided force of truth—were not denying adoration to the image of her whom the morning stars extol, and whose beauty amazes the Sun and Moon, (though some, who vainly claim to follow Christ and to be ministers of the Gospel, impudently abuse her, and are thus worse than the very Musalmans).

Another discussion

A discussion arose amongst the King's religious doctors regarding Bathsheba, the wife of Uriah; whereupon the King had the priests summoned and asked them for a true account of that affair. This was the signal for a discussion which lasted till midnight.

---

261 Abdul Saman. This is the name of the office, meaning custodian of the royal effects—Author's note.

262 This is the famous Jharokha, whence the King used to hear petitions also. In the interests of order such a practice was vitally necessary to afford incontestable proof that the King was alive. The demise of a king in those days was usually followed by civil war and confusion. To the Hindus this was a sacred sight, for the King according to their ideas is the representative of God on earth. Akbar would have been the last to discontinue such a practice. Aurangzeb discountenanced it as smacking of idolatry (see also *note* 291)

I will merely summarise its main heads. First of all the priests asked how Muhammad's statement in the second chapter of Alcoranus (*i.e.*, in the chapter called Albaccara, or 'The Cow') is to be interpreted, where he declares that everyone can be saved in his own religious law. For in many other passages he condemns those who do not believe in Alcoranus and himself, calling such men wicked unbelievers and outlaws. The Musalman doctors were greatly perplexed by this question, they had no answer ready, and indeed at first denied that Alcoranus contained such words. For they are not enough devoted to religion to make themselves thoroughly acquainted with their own book. Upon a copy of Alcoranus being produced, the priests showed the passages openly to everyone present. The doctors then made various silly, absurd and irrelevant attempts to interpret the words. One of them said that for ten years he had diligently and carefully endeavoured to discover the meaning of that saying, but had not been able to do so. The rest followed the explanation of the priests, namely, that it was a rash and false statement. Another doctor interposed that the following words must have been omitted, "if they believe in the prophet and in one God without a rival, and cry, 'Laillah, illallah, there is no god but God." To this Rudolfus replied, "If that is true, there is no use in repeating the watchword of Muhammad 'Muhammad rassul allah,' *i.e.*, Muhammad is the messenger of God." This was not only approved but even applauded by all those present, especially by the King, who could not bear the name of Muhammad to be invoked; for he himself was rightly of the opinion that Muhammad was not only unworthy of being praised as a saint, but was a wicked and impious villain. Rudolfus' opponent was silenced by this logical consequence of his own suggestion, and was too much abashed to continue the discussion. And indeed his attempted explanation was plainly inept. For if anyone rejects his own religion and becomes a Musalman and then dying obtains salvation (conditions which we allow only for the sake of argument), he is still not saved in the religious law which he broke, but in that of Muhammad to which he was converted. Hence Muhammad is inconsistent when he asserts that no one can be saved who has not kept his own law, and that each religious law can confer salvation upon its faithful followers, even though they are not Musulmans. If the explanation suggested by Rudolfus' opponent is correct, it is clearly proved that Muhammad was the most ignorant and clownish of mankind in holding this wild notion,that a religious law can save a man who has rejected it. The truth is that Muhammad made this assertion that everyone can be saved in his own law partly as a confession that the books of the various laws (*i.e.*, the Thorah or Pentateuch, the Zabur or Psalms, and the Injil or Gospel) have come from God, and partly to avoid estranging from himself the sympathy of Jews and Christians. And we must believe him to have written that no one could be saved who had not sworn to obey his own law, in order that he might definitely secure the men for whom he had been angling and who were then as it were on the hook.[263]

The priests contended, as an outcome of the above discussion, that Alcoranus contains many patent inconsistencies and contradictions. This they proved by many quotations, and their opponents were compelled to admit the fact, though much against their will. Seeing this, Rudolfus said to them, 'Why are you so deeply concerned about a matter which is perfectly plain and manifest?' The King approved of this remark, and the doctors were silenced. They would have to wait for an explanation till they met Muhammad in Hell, and could ask him in person. Rudolfus added that the passage in Alcoranus is false which declares that from the foundation of the world there has been but one law given to men by God and explained by God Himself in different way at different

[263] One or two lines missing here ... Tr.

times. For in the earliest times Adam and Noah, who were the first interpreters of the Law, taught their descendants a few of its precepts. Afterwards Moses announced to posterity the revelation which he received upon the mountain, when God appeared to him in a glowing flame. Finally Christ, the Son of God, our Liberator and Saviour, revealed to us the Word of God, as He had learnt it from His Father, whom He perpetually and without beginning listens to and obeys; and His revelation is contained in the Gospel in which we Christians believe. To this not one word could the Musalmans answer. The priests were then asked to explain some of their teachings; for instance, whether proof is needed of things which must be believed. To this the priests replied that faith takes the place of proof in the case of things which God enjoins us to believe, and that it is both foolish and impious to seek for proof of things that are too high for us grovellers on the ground to perceive. The King, Abdulfasilius and the chief of the doctors[264] agreed with this, but the two former would not admit that faith is the gift of God, insisting vehemently that faith and grace are the same virtue. The priests were hard put to it for want of vocabulary and a suitable interpreter, for the others made use of certain Arabic terms. Hence, finding that the question was one merely of terminology, they did not think it advisable to dispute the point, especially as they would obtain another opportunity of explaining their position. The doctors then declared that it was very difficult to say that God has a Son and that Christ is the Son of God; but the priests replied that it was more difficult to call Christ 'Rhohallah' (*i.e.*, the Breath or Spirit of God) than 'Ebenallah' (*i.e.*, the Son of God). For not only the Gospel, but Alcoranus itself in its fourth chapter (Elnessa), affirms that Christ is 'Quel-

264 I am unable to identify this chief of the doctors. The doctors whose names I would like to suggest are Abdun-Nabi, Shaik Mubarak, and Sultan Khwaja Abdul Azim. But I doubt if Abdun Nabi was present at these discussions.

emetollah' (*i.e.*, the Word of God); and hence it is easier to show that He is the Son of God than that He is the Breath of God (provided at least that a certain foundation of faith be first laid on which to build), since God has no body to contain his breath, nor chest, nor lungs with which to breathe. Moreover in calling Christ 'Calametollah' (*i.e.*, the Word of God) Alcoranus so far agrees with the first words of the Gospel, 'In the beginning was the Word.' All this Rudolfus put into Persian, and added that God has no incidental attributes, since everything that is in God is God Himself.

This discussion went on till very late. The King approved of all that the priests said and finally retired to rest. At the beginning of the discussion he had whispered into the ears of the priests, 'For the sake of these doctors I beg that there may be no slandering of Muhammad in this discussion.' This hint the priests took great care to follow.

The King was always pondering in his mind which nation has retained the true religion of God; and to this question he constantly gave the most earnest thought. He devised the following ingenious method of settling the problem. On a certain night he ordered all the nobles, the religious leaders both of Hindus and Musalmans, and the Christian priests to be summoned to the inner palace. He placed the nobles in lines according to their rank, bade all the wise men and doctors of religion take their places before him, and then asked them questions on various points. The Christian priests, in accordance with a previous decision, brought up for discussion the following very knotty point. 'Alcoranus says that if this book is taken to a mountain, the mountain will be split in twain. In regard to this we have two questions to ask. Firstly, of what book is this to be understood? Is it the one which is said to have fallen from heaven and to have been given to Muhammad by Gabriel? Or does it apply to all the copies of that original book? If the latter is the case, why is this mountain on which we stand not split in twain, if Muhammad is to be regarded as a true prophet? For there are many copies of Alcoranus on this mountain. But if the saying is to be understood as applying only to the original book which was brought from heaven, then we ask our second question—Where is that original book and has it ever split a mountain?' The doctors readily agreed that the words in question were not to be understood of the copies of Alcoranus in common circulation. But they dared not acknowledge where the original copy was, though they knew well enough. They tried to evade the question by various devices and fictions. A certain man[265] who was known as the Sultan of Mekka because he had lived for long in that city, was asked by the King whether the original was not kept at Mekka: but replied unblushingly that he did not know. The King then remarked to the priests, 'Do not suppose, Fathers, that my doctors will answer you accurately according to the genuine words of Alcoranus. For every one of them answers merely according to his own opinion or prejudice'. The priests then said, 'We give all who are here present free leave and opportunity to go and look for that original book, to bring it when found to the foot of this mountain, to retire to some distance on the plain, leaving us on the mountain, and then to send the book up to us on the mountain. We are prepared to run the risk of the mountain splitting. If it does not split, they must confess that the book is a tissue of fraud and lies, and was never sent from God, since it does not fulfil the engagement which it contains, and by which it was to be proved the book of God, nor does it vindicate the good faith of him who made this promise.' Someone then suggested that the saying was hyperbolical. Rudolfus replied that, if this was so, then that other passage must also be understood hyperbolically in which it was said that Muhammad

---

265 This probably refers to Sultan Khwaja Abdul Azim, *Mir Hajj* (*J.A.S.B.* Vol. LXV. 1896 p. 48) He returned from Mecca in 1578, and died in 1584.

had caught half of the moon in one of the sleeves of his linen shirt, and had tossed it into the sky by means of the other sleeve, in order that it might be united to the other half of the moon. This is regarded by the Musalmans as one of the chief miracles of Muhammad. Rudolfus maintained that if there is no hyperbole in this latter passage, then none can be suspected in the former.

At the conclusion of this discussion the King briefly addressed all who had been present. He said, "I perceive that there are varying customs and beliefs of varying religious paths. For the teachings of the Hindus, the Musalmans, the Jazdini,[266] the Jews and the Christians are all different. But the followers of each religion regard the institutions of their own religion as better than those of any other. Not only so, but they strive to convert the rest to their own way of belief. If these refuse to be converted, they not only despise them, but also regard them for this very reason as their enemies. And this causes me to feel many serious doubts and scruples. Wherefore I desire that on appointed days the books of all the religious laws be brought forward, and that the doctors meet together and hold discussions, so that I may hear them, and that each one may determine which is the truest and mightiest religion." He then turned to the priests and asked which day is auspicious and destined to be good (as he put it). They answered that no day is inauspicious and evil, although some may happen sometimes to be better than others. 'For since the light of every day is bestowed by the mandate of God, who does no evil, no day can be called evil in itself alone. Yet it is written in the Gospel, (by which name the Musalmans with whom the discussion was being held call the New Testament), 'See to it then, brethren, that ye walk circumspectly, not as fools, but as wise, redeeming the time because the days are evil.' The reason for this statement is that the men of that age were evil, or that being close to the

266 Gabræi (Parsis)—*Author's note* (see note 22)

coming of Anti-Christ the age itself was disastrous to those who believed in Christ. It is a common saying moreover that he who befouls himself with crimes was born on an ill day; but in so saying we blame the man, not the day. Christ also said, as if in paradox, 'Sufficient unto the day is the evil thereof.' By the same figure of speech days are called good or better from the events which happen to us on them. When enterprises are to be begun which redound to the praise and glory of God and to the benefit of souls, there is no need to investigate whether the day is auspicious and good, or inauspicious and evil. For in truth there is no such thing as a day which is evil and inauspicious by its own nature, as the saying is, and not by reason of the deeds done on it.' These views appeared very extraordinary to all who heard them; for they believe that an inexorable fate has decreed that some days shall be evil and inauspicious, wherefore they cast lots and take the advice of soothsayers and diviners with most superstitious zeal and an almost incredible anxiety, in order to find out whether a given piece of business should be started today or tomorrow. However, no one dared to oppose Rudolfus; and so the King dismissed the assembly and retired.

On the next day he again ordered several doctors belonging to other sects to be summoned together with the priests. When they had arrived, he said to the priests, 'I desire that we should now begin to carry out my proposal of yesterday: and I beg you to do your part readily: for the Most High God has given me the desire to take the step you wish, and which you have so often pressed upon me. God knows that I am sincere in my will and intentions regarding this determination which I have made.' At the moment when he said this his two eldest sons were sitting by his side and several chieftains and petty kings were standing around him. The priests replied that they would not hinder or delay his satisfying his desire, and at once began the proposed course of lectures and discussions with an exposition of the Gospel. However the others gradually ceased coming to the appointed place, and the Christians alone gladly obeyed the King's desire. They also brought him what they wrote, on the days arranged: and he asked them a few questions, rather to avoid appearing changeable in his intentions than because he was still interested in his original proposal. However the priests began to suspect that he was intending to found a new religion[267] with matter taken from all the existing systems; and hence they also gradually withdrew themselves from the meetings. For at this time the King was daily showing greater and greater favour to the Hindus, at whose request he had forbidden the sale of buffalo-flesh in the meat market. Hence the priests did not feel it right to give him the pearls of the Gospel to tread and crush under his feet. Furthermore he had caused a wooden building of ingenious workmanship to be constructed, and had it placed on the very highest point of the palace-roof: and from this he watched the dawn and worshipped the rising sun. Nevertheless the priests continued to pray for better things, and did not feel they should refuse to go on the projected embassy.

The Embassy Starts

At last, after long delays, one of the priests set out from Agara for Goa with the ambassadors, and by the grace of God, for whose sake it had been undertaken, accomplished the long journey safely, though he was at times in great danger. For Saydius Musapharus[268] had been compelled by the King to go upon the embassy against his own will. He regarded it as so long and interminable a journey as to be almost the same as banishment. He had heard moreover that a sealed letter had been given to the Priest, which was to be opened at Surat, and he was afraid that this letter

---

[267] Known as the Din-Ilahi. It was based chiefly on Hinduism, Zoroastrianism and Jainism. Devotion to Akbar was its main tenet.

[268] Sayyid Muzaffar

contained orders for his execution, for the King had not long before been informed that he had been implicated in Xamansurus' conspiracy. Hence Saydius Musapharus frequently urged the Priest to open the letter, which by the command of Rudolfus the Priest refused to do. Hence Saydius Musapharus tried not once or twice only to persuade his colleague to help him in secretly making away with this Priest, which might quite easily have been accomplished. The embassy would have been prevented from proceeding by his murder; for the King had foolishly, and moreover falsely, told Musapharus that its being sent was due to the efforts of the two priests; and hence the two Mongol ambassadors would have been able to return home. However, by the mercy of God, the other member of the embassy was friendly to the Priest, and did not object to acting as an ambassador merely to the Viceroy of India.[269] Hence he prevented his colleague's committing the crime. For he declared that it was unworthy of the good faith of a Musalman to murder an innocent and upright man, who relied confidently on their friendship, for no other reason than that he was obeying the King's orders; moreover they knew that the intended victim had no evil intentions against themselves. He also pointed out that, since the sealed letter was to be opened at Surat, Saydius Musapharus could then decide, according to the nature of its contents, whether or no it would be dangerous for him to proceed.

Saydius Musapharus was mollified by these considerations, and was dissuaded from his intention. He decided to go to Cutubdicanus, the governor of Baroccium, who was his kinsman, and ask him for advice as to the best course to pursue. The Priest had to hasten to Damanum at the utmost speed in order to arrange for a ship to be ready there for the use of the embassy; and hence Saydius Musapharus gave him eight of his

---

269 Dom Francisco de Mascarenhas arrived in India in April 1581—he being the first Viceroy of Goa appointed by Philip II after the subjection of Portugal. (Danvers II, 28, 40).

servants as an escort, though only as far as Mandhoum. On proceeding without this escort beyond Mandhoum, the Priest unexpectedly fell into the greatest danger. For the roads were infested on all sides by robbers; and to Musalmans the mere name of Christian or Frank is horrible and hateful. Hence they are easily induced to put Christians to death. Besides this, in accordance with the King's orders, the governor of Mandhoum had directed a certain Mongol soldier to escort the Priest as far as Angertum. Four other soldiers were ordered to accompany the two as far as the Narvada, and to see them safely across the river.

After crossing the Narvada, the Mongol thought that a good opportunity offered itself to murder the priest and to take away any money he might have. It was only needful to get him as far as possible away from the road. He pretended therefore that he had some business to perform in one or two villages, and he tried to persuade the Priest to go with him. However, although the latter had no idea of these evil intentions, he felt in his mind a divinely implanted instinct against allowing himself to be inveigled far away from his companions and especially from a certain young Christian who was with him. Hence neither the Mongol himself nor the robbers whom he had encouraged to station themselves in ambush in well chosen places, dared to attack the Priest and his little band of companions. Thus, by the help and protection of God, Angertum was safely reached, where he was received with the greatest possible kindness by the adopted son of the governor of Mandhoum. Having arrived at Angertum the aforementioned Christian youth reproved the Priest for having allowed himself to be decoyed some little distance away from the rest by the Mongol soldier. Furthermore the youth informed him that, on learning from someone in the inn the previous day that the priest was a Christian and had been summoned by the King to teach him Christianity, this soldier had plainly declared that, if he got a chance, he would kill not only the Priest but the King as well.

In the pass over the Avazus range a band of robbers was met with, but by collecting his company closely together and telling them to march as it were hand in hand the Priest escaped this danger also. The robbers were hiding in the thickets of the forest. Glimpses could be caught of them through the bushes which almost blocked the road. They were planning to attack the travellers from behind out of their ambush. However, when they saw how closely their intended victims kept together, they ceased to follow them.

The territory of Surat was at length reached, exactly at the time when the Portuguese, incensed at the outrages of the Mongols, were blockading the mouths of the Taphtius river with a fleet, in order to cut off any ships sailing for Mekka without a safe-conduct. This coincidence caused the Priest no little trouble. For he was arrested by the governor of Beara and sent to Surat under a guard of three soldiers. When he arrived there, instead of being hospitably welcomed, he was imprisoned (though in honourable confinement) in some buildings surrounded by a very strong wall, where he was guarded by several soldiers and a janitor. The governor of the city accused him of trying to avoid returning to Surat. On hearing the reason for this, the governor was somewhat mollified, but again objected that the Priest had shown him no certificate or order from the King to prove the truth of what he said. The Priest then exclaimed, 'Here is my original certificate, which may be confirmed by the testimony of my colleagues. See, here on this other letter is the King's seal, can you not recognise it? I freely hand it to you. Take it away with you and carefully examine it. You will find that I am telling the truth.' 'Still,' said the other, 'You refused at first to come to Surat.' 'But I came nevertheless,' replied the Priest. The governor of the city then said, 'Well, you are welcome;' and went away. However, he afterwards sent large and liberal gifts of corn to the Priest as a sign (or rather a pretence) of friendship. By the gracious interposition of Providence, the young Christian mentioned above arrived from Daytanum[270] three days after the Priest's arrest, having arranged for a horse to be supplied from that city (which belongs to a petty chief). From him and his servants the governor and the chief police officers and the other councillors learnt that the Priest's statements were true. Whereupon they decided to release him with every sign of respect, in order that his anger might be appeased in case he were offended by his thinly disguised imprisonment, and that he might not report the affair to the King, whom they knew to regard him very affectionately. They also wished, in case he protested at the way in which he had been treated, to be able to pretend that they had kept him indoors until a suitable opportunity offered itself of giving him a welcome marked by the dignity and honour which should be shown to one coming straight from the royal presence. Yet before this they had more than once held a council to decide whether or no the priest should be murdered.

This crime they would perhaps have committed, had not a Greek Turk (or Rumes as they call a Greek) withstood them, and said that it would be better to honour this innocent stranger, who came directly from the King, than to punish him simply because he was a Christian, even though the Portuguese fleet was threatening the mouth of the river. Hence the governor[271] invited the Priest to a banquet on a certain date. On that day the citadel was decorated with flags, soldiers were stationed in rank along the wall, the whole of the cavalry was led out on to the plain, squadrons of elephants were drawn up, and the governor himself came forth to meet the Priest on the plain in front of the citadel, attended by a large cavalcade. He awaited his guest sitting in a pavilion, whence he sent the chief of

---

270 Daytan, near Surat, (mentioned by Peter Mundy in his Travels).

271 His name was Miram Sultan—*Author's note.*

his household with a small escort of cavalry to summon and conduct the Priest to his presence. The Priest came with this escort, and perceiving the governor from a distance dismounted from his horse, and saluted him and those who were sitting with him. He then took his seat, whereupon a salute was fired first from the big guns of the citadel, then from the smaller guns, and finally from the muskets of the garrison. Lastly the whole army shouted 'Allah' thrice over. The governor then rose, and the Priest followed his example. The company mounted and proceeded to the governor's palace, where the Priest was entertained to a most sumptuous banquet. He was totally unaware of the motive for all this honour and hospitality: and was indeed overcome by grief at the time. For on the day after reaching Surat he had heard that two young men had been murdered on the day of his arrival. They had been betrayed by two renegades and apostates from the faith, and on being asked whether they were spies, had openly confessed that they were. They were given the choice of death or of abjuring Christianity and becoming Musalmans. However, they bravely replied that they would a thousand times rather be murdered than desert the Christian faith, the religion of God. Though a ransom of a thousand pieces of gold was offered for them by the Vanianes,[272] and actually counted out on the spot, they were by the governor's orders immediately put to death. These Vanianes are Hindus, but resemble the Pythagoreans. They eat no living creature, and ransom from death, if they can, everything that breathes, even fleas, bugs, worms, and small birds. I believe they were formerly called Germanes,[273]

---

272 Obviously the author means the Banias (traders). They were Jains.

273 Father Monserrate here refers to Strabo. But here the Vanianes were Jains, whereas the Germanes of Strabo have been identified by eminent scholars with Buddhists—the word Germanes being an 'erroneous transcription' of Sarmanes or Sramans, *i.e.*, Buddhist monks.

because they disagree with the religious system of the Brachmanae. They call themselves Vaniaa: and the Brachmanae call themselves Bamen.

On board the Portuguese flag-ship.

After the banquet was over the Priest was given a safe-conduct to proceed to the Portuguese fleet. On reaching it he was received with great honour, much against his will, in order that the Musalmans might perceive how greatly the Portuguese honour their priests. For Fernandus of Miranda, the admiral, with whom the Priest had a close and long-standing friendship, begun in Portugal, welcomed him with a salute of the fleet's guns. The ships were also gorgeously decorated with flags. After an all-night consultation with the admiral on a large number of subjects, the Priest returned to Surat at early dawn, greatly to the surprise of the inhabitants who said, 'This is a man wholly without falsehood or deceit: for he has returned hither, though he might safely have remained with his countrymen.' Hence, whilst he was preparing for his journey to Damanum, the governor and the chief of the police vied with each other in entertaining him. Finally, after bidding them an affectionate farewell, he reached Damanum. Whilst he was awaiting the arrival of his colleagues at this place, the admiral captured a ship sailing from Mekka to Surat. She surrendered to him on the condition that all on board, except Turks, deserters and Christian renegades, should be allowed to go in safety. However, the admiral delayed fulfilling this condition; and many of the prisoners died of starvation, thirst and hardship. Others were kidnapped and unjustly sold into slavery by certain wicked Christians. Seeing this the Priest felt it his duty to persuade the admiral to keep his promise. The admiral gladly listened to his advice and commissioned him to find out who amongst the prisoners were Turks, and who Christian renegades. This, the priest did, making a very careful inquiry which lasted for two days. The Mongols were allowed to go free; but a number of Turks and Christians were retained in prison.

It has been mentioned above that Muzapharus had come on the embassy against his will, and that he had gone to Cutubdicanus to ask for advice. However, the latter refused to have anything to do with him unless he obeyed the King's orders ; for the old man wisely refused to run the risk of furthering Muzapharus' disloyalty. Hence Muzapharus, leaving all his property, fled secretly to the king of the Sedani,[274] who are now called the Decanii. However Ebadullas, the other ambassador, reached Damanum whence he sailed with the priest to Goa.

Monserrate's return to Goa.

The Viceroy of India received first the Priest and then the ambassador very courteously and affectionately. On learning the reason for the latter's coming and the importance of the embassy, the Viceroy, after conference with the nobles, generously made an offer to provide all necessary expenses for the voyage. The Provincial also communicated the matter to the Fathers of the Society, in accordance with the regular procedure, and granted the Priest leave to proceed with the ambassador. However, that year only one ship had arrived in India from Portugal; and hence all were united in the opinion that it would consort ill with the dignity of such great kings for the ambassador to make the voyage to Portugal in that ship, for it was but small and had already many passengers. It was hence agreed that the embassy must be put off for a year. Thus the Priest transferred his attention and thoughts to the duties of his ministry. When the next year arrived, the state of affairs had occasioned such changes of plans and policy that the project of the embassy was entirely abandoned and delivered over to eternal oblivion.

Rudolf's return and Martyrdom.

Meanwhile Rudolfus had grown weary of the King's fickleness, for he changed himself into more numerous shapes even than Proteus. Moreover the Provincial sent frequent letters bidding him to return. Hence he obtained

[274] See note 301

leave to depart, though only with considerable difficulty, and after giving a promise to return if he could. He arrived at Goa during the following year (1583); and the next July was murdered at Conculinum, in the district of Salsetum, by idolators. When he heard of his death, Zelaldinus was deeply moved and putting his finger into his mouth is reported to have said, 'Alas, Father, my advice was good that you should not go; but you would not follow it.'

This marks the end of the first Mission to the Mongols (the subject of this book) and of the proposed embassy to Portugal. It came to a conclusion so unfortunate that the writer of this book has made no second attempt.[275] Hence we may justly suspect that Zelaldinus had been led to summon the Christian priests not by any divine prompting but by curiosity and too ardent an interest in hearing new things, or perhaps by a desire to attempt the destruction of men's souls in some novel fashion. For if this enterprise had been of God, it could have been hindered by no hardships or obstacles. Since it was not of God it collapsed of itself, in spite of the King's obstinacy.

Rudolfus was gentle and simple, and thought all others to be like himself in these respects. He was devoted to the study of religious treatises and to prayer. Indeed the only thing that would tempt him away from these pious pursuits was the necessary study of Persian or of some other similar subject. He was perpetually conscious of God and seemed to dwell in His presence. 'My eyes are ever on the Lord.' Lest he should become weary he used to chant in a low voice, whilst walking, those brief prayers which we call ejaculations. He was entirely forgetful of himself, frequently sleeping the whole night in his clothes and in the attitude of prayer, or perhaps sitting in his chair, or—if his need of

---

275 This sentence was originally written, 'and no second attempt has been made to send a Mission,' but was altered after the sending of the second and third Missions in 1591 and 1596.

sleep was such as to cause him to lie down—in an attitude more suited to bearing punishments or to doing penance than to taking rest. He used to wear a hair-shirt, to flog himself, and very frequently to fast. He often imposed upon himself a rule of silence and solitude, only coming out of his cell for purposes of religion. He was devoted to perpetual chastity, and invoked the aid of the Virgin Mother of God to enable him to keep this resolution. He had given himself into her keeping, and vowed to extol her whenever opportunity offered. He used to take pleasure in singing softly to her honour little extempore songs, which he improvised. He was most particular in his observance of the rules and discipline of the Society, especially as regards poverty. He was glad to wear old worn-out garments and shoes. His mind was continually fixed on God, so that he often forgot what he was about. Very frequently he could not remember where he had left his hat, his spectacles, his books and the like. He was of virgin modesty. For whenever he spoke to the King he blushed deeply. He was of marvellous patience and extreme humility. He used to call himself, in jest, a fool by birth and nature. However in the space of six months he learnt the Persian language (in the polished literary form which is used by men of learning and is mixed with Arabic) so perfectly that he was able to express his thoughts with the greatest precision and felicity, to the admiration of all who heard him. For this reason he obtained a great name for extraordinary genius and learning, both with the King and with the erudite Mongols so that, as he himself used to say, none of them dared to oppose him in argument even about their own religion and book. Nay more, every one, even Abdulfasilius, who easily excelled all the rest in keenness of intellect, purposely waited for Rudolfus to express his opinion, being afraid lest otherwise they would have to retract their statements when Alcoranus was produced, or be forced to acknowledge with shame the force of his arguments.

He had given much study to philosophy and theology, and was a distinguished scholar in these subjects.

It was remarkable with what zeal he longed that Zelaldinus should be converted from a wicked life to the worship of God. He left no stone unturned in order to bring him to the faith. When the King understood this, he began to love Rudolfus warmly, not because he had any idea of becoming a Christian, or had much of an opinion of our religion, but because (as he used to say himself), knowing that Rudolfus regarded Christianity as the best of all religions, he perceived his love for himself (the King) in the fact that he tried so earnestly to induce him to accept this best of all paths to salvation.

God the Most High from His throne in Heaven perceived the designs and ambitions of this excellent priest, and gave him the highest reward and the most splendid honour. For he was delivered unscathed by God from the midst of barbarous and ferocious Musalmans, from many threatenings of death and destruction, from peril of his life by chance and accident, only to be slain at last almost in his own country, and by tributaries and subjects of his own King. For once at Surat and again at Fattepurum the carriage in which he sat, and which was being driven at a rapid pace, collapsed and was smashed to pieces. On both occasions Rudolfus was violently flung out, running a grave risk of being crushed to death, or of falling so heavily upon the ground as to lose his life. Bruised and shaken he rose only with the greatest difficulty, and returned pale and half-dead to his place of residence. Twice also he was in great danger of being crushed by elephants; for at the King's command he used to descend into the Circus, where the King was, and where maddened elephants were flinging themselves upon each other in battle. Now the nature of the elephant is such that his ferocity becomes dangerously aroused in combat. For when they first catch sight of the other elephants which have been sent into the arena to fight them, they attack blindly any men who may happen to be in their way. Moreover, when they have been defeated and are in flight, they rush upon any one they may see, snatch him up and destroy him. At such times they are entirely beyond their drivers' control. Once a fugitive elephant rent in twain a cloak which had become entangled in Rudolfus' legs and was hindering his flight. On another occasion he would certainly have been killed by an elephant, had not his companion called him back from a place to whichthe was hastening as a refuge, (but where an elephant was standing, which struck him with its trunk and almost succeeded in seizing him).[276] He burned with a great desire for a martyr's death. For he often said, "Will these Musalmans never martyr us?" To which the other priest used to reply, "The King is too fond of us; no one dare touch us." At this Rudolfus used to frown as if in deep chagrin.

However God, of His own hidden purpose, denied Rudolfus martyrdom when he was expecting and longing for it so eagerly, and then gave it to him when he expected it not at all—though perhaps I should not say that he was not expecting it; for when it came suddenly upon him, he gladly stretched out his neck and offered his throat to the savages who slew him. And from this I conclude that he was wont frequently to meditate on martyrdom and to pray for it. When he was attacked by the swords and spears of outlaws and traitors I think he must have said,[277] 'Lo, what I have desired that I now see: what I have hoped for, that I now obtain: I am united in Heaven to Him whom on earth I loved with my whole soul.'

This excellent young man was pierced by five great wounds, two at the back of his knees, one in his throat, one on the crown of his head, and one in his breast. From the last-named wound uncorrupted blood was still flowing on the fourth day after his death. He

---

276 One or two lines missing here.—Tr.

277 After the fashion of the Roman maiden Agnes.—*Author's note.*

was murdered in the thirty-third year of his age, on July 15th, 1583, at Conculinum. He had spent his whole manhood in the Society of Jesus. There died with him Alphonsus, Antonius and Petrus, priests, and Franciscus, a novice of the same Society not yet admitted to the priestly office. These received wounds similar to those of Rudolfus. He was killed on the same day on which, thirteen years before (*i.e.*, 1570) Ignatius Azevedius and his forty-nine companions had been murdered by Jacobus Soria on the island of Palma. Rudolfus was the son of the Duke of Atria, and nephew of Father Claudius Aquaviva, General of the Society.

Characteristics of Akbar.

To return to Zelaldinus, from whom we have been for a time led away by this account of Rudolfus' death. This Prince is of a stature and of a type of countenance well-fitted to his royal dignity, so that one could easily recognise, even at the first glance, that he is the King. He has broad shoulders, somewhat bandy legs well-suited for horsemanship, and a light-brown complexion. He carries his head bent towards the right shoulder. His forehead is broad and open, his eyes so bright and flashing that they seem like a sea shimmering in the sunlight. His eyelashes are very long, as also are those of the Sauromates,[278] Sinae,[279] Niphones[280] and most other north-Asiatic races. His eyebrows are not strongly marked. His nose is straight and small, though not insignificant. His nostrils are widely opened, as though in derision. Between the left nostril and the upper lip there is a mole. He shaves his beard, but wears a moustache like that of a Turkish

278 A sub-division of the Scythian tribe inhabiting lands above the Danube and the Black Sea and north of the Caucasus, (Strabo I, 470, 480; II 226-'27).

279 Chinese. 'Seres was the name of the great nation in the far east as known by land, and Sinae as known by sea,' (Yule's *Marco Polo,* Introduction p. 11).

280 Japanese. (Japones or Niphonzi—*Author's note*).

youth who has not yet attained to manhood (for on reaching manhood they begin to affect a beard). Contrary to the custom of his race he does not cut his hair; nor does he wear a hat, but a turban, into which he gathers up his hair. He does this, they say, as a concession to Indian usages, and to please his Indian subjects. He limps in his left leg, though indeed he has never received any injury there. His body is exceedingly well-built and is neither too thin nor too stout. He is sturdy, hearty and robust. When he laughs, his face becomes almost distorted. His expression is tranquil, serene and open, full also of dignity, and when he is angry, of awful majesty. When the priests first saw him he was thirty-eight years of age. It is hard to exaggerate how accessible he makes himself to all who wish audience of him. For he creates an opportunity almost every day for any of the common people or of the nobles to see him and converse with him; and he endeavours to show himself pleasant-spoken and affable rather than severe toward all who come to speak with him. It is very remarkable how great an effect this courtesy and affability has in attaching to him the minds of his subjects. For in spite of his very heterodox attitude towards the religion of Muhammad, and in spite also of the fact that Musalmans regard such an attitude as an unforgivable offence, Zelaldinus has not yet been assassinated. He has an acute insight, and shows much wise foresight both in avoiding dangers and in seizing favourable opportunities for carrying out his designs. Yet all these fine qualities both of body and mind lose the greater part of their splendour because the lustre of the True Faith is lacking.

Zelaldinus is greatly devoted to hunting, though not equally so to hawking. As he is of a somewhat morose disposition, he amuses himself with various games. These games afford also a public spectacle to the nobility and the common people, who indeed are very fond of such spectacles. They are the following:—Polo, elephant-fighting, buffalo-fighting, stag-fighting and cock-fighting, boxing contests, battles of gladiators, and the flying of tumbler-pigeons. He is also very fond of strange birds, and indeed of any novel object. He amuses himself with singing, concerts, dances, conjurer's tricks, and the jokes of his jesters, of whom he makes much. However, although he may seem at such times to be at leisure and to have laid aside public affairs, he does not cease to revolve in his mind the heavy cares of state. He is especially remarkable for his love of keeping great crowds of people around him and in his sight; and thus it comes about that his court is always thronged with multitudes of men of every type, though especially with the nobles, whom he commands to come from their provinces and reside at court for a certain period each year. When he goes outside the palace, he is surrounded and followed by these nobles and a strong body-guard. They have to go on foot until he gives them a nod to indicate that they may mount. All this adds greatly to the wonderful majesty and greatness of the royal court.

According to the instructions of the worthless Muhammad and the custom of the Musalmans, the orthodox must wear a long robe coming down to the calf, together with shoes very low at the ankle. Their dress must be made of wool, linen or cotton: and must be white. The shoes must be of a certain fixed pattern. However, Zelaldinus is so contemptuous of the instructions given by the false law-giver, that he wears garments of silk, beautifully embroidered in gold. His military cloak comes down only as far as the knee, according to the Christian fashion; and his boots cover his ankles completely. Moreover, he himself designed the fashion and shape of these boots. He wears gold ornaments, pearls and jewellery. He is very fond of carrying a European sword and dagger. He is never without arms: and is always surrounded, even within his private apartments, by a body-guard of about twenty men, variously armed. He much approves the Spanish dress, and wears it in private. He himself can ride and control elephants, camels and horses. He drives a two-horse chariot, in which his appearance is very striking and dignified. He generally sits, with crossed legs, upon a couch covered with scarlet rugs. However, he has a velvet throne of the Portuguese type carried with him on a journey, and very frequently uses it.

His table is very sumptuous, generally consisting of more than forty courses served in great dishes. These are brought into the royal dining-hall covered and wrapped in linen cloths, which are tied up and sealed by the cook, for fear of poison. They are carried by youths to the door of the dining-hall, other servants walking ahead and the master-of-the-household following. Here they are taken over by eunuchs, who hand them to the serving girls who wait on the royal table. He is accustomed to dine in private, except on the occasion of a public banquet. He rarely drinks wine, but quenches his thirst with 'post' or water. When he has drunk immoderately of 'post,' he sinks back stupefied and shaking. He dines alone, reclining on an ordinary couch, which is covered with silken rugs and cushions stuffed with the fine down of some foreign plant.

His palaces.

The splendour of his palaces approaches closely to that of the royal dwellings of Europe. They are magnificently built, from foundation to cornice, of hewn stone, and are decorated both with painting and carving. Unlike the palaces built by other Indian kings, they are lofty; for an Indian palace is generally as low and humble as an idol-temple. Their total circuit is so large that it easily embraces four great royal dwellings, of which the King's own palace is the largest and the finest. The second palace belongs to the queens, and the third to the royal princes, whilst the fourth is used as a store house and magazine. The roofs of these palaces are not tiled, but are dome-shaped, being protected from the weather on the outside by solid plaster covering the stone slabs. This forms a roof absolutely impervious to moisture.

The palaces are decorated also with many pinnacles, supported on four columns, each of which forms a small covered portico. Not a little is added to the beauty of the palaces by charming pigeon-cotes, partly covered with rough-cast, and partly showing walls built of small blue and white bricks. The pigeons[281] are cared for by eunuchs and servant-maids. Their evolutions are controlled at will, when they are flying, by means of certain signals, just as those of well-trained soldiery are controlled by a competent general by means of bugles and drums. It will seem little short of miraculous when I affirm that when sent out, they dance, turn somersaults all together in the air, fly in orderly rhythm, and return to their starting point, all at the sound of a whistle. They are bidden to perch on the roof, to conceal themselves within their nesting-places, or to dart out of them again; and they do everything just as they are told.

There is another great building, as large as the palace, in which is the tomb of Pirxecolidezcamus,[282] the philosopher who persuaded the King to remove his residence to Siquiris, and who—with the greatest stupidity—is worshipped as a saint, although he was stained with all the crimes and wickednesses of the Musalmans.

The other buildings erected by Zelaldinus in various parts of his dominions are of equal magnificence. These have been built with extraordinary speed, by the help of a host of architects, masons and workmen. For instance he built a very large peristyle, surrounded with colonnades, two hundred feet square, in three months, and some circular baths three hundred feet in circuit, with dressing-rooms, private apartments and many water-channels, in six months. Here he himself bathes. In order to prevent himself being deafened by the noise of the tools with which stones are shaped and beams

---

281 Akbar was a great pigeon-fancier. More than 20,000 pigeons, divided into 10 classes, were kept at court, (Blochmann I, 298-301).

282 The reference here is to 'Pir Shaikh-ul-Islam,' *i.e.* Selim Chisti, (Hosten). See note 67.

and other timber cut, he had every thing cleverly fashioned elsewhere, in accordance with the exact plan of the building, and then brought to the spot, and there fitted and fastened together. The Priests gave close attention to all this, and were reminded of what is said to have happened at the building of the temple in Jerusalem, when no iron instruments of the builders were heard. They saw that this could have been true without the intervention of a miracle.

Zelaldinus is so devoted to building that he sometimes quarries stone himself, along with the other workmen. Nor does he shrink from watching and even himself practising, for the sake of amusement, the craft of an ordinary artisan. For this purpose he has built a workshop near the palace, where also are studios and work-rooms for the finer and more reputable arts, such as painting, goldsmith-work, tapestry-making, carpet and curtain-making, and the manufacture of arms. Hither he very frequently comes and relaxes his mind with watching at their work those who practise these arts.

Akbar a great patron of letters.

He is a great patron of learning, and always keeps around him erudite men, who are directed to discuss before him philosophy, theology, and religion, and to recount to him the history of great kings and glorious deeds of the past. He has an excellent judgment and a good memory, and has attained to a considerable knowledge of many subjects by means of constant and patient listening to such discussions. Thus he not only makes up for his ignorance of letters (for he is entirely unable either to read or write), but he has also become able clearly and lucidly to expound difficult matters. He can give his opinion on any question so shrewdly and keenly, that no one who did not know that he is illiterate would suppose him to be anything but very learned and erudite. And so indeed he is, for in addition to his keen intellect, of which I have already spoken, he excels many of his most learned subjects in eloquence, as well as in that authority and dignity which befits a King. The wise men are wont every day to hold disputations on literary subjects before him. He listens with delight, not to actors, but to mimics and jesters, thinking their style of speaking to have a literary flavour. For the lawgiver (Muhammad) forbade all kinds of plays, both tragic and comic, and all acting, being such an impostor that, in order to gain a reputation for goodness and sanctity, he forbade things which are not in themselves wrong. And having once gained this reputation he found the way easy to a position from from which he could issue those precepts of his which are alien not only to the innate dignity of human nature but also to the general conscience of mankind. For, to draw attention to one or two such points, he allowed incestuous unions with closely-related women, excepting only the mother and the sister. He also invented and introduced amongst the Musalmans two forms of marriage, first that with regular consorts, who may number four: and second that with those who are merely called wives, and who may be as numerous as a man's resources allow. Musalman kings employ this sanction and licence of the foulest immorality in order to ratify peace and to create friendly relationships with their vassal princes or neighbouring monarchs. For they marry the daughters and sisters of such rulers. Hence Zelaldinus has more than 300 wives, dwelling in separate suites of rooms in a very large palace. Yet when the priests were at the court he had only three sons and two daughters.[283] His sons' names are as follows:—the eldest is Xecus,[284] called after the Xecus by whose advice, as has been mentioned, the King built Sequiris; for this boy was the first born after the change of capital, and thus survived infancy. The second son is Paharis, and the third Danus or Danialus.

---

283 The three sons were Selim (Jahangir), Murad (Pahari) and Danyal; for daughters see note 121.

284 Selim was called by Akbar the Shaikh Baba.

Zelaldinus has about twenty Hindu chieftains[285] as ministers and counsellors to assist both in the work of governing the empire and in the control of the royal household. They are devoted to him, and are very wise and reliable in conducting public business. They are always with him, and are admitted to the innermost parts of the palace, which is a privilege not allowed even to the Mongol nobles. However, he is wont to entrust the provincial governorships to chiefs of the Xacattaei who are related to him. Some of these chiefs also act not only as tutors but also as guardians to his sons. His object in arranging this is to attach the chiefs to himself by a yet closer bond of affection, and also to provide protectors for his children from the malice of his life-long enemies. Their literary education is committed, according to the Persian custom, to learned old men,[286] of a spurious virtue (but really of a character as wicked as that of the most abandoned amongst these Musalmans), and of an empty and ostentatious kind of piety and excellence. The princes have also trainers to teach them the use of arms, riding-masters, and instructors in archery. He gives very great care and attention to the education of the princesses, who are kept rigorously secluded from the sight of men. They are taught to read and write, and are trained in other ways, by matrons.

Counsellors.

The following is the method the King employs in deliberation—he asks each counsellor privately for his own opinion, and then himself decides upon the course which seems to be supported by the largest number and the most experienced. He asks their advice even about subjects upon which he has already made up his

---

285 It would be interesting to know the names of all these Hindu chieftains. From Abul Fazl's list (1590) it appears that there were 31 Hindus among 252 Commanders of Mansabs from 5000 to 500 Of 163 Commanders of Mansabs from 500 to 200, 26 were Hindus (*Calcutta Review* Vol. LII, 1871, Blochmann's article on *The Hindu Rajas under the Moghuls*).

286 See note 99. Shaikh Faizi had been employed as tutor to the princes.

mind, saying to the nobles, 'This is what I think should be done, do you agree?' They reply 'Salaam, O King;' whereupon he says, 'Then let it be carried out.' If however any of them do not agree with him, he listens patiently, and sometimes even alters his own opinion. Seven of his chief counsellors are chosen for the following purpose. One of them is on duty each day to attend to the business of those who crave an audience, to bring forward their petitions, and to note down and transmit the King's replies. It is the duty also of these chief counsellors to act as masters of the ceremonies, to usher forward those who are admitted to do homage to the King, to conduct them back again, to station them in the places to which their dignity entitles them, and to present their petitions before the King.

Conduct to Embassies.

Zelaldinus receives foreigners and strangers in a very different manner to that in which he treats his own fellow-countrymen and subordinates. For he behaves with marked courtesy and kindliness to foreigners, especially to the ambassadors[287] of foreign kings, and to princes[288] who have been driven from their dominions and appeal to him for protection. Such princes he furnishes with troops and resources, on one condition only, namely that they shall employ only his own weights and measures and money coined by himself. However he received the envoys of the Turkish Viceroy of Arabia Felix, whose capital is Senaa, so ungraciously that the embassy

---

[287] There were no less than four embassies from Abdullah Khan, king of Turan,—in 1572, 1577, 1586 and 1596. Akbar no doubt courteously received them all. But his letter (in reply to the embassy of 1586) proposing alliance with Abdullah Khan against the Turks, is 'full of contempt veiled under the mask of courtesy' (*A. N.* III. pp. 753—761). The embassy from Abdul Mumin, son of the king of Turan, requesting the hand of Akbar's daughter and demanding the surrender of the *Aimaqs* of Badakshan was contemptuously treated. Embassies also passed between Akbar and the Shah of Persia.

[288] *e.g.* Shahrukh Mirza, who married Akbar's daughter Shukrunnisa in 1592.

'vanished in a cloud of smoke.' For the chief ambassador was put in irons and banished for a long period to Lahore, whilst his attendants made good their escape secretly. The reason for this is said to have been his resentment at the arrogance both of the ambassadors themselves and of the king who sent them, and the endeavour which they made to persuade him to wage war against the king of Spain and Portugal

When his aunt returned from Mekka, the King had the street-pavements covered with silken shawls, and conducted her himself to her palace in a gorgeous litter, scattering largess meanwhile to the crowds.

In brief, Zelaldinus behaves so sternly towards the nobles who are under his proud sway that each one of them believes himself to be regarded not only as a contemptible creature but as the very lowest and meanest of mankind. For instance these nobles, if they commit offences, are punished more severely and relentlessly than the rest of the people, even those of the meanest degree.

His officers.

I have already mentioned that Zelaldinus has seven chief counsellors, one for each day of the week. In the same way he appoints four or five secretaries, out of a body of scribes, for duty each day. These secretaries[289] write down all the business transacted by the King, all the measures he takes, and all the orders he issues. They take down what he says with such speed that they appear carefully to catch and preserve his words before they can fall to the ground and be lost. This somewhat superstitious custom would seem to have come down from the days of those old Persian kings who—according to the

289 They were called Waqiah-nawis or News-writers. According to Abul Fazl they were fourteen in number, 'two of whom did daily duty in rotation so that a turn of each came after a fortnight'; and Blochmann commenting on this writes: "First day, first and second writers; second day, second and third writers; third day, third and fourth writers, and so on" (Blochmann I 258 n. 2.).

books of Daniel, Esdras and Esther in the Holy Scriptures—maintained the same system of scribes: in their case indeed these scribes were called chroniclers, because it was their function accurately to record in their journals and note-books every event which happened. Such is the childish folly of these scribes that the fools think it the act of a boor and a savage even to tread upon the King's shadow.

The officers mentioned above, together with the captains of the bodyguard, and the guard itself (which is on duty for 24 hours and receives rations of grain from the King) are changed in rotation .every day. The same applies to the janitors, servants and orderlies of the palace. The chief police-officer, the confidential counsellor, the chief paymaster, the comptroller of accounts, the head of the public works, the chief justice, the lord chamberlain, the governor of the palace, who has charge of the King's household, the officer in charge of the royal camp, the superintendent of the treasury, the chief janitor, the chief jailor, the chief executioner, and the head cook, etc.. etc., are all permanent officials always at hand in the palace. Men of low birth, upstarts, and (as the Mongols say) 'men who have risen,' together with those of alien birth, are given posts in the royal household if the King finds them capable and efficient, and are gradually promoted. But if such men practise mean and contemptible tricks or intrigues, he bids them always carry about with them the tools of their original handicraft, lest in their vulgarity and insolence they ever forget the low station from which they have sprung.

In order that the officers who are permanently on duty in the palace may be able to perform their duties conveniently and thoroughly, the King has had a small private office built for each of them within the precincts of the palace. In these offices they can work undisturbed; and hence the name of iataxqhana [290] (i.e. house of solitude or house of quenching thirst) has been given to them.

290 Yatash Khana.

Zelaldinus maintains, and gives a liberal education to, many noble boys and youths who have lost their fathers; and in this he might well be imitated by other princes.

Sources of Revenue.

The King exacts enormous sums in tribute from the provinces of his empire, which is wonderfully rich and fertile both for cultivation and pasture, and has a great trade both in exports and imports. He also derives much revenue from the hoarded fortunes of the great nobles, which by law and custom all come to the King on their owners' death. In addition, there are the spoils of conquered kings and chieftains, whose treasure is seized, and the great levies exacted, and gifts received, from the inhabitants of newly-subdued districts in every part of his dominions. These gifts and levies are apt to be so large as to ruin outright many of his new subjects. He also engages in trading on his own account, and thus increases his wealth to no small degree; for he eagerly exploits every possible source of profit.

Moreover, he allows no bankers or money-changers in his empire except the superintendents and tellers of the royal treasuries. This enormous banking-business brings the King great profit; for at these royal treasuries alone may gold coin be changed for silver or copper, and vice versa. The government officers are paid in gold, silver or copper according to their rank. Thus it comes about that those who are paid in one type of coin need to change some of it into another type.

Such means of increasing the revenue may be thought base, but they have two distinct advantages; for the coinage cannot possibly be debased or adulterated; and the rate of internal exchange is kept constant, since it cannot be manipulated by fraudulent money-changers. Moreover, as all the money in circulation comes eventually to the royal treasuries, there can be no scarcity of money with consequent high prices.

There is a law also that no horse may be sold without the King's knowledge or that of his agents. He allows auctions to be freely held, but buys up all the best horses for himself, without however interfering with the bidding, or taking offence if any one tries to outbid him. In order to avoid any suspicion of oppression, the money is publicly counted out on these occasions, and the seller receives several gold pieces beyond the actual price.

Zelaldinus is sparing and tenacious of his wealth, and thus has become the richest Oriental king for at least 200 years. This fact the chieftains who surround him at his court are continually dinning into his ears, in order to ingratiate themselves with him. With the object of exhibiting his wealth[291] four times every year he has sacks of minted copper money publicly piled up (I think in the palace courtyard) into a heap ten feet wide and thirty feet high. By the side of this pile sit the superintendents and tellers of the treasury. They supervise the counting of the money, which is paid out to those who are entitled to receive it, after deduction of the profit which an ordinary banker would have made if it had been deposited with him. Each sack holds about four thousand copper coins.

The crowd of officers, secretaries and paymasters, who administer the royal supplies, and grant safe-conducts, passes, contracts, etc., are accommodated in a very large hall. This secretariat is presided over by a chieftain of great authority and ability who signs the

---

[291] The Fathers of the Third Mission record that once they found the king "busy counting a large sum of gold coins of many different values which he had ordered to mint. Behind him were some hundred and fifty plates full of them, and a good number of bags, with others that had already been examined or were still to be seen. He examines them by himself or by others and it is his chief distraction every day, when he has retired, that is during the leisure left him after he has shown himself three times to the people; and when the money has been counted and put in bags, he has it placed among his treasures, which are very great" (*The Examiner*, Nov. 22, 1919., pages 469-70).

royal 'farmans.' These are eight days afterwards sealed by one of the queens, in whose keeping is the royal signet-ring and also the great seal of the realm. During this eight days' interval every document is most carefully examined by the confidential counsellor and by the King himself, in order to prevent error and fraud. This is done with especial care in the case of gifts and concessions conferred by the royal favour.

Justice.

The King's severity towards errors and misdemeanours committed by officials in the course of government business is remarkable, for he is most stern with offenders against the public faith. Hence all are afraid of his severity, and strive with all their might to do as he directs and desires. For the King has the most precise regard for right and justice in the affairs of government. In accordance with Musalman practice cases are decided by a double process before two judges. However by the King's direction all capital cases, and all really important civil cases also, are conducted before himself. He is easily excited[292] to anger, but soon cools down again. By nature moreover he is kindly and benevolent, and is sincerely anxious that guilt should be punished, without malice indeed, but at the same time without undue leniency. Hence in the cases in which he himself acts as judge the guilty are, by his own directions, not punished until he has given orders for the third time that this shall be done. During the campaign against the king of Chabulum, twelve deserters to the enemy were captured in an ambush near the Bydaspes and brought before the King. He pronounced judgment upon them; some were to be kept in custody in order that their case might be more thoroughly investigated, whilst some were convicted of treachery and desertion and handed over for execution. One of these latter, as he was

292 Father Monserrate in his other book says 'He seldom gets angry but then violently; yet he cools down quickly for he is naturally kind' (*J.A.S.B.* Vol. VIII. 1912 p. 192).

being hustled off by the executioners, begged for a chance to say something. 'O King,' he said, 'order me not to the gibbet, for nature has bestowed upon me marvellous powers in a certain direction.' 'Well,' said the King, 'in what direction do you thus excel, O miserable wretch?' 'I can sing beautifully.' 'Then sing.' The wretched fellow then began to sing, in a voice so discordant and absurd that everyone began to laugh and murmur, and the King himself could scarcely control his smiles. When the guilty man perceived this, he put in, 'Pardon me this poor performance, O King. For these guards of yours dragged me along so roughly and cruelly, on a hot and dusty road, and pummelled me so brutally with their fists, that my throat is full of dust, and my voice so husky that I cannot do myself justice in singing.' The King rewarded this witty saying with such signal grace that for the sake of this one man he pardoned both the fellow himself and his companions.

The following are the ways in which the guilty are punished. Those who have committed a capital crime are either crushed by elephants, impaled, or hanged. Seducers and adulterers are either strangled or gibbeted. The King has such a hatred of debauchery and adultery, that neither influence nor entreaties nor the great ransom which was offered would induce him to pardon his chief trade commissioner,[293] who although he was already married had violently debauched a well-born Brahman girl. The wretch was by the King's order remorselessly strangled. Although Muhammad did not forbid unnatural crimes, yet Zelaldinus punished those who are guilty of such crimes by savage scourging with leather thongs.

There are two ministers of justice, one primary, and the other for appeals. There is also a chief magistrate. Judgment is delivered only verbally, and is not recorded

93 Beveridge identifies him with Jala who was executed for rape. 'He was Akbar's broker's son and perhaps the son of Rumi Khan, if not Rumi Khan himself.' _ (*A.N.* III 390, 391).

in writing. Ordinary criminals are kept under guard in irons, but not in prison. Princes sentenced to imprisonment are sent to the jail at Goaleris,[294] where they rot away in chains and filth. Noble offenders are handed over to other nobles for punishment, but the base-born either to the captain of the despatch runners, or to the chief executioner. This latter official is equipped even in the palace and before the King with many instruments of punishment, such as leather thongs, whips, bow-strings fitted with sharp spikes of copper, a smooth block of wood used for pounding the criminals sides or crushing to pieces his skull, and scourges in which are tied a number of small balls studded with sharp bronze nails, (this latter weapon must I think be the one called by the ancients the scorpion). However no one is actually punished with these instruments, which seem to be intended rather to inspire terror than for actual use. For the same reason various kinds of chains, manacles, handcuffs and other irons are hung up on one of the palace gateways, which is guarded by the afore-mentioned chief executioner. The other three gateways are guarded by the chief doorkeeper, the chief trainer of gladiators, and the chief despatch-runner respectively.

It is the duty of the orderlies to manage the water-clocks and to strike the time on bronze gongs. These water-clocks consist of a brazen vessel filled with water, and a hollow bronze cone of such a size that exactly a quarter of an hour is taken for the water to fill it through a small hole in the bottom. This cone is placed on the top of the vessel filled with water, and the water runs in through the hole in its bottom. When the cone is full, it sinks, and thus shows that a quarter of an hour has elapsed. Everything that goes on in the palace is regulated by this clock. At fixed hours, namely before dawn when the cocks begin to crow, and in the evening, a barbaric din[295] is kept up for the space

[294] Gwalior. See note 55.

[295] From the *Naqqarah-Khana* (Blochmann I pp. 50-51)

of a full hour by means of trumpets, bugles, drums, rattles, bells and the like.

Amongst the despatch-runners are certain couriers[296] who in one day can run on foot as far as a horseman can ride at full speed. They are said to have their livers removed in infancy, in order to prevent their suffering from shortness of breath. They practise running in shoes made of lead, or train themselves by repeatedly lifting their feet and moving their legs (whilst remaining standing still in one place) till their heels touch their buttocks. When their leaden shoes are removed, they are seen to be magnificent runners, by the help of whose swiftness the King can very rapidly and regularly obtain news or send orders on any matter touching the peace of his realm.

Extent of the Empire.

And this realm is indeed a vast one. On the north in the direction of the Circius it is bounded by Mount Imaus[297] (which is now called by its inhabitants Cumaunius[298]), by the river Indus, and by the Paharopanisus. In the south its limits are the Gangetic gulf and various inland regions which adjoin the territories of Narsinga and Bisnaga[299] to the north of the Pandae.[300] Further west its southern boundary is found by Ariacum,[301]

---

296 Greek *Okypodes* (Strabo lib. 15); Hindustani '*Gelabdares*' which may not inaptly be rendered Pegasi.—*Author's note* (See Strabo's *Geography* Vol. III. p. 108).

297 See note 227

298 Kumaon.

299 Kingdom of Vijayanagar. Narasingha Saluva, governor of Chandra Giri deposed in 1486 or 1487 the Raja of Vijayanagar, and assumed the government. He made extensive conquests in the Tamil country and so successful was his administration that to Europeans the Vijayanagar kingdom was known as the 'Kingdom of Narsingh.' (See Sewell's *A Forgotten Empire.*, pp. 107-9).

300 The Pandyas occupied the modern districts of Madura and Tinnevelly.

301 This is *Ariake* of Ptolemy. "Ariake corresponded nearly to Maharastra. It may have been so called because its inhabitants being chiefly Aryans and ruled by Indian princes were thereby distinguished from their neighbours who were either of

which lies next Goa, and Cuncanum,[302] which is now called Canara, and the country of the Sedani, who live close to Xeulum and are called Deccanici. In the west it is bounded by the coast of Gedrosia and the Indian Ocean, and in the east by the regions of the Emodi[303] which extend far towards the sunrise, and by the great estuary of the Ganges, which flows from the same mountains as the Jomanes, but from a different fountain-head and by a different course. However I must remind the reader that my task is not a general description of India, but merely an account of the empire of Equebarus.[304] Of late he has added to that empire, partly by force of arms and partly by voluntary surrender, most of Gedrosia. Hence it may well be believed that the circuit of the whole of his dominions is more than 20,000 miles, and that they lie in the heart of what the ancients called 'India within the Ganges,'[305] the land which according to the historians of antiquity, was reached by Alexander the Macedonian, and which was first evangelized, according to the Christian Fathers, by St. Bartholomew. St. Thomas is said also to have lived in the coastal district.

This empire is very beautiful and healthy, although in many places not well provided with fruit trees. On

---

different descent or subject to foreign domination. The territory was in Ptolemy's time divided among three potentates, one of whom belonged to the dynasty of Sadines and ruled the prosperous trading communities that occupied the sea-board." From the 'Periplus of the Erythraean Sea' we learn that Sandanes conquered Kalyan and subjected its trade to the severest restriction. The Sedani of Father Monserrate is the dynasty of Sadines (Ptolemy, pp. 39 to 40. See Map No. XI of *Geographi Graeci Minores: Mar. Eryth*).

302 Konkan.

303 See note 227.

304 Akbar. (For if God permit, I shall add to this work another containing all the information I have been able to collect concerning the whole of India—*Author's Note*).

305 Between Kabul on the west and the Ganges on the east and between the mountains on the north and the ocean on the south. (Ptolemy p. 33).

account of the diversity of the climate in different parts it produces many and various types of crops. Thus in the southern area or zone (as geographers would call it), the same crops are found as in the maritime district (near Goa). But the farther one goes towards the north the more similar does one find the staple products to those of Europe, though indeed the following are the only representatives of the long list of European fruits and trees which grow in India with real exuberance (and these only on the Himalaya range), viz. the grape, the peach, the mulberry, the fig (in a few places), and the pine tree. The whole country bears pomegranates in abundance. The Cotonian apple, the pear and similar fruits are imported from Persia. Rice, wheat, millet and pulse are produced in great quantities. Amongst a great number of non-fruit-bearing trees, I recognised as European only the plane, though there are willows in Indoscythia. In many places in the neighbourhood of the Indus flax and hemp are sown. The plant which is commonly called 'bangue,'[306] and which when used as a drink produces intoxication and stupefaction of the mind and senses, has leaves very similar to those of the hemp-plant. It does not however grow on one stalk only, but has a low stem, from which spring a number of other branches, like a bush. Indigo and opium are largely grown in the south, and bring no small profit to the royal revenues. Indigo is a plant from which a juice is extracted yielding a blue dye when it hardens. The vernacular name means (as in Persian also) 'blue,' but the Portuguese have added a letter, calling the plant 'anilum' instead of 'nilum.'

Relics af ancient Christianity.

This empire of India, which the Turks call Industan, used in times past to be ruled by Christian kings. Our ancestors, owing to their ignorance of India before it was explored by the Portuguese, used to call these kings the Indian Presbyter Johns; and there were many

306 Bhang.

silly and superstitious tales told concerning them. The fact that no single trace of Christianity remains in all this vast area, comprising so many different regions, shows with what bitter hostility the Musalmans treat Christians, their religion, and their sacred buildings and institutions. For in the time of Timur Beg, i.e. 187 years ago, this Christian dynasty was still established in India. Indeed there are still relics of Christianity to be found in the recesses of the Himalayas, where the Musalmans have never penetrated: at least so say the Jogues,[307] who are great travellers, though indeed they are untrustworthy witnesses, telling many downright falsehoods, and mixing a little truth with much fiction. For some of these Jogues, who were questioned by the priests about the Himalayas, said that the range was steep and hard to climb, but at the top flat and suited to human habitation. They also declared that on the bank of a certain lake, which is called by the local inhabitants Mansariior,[308] there is a very ancient city, in which lives a race of people who meet together in a special building every eighth day to offer the sacrifices and prayers which form their religion. The men sit, with crossed legs (as is the custom of the country), on the right-hand side of the sacred building from the door-way to the shrine, and the women on the left-hand side. A man clothed in a linen garment sits, also with crossed legs, in a higher place at the middle of the top end of the building; and in front of him is placed a low table bearing two golden vessels, one of which contains wine and the other bread. This man reads something from a book, to which the others give replies; he then delivers an address and finally the people rise one after the other from their places, first the men and then the women, making no noise and preserving due order. They approach the priest and receive from him a small crust of bread and a draught of wine. Then they return to their seats. When all

307 Yogis or Ascetics.

308 Manasarowar.

has been accomplished, each returns home. The priests would have carefully examined this whole matter, had not the end of the mission frustrated their design.

The ancestors of Akbar.

Zelaldinus the Great acquired his empire partly from his ancestors and partly from many petty chieftains whom his own conquests overthrew. This matter is worth going into further. The grandsons of Temur were compelled, by financial difficulties, by frequent rebellions of their miscellaneous and ill-regulated army (which was forcibly enrolled from the lands they had conquered), by constant attacks from Persians, Parthians, and Turks, and finally by continual treachery amongst their own adherents, to retreat to the territories whence their grandfather Temur had burst forth—that is to the region of Bactria and Sogdiana, whose chief cities are Samarcanda,[309] Boccora[310] and Balcum.[311] When their affairs somewhat improved, they began—as is the way with kings—to plan fresh conquests. They were prevented by the power of the Turks and the Persians from attacking Media, Asia Minor or Armenia; and hence began to harry Paharopanisus, Indoscythia and India, regions then ruled by the Patanaei. The Patanaei of the Paharopanisus and Indoscythia were first subdued, and the descendants of Temur established their capital at Chabulum in order to be the better prepared for crushing the remainder of the Patanaei. In this enterprise Baburus,[312] the grandfather of Zelaldinus, and a great and famous soldier whose warlike prowess rivalled that of his ancestor Temur, was so markedly successful as to drive the Patanaei from almost the whole of their Indian dominions, confining them to a few small outlying principalities. However, being somewhat rash and improvident, Baburus suffered a disaster

309 Samarkand.
310 Bokhara.
311 Balkh.
312 Babur.

at the hands of his own subjects not less crushing than that which he had inflicted on the Patanaei. For he was deprived of the realm of Samarcanda by a traitor,[313] whom he had appointed governor with full powers during his own absence. Baburus was succeeded by Emaumus, who was attacked by the Patanaei whilst he was carrying on a war in Gedrosia. For these Patanaei, who are great warriors, were mindful of the disaster which they had suffered at the hands of Baburus. They were longing also to return to their native land, from which they had been exiled in great numbers, and were incited by the hope of certain victory. Their attack was so successful that they recovered all that Bàburus had conquered, and even compelled Emaumus to treat with them about the whole position of affairs. Being in these acute difficulties Emaumus went as a suppliant to the king of Persia,[314] the founder of the new sect already mentioned, and begged him for assistance. The said king gave him troops, under a famous general,[315] on condition that Emaumus gave him his own name and assumed the Persian type of turban. These conditions Emaumus accepted, and with the resources thus acquired re-conquered all that the Patanaei had occupied, and moreover kept these Patanaei in check through the courage of his Persian general. However he died as the result of the fall at Delinum, which I have already mentioned, at a time when his son Zelaldinus was at Agra. The Persian general[316] had been rendered insolent by the favour of the dead king, who used to declare that he owed all his recovered good fortune to him alone, and was even accustomed to call him his father. He thus endeavoured to usurp the throne.

---

313 So far as I know history does not verify this statement of Father Monserrate.

314 Shah Tahmasp.

315 The reference here is to Budagh Khana commander of the Persian auxiliary force sent by Shah Tahmasp to help Humayun.

316 Here the reference seems to be to Bairam Khan. The whole thing is hopelessly confused. See *note* 238.

Hearing that Zelaldinus had been hailed as king by the citizens of Agra, he was greatly annoyed, and began to favour the accession of Mirsachimus, the second son of Emaumus, who had become king of Chabulum. However whilst he was meditating these designs, Zelaldinus, who was a resolute and vigorous young man, anticipated his treachery, and learning that the Persian was hesitating attacked him unawares and captured him after a pitched battle. He did not however put the prisoner to death, but spared him on account of his services to his father and himself in restoring to them their kingdom when it had been overrun by the Patanaei. This clemency led to the revolt of many of his father's vassal-chieftains. However after the defeat of the Persian, it was easy for Zelaldinus to finish off the war which had been originated by his grandfather and successfully continued by his father. For by combining his original army, by whose help he had defeated the Persian, with the latter's troops, who had gladly transferred their allegiance to himself, he conquered the Gaccares, the Cambovi,[317] the Baloches, the Rattoi,[318] the Rasputes, the Geratae,[319] and the Patanaei (whose king David was slain in battle). Afterwards he also subdued the Indoscythians and Mongols who supported his nephew. Finally he defeated the Caspirii. I shall forbear to enumerate the cities, towns and districts which he occupied, and the other princes whom he conquered; for their names are outlandish and unpronounceable.

---

317 I am unable to ascertain the identity of the Cambovi. They may be Gujaratis or they may be the people of Camboja. But here again a difficulty arises in the identification of the country of Camboja. According to Arrian the Hydraotes (Ravi) flows through Cambistholes, which has been identified with Camboja. In *Hobson-Jobson* we read that Camboja was situated about the locality of Chitral or Kafiristan. For a different opinion see *J.A.S.B.* Vol. VII 1911, p. 619.

318 Perhaps Mahrattas,

319 The identification of the Geratae with Getae or Jats does not seem to me to be probable.

Indian towns.

To say something about Indian towns:—they appear very pleasant from afar; for they are adorned with many towers and high buildings, in a very beautiful manner. But when one enters them, one finds that the narrowness, aimless crookedness, and ill-planning of the streets deprive these cities of all beauty. Moreover the houses are purposely built without windows on account of the filth of the streets. None the less the rich adorn the roofs and arched ceilings of their houses with carvings and paintings: plant ornamental gardens in their courtyards: make tanks and fish-ponds, which are lined with tiles of various colours: construct artificial springs and fountains, which fling showers of water far into the air: and lay down promenades paved with brickwork or marble. Yet such houses will show nothing in their facades or entrances by which the eye of the passer-by might be attracted, and nothing by which it might be known that inside is anything out of the ordinary. The Brachmanae have another style of architecture; but they also beautify their houses with cleverly executed statues and sculptures of fabulous heroes and monsters either in wood or stone. They never forget to carve or paint somewhere on their buildings (generally on the capitals of the columns) the crested snake, which is called by the Portuguese the 'cuckoo-serpent,' and which I believe to be the Egyptian asp.

The common people live in lowly huts and tiny cottages: and hence if a traveller has seen one of these cities, he has seen them all.

The ideas of government entertained by the Brachmanae and the Musalmans in Zelaldinus' empire differ widely. For the Brachmanae govern liberally, through a senate and council of the common people: but the Musalmans have no council or senators, everything being decided by the arbitrary will of the governor appointed by the King.

[Here follow 23 pages of somewhat unreliable tales concerning Chingiz Khan, Timur, the Scythians, etc. See Appendix.]

Thus I have written an account as full and careful, and (be it said without pride) as accurate as the demands of brevity and clearness would allow, of the purpose of Zelaldinus in summoning the priests, of their transactions with the King and his religious doctors, of the cause and conduct of the war with Mirsachimus: then of the return of the priests, and of the murder of Rudolf: next of the King's character (both at home and in the field), of his intellectual gifts, of his majestic deportment, and of his wars. Finally I have described his native land, and the brave and warlike stock to which he belongs. Thus I seem to have reached the end of my labour: and may it prove to have been to some at least a useful labour.

THE END.

PRAISE TO THE MOST HIGH GOD.

I finished this commentary at Eynanum in Arabia on the feast of St. Antony of Padua in the month of June, 1590.

The manuscript was taken from me by the Turks at Senaa, but given back again at the feast of the Eleven Thousand Virgins in the month of October of the same year.

I finished copying and revising the manuscript at Senaa in Arabia on the feast of St. Damasus in the month of December, 1590 A.D.

APPENDIX.

FATHER MONSERRATE'S ACCOUNT OF JENGHIZ KHAN, TIMUR, Etc.

JENGHIZ KHAN AND HIS SONS.

Zelaldinus was descended on the mother's side from Cinguiscanus,[1] as the King himself informed the Fathers. Cinguiscanus was a native of European Sarmatia.[2] The Alauni,[3] Scythians and other peoples were then settled in the part of Sarmatia lying beyond the Tanais[4] and that Mount Belia which Alexander the Macedonian is recorded to have reached and where he set up altars. These tribes, which up to that time had been obscure, and had paid tribute to their neighbours, were first led out of their hiding-place, as it may be called, into the light and on to the stage of world-history by Cinguiscanus. This violent movement occurred about the year 1242 A.D.[5] The tribes were called by the Scythian or Sarmatian names of Mongols and Tartars.

It is uncertain whether this name of Mongol was given them by the first ancestors of their tribe or by the judges and arbitrators who settled their quarrels before Cinguis led them out into the light: or whether it is derived from the district they inhabited, or finally from the river Mongus, into which runs the Arethusius, and on the banks of which the Tartars used to live in the winter-time as far down as its mouth in the Sea of Sarmatia.[6]

The Tartars were called Tattars by their neighbours, in consequence of a defect in their language and idiom, for they rasp out, rather than pronounce, the single-syllable words of which their gabbling speech consists, running their consonants together so as to produce sharp harsh

---

1 Jenghiz Khan

2 District west of the Don.

3 Alans.

4 The Don.

5 The real date of Jenghiz Khan is 1162-1227.

6 The Baltic.

A

sounds. The Mongols, on the other hand, speak a language very similar in vocabulary and sound to Turkish.

Cinguiscanus is said to have been raised to the great dignity which he attained in consequence of an oracle, invented no doubt by himself, or provided by some evil spirit. His tribesmen the more readily believed in this oracle because they greatly resented having to pay a tax to their neighbours for their pasture-lands, and hence they made Cinguis their leader as the oracle directed. He was a man of shrewd wisdom, born to rule, and hence, before the neighbouring Scythian hordes could learn what was on foot, he took care immediately to bind the common people to himself by an oath, lest they should wish to revoke their choice of him as their leader. He also made a bargain with the soldiers. Next, in order to test the fidelity of his officers, he ordered seven of them, who had been the popular leaders before he himself came into power, to butcher each his own children. It was a horrible crime. Yet, through fear of the common people, and having had their superstitious fears aroused by the oracle, the seven officers did as they were bid. His reign being thus inaugurated with parricide, Cinguis divided his forces into companies of ten, one hundred, one thousand, and ten thousand.

Officers were assigned to each company. The Scythians afterwards adopted the same system.

First of all Cinguis brought the neighbouring Scythians under his yoke, making them his tributaries, and exacting from them both money and troops. When he saw that he had raised an army large enough for foreign aggression, he marched against David, the Christian king of India, to whom the Scythians paid tribute, and easily defeated him by means of an unexpected attack on both flanks. David was captured and promptly massacred with his children and household. One daughter only was spared, whom Cinguis is said to have married.

After the successful conclusion of this war, having gained great riches and resources from his spoils, Cinguiscanus began carefully to plan attacks on more distant peoples. He divided his forces into three parts. Baiothnoyus was put in command of one of these armies, with which he overran Persia, subdued greater Armenia, and penetrated as far as Iconium,[1] a city of Lycaonia, which had been the original capital of the Turkish empire. Another army was given to Bacco,[2] who crossed the Tanais, advanced beyond the Euxine Sea, and brought defeat and ruin upon the Jazigae,[3] Rhutheni,[4] Poloni,[5] and Pannones.[6] He himself is believed to have led another army towards the south, but to have met with little success. He never spared himself, nor avoided labour and danger. It is said that on one occasion his army having been defeated and routed in a great battle, he was obliged to seek a hiding-place amongst some bushes, and was saved from destruction by a miracle. For when the enemy, who had followed his flight, reached the thicket where he had taken refuge, and began carefully to search it, an owl—a bird regarded as ill omened by the superstitious—flew out terrified by the noise of their approach, and thus convinced them that no one could recently have taken refuge there. Thus they ceased their search for the king. The owl has ever since been held in great honour by the Mongols.

After being delivered from this danger and having obtained many subsequent victories, Cinguiscanus became so overweeningly proud and infatuated as to dare to arrogate divine honours to himself. Being, like a second Alexander of Macedon, a scourge to the whole earth, he began to regard himself as of more than human greatness, and with no less folly than impudence gave orders that throughout the army he should be publicly proclaimed as the sole master of the world and the son of God, in the same manner as the Musalmans publicly call upon Muhammad as the messenger of God. Moreover he caused a statue of himself to be carved, and had it placed in a public position, where, like Nabuchodonosor,[7] he ordered that it should be worshipped.

---

1 Konia.
2 Batu.
3 A tribe living between the Theiss and the Danube.
4 Ruthenes.
5 Poles.
6 The people of Hungary.
7 Nebuchadnezzar. (Dan. 3).

He is said on one occasion to have summoned his sons to him, and to have exhorted them to peace and concord in the following manner. He bade them each bring to him an arrow. When they came with these arrows, he ordered them to be gathered into one bundle, and then told his eldest son to break the bundle. This he attempted to do, but in vain: and likewise the younger sons. Cinguiscanus then pointed out to them that if they preserved concord in their guardianship of the empire, it would remain firm and unshaken, but if not, it would decay and became liable to ruin at the hands of its enemies.

Having extended his empire far and wide, Cinguiscanus began to desire rest, and hence founded the city of Darganxus[1] in central Scythia, where he established the seat of his government. However he persisted in his insane claim to a false divinity, and in the midst of his victories was punished for his folly and madness by a stroke of lightning, which destroyed him miserably. During his lifetime he had begotten twelve sons, to whom (with true paternal indulgence) he granted free permission to follow whatever religion they liked, although all his other subjects were compelled on pain of dire punishments to worship himself. One of these sons, by name Otthodayus,[2] had as his mother the daughter of the King of India, and was a Christian. The rest remained idolaters. The names of four of them, who were born of another wife of Cinguiscanus, still survive, viz., Gabyrius, Xacattaas,[3] Osbequis,[4] and Chareas. The names of the rest have perished. Cinguiscanus gave the military command of Samarcanda and an army to Xacattas. His soldiers began to be called Xacattaei after their commander, to distinguish them from the rest of the Mongol hordes. Xacattas had three sons, Jachis,[5] Batto,[6] and Tagladayus.[7] Next Cinguiscanus handed over the government of Boccora and the city of

---

1 ? Karakoram.
2 Ogotai (Ogdai).
3 Zagatai (Chagatai).
4 Uzbeg.
5 Juji (Hosten).
6 Batu.
7 Tagladay (Hosten).

Balcum, together with suitable forces, to Osbequis, whose troops in a similar manner were called Osbequii. This tribe still exists and bears the same name. The rest of the Tartar and Mongol hordes, and Scythia itself, and the city of Darganxus, which he had founded, Cinguiscanus gave to Otthodayus. His other sons received governments in other districts which he had conquered.

Next Xacattas, the emperor of Samarcanda, living as he did not far from Media and Asia Minor, despatched his sons to attack those countries. Jachiscanus[1] was sent westward, Battocanus northward, and Tagladayus southward. Xacattas himself marched against the Christian Serae[2] with the pick of his armies.

Batho's impetuous advance carried him as far as Austria. He devastated cruelly the countries which he invaded; but was finally drowned in the river Dravus together with a large number of his soldiers. The officers of his army who escaped this disaster rallied round his sons, whom he had appointed governors of his conquests.

Tagladayus was routed by the Aethiopians, and united his remaining forces to those of his brother Jachiscanus, under whose command he placed himself also. Jachiscanus carried on operations in Persia, from which country and from Mesopotamia he drove out the Turks.

Xacattas was killed at Samarcanda in consequence of a conspiracy of the Sogdians, which had been brought about by the quarrels and civil wars of himself and his brothers, (as had been foretold by his father). After his death the people of Samarcanda chose for themselves a ruler of Sogdian race, who gave instructions that his own soldiers should be enrolled and returned as Xacattaei. His object in this was to bind more strongly to himself the real Xacattaei, who formed the flower of his forces, and whom he had already conciliated with liberal gifts. He also wished to show how highly he esteemed their warlike prowess and the prestige of their name. By this politic action was removed the fatal danger of those discords which are apt to arise between foreigners and native-born when they differ not only in race but in name also.

---

1 Juji Khan.
2 Chinese.

The sons and grandsons of Xacattas, together with their remaining hordes of Xacattaei, were again and again heavily defeated by the people whose territories they had wantonly overrun; and were finally driven back once more into Scythia, where they took up again the wandering life of their forefathers under the name of Xacattaean Tartars. This is the reason why the habitat of the Xacattaei is described as being both in Sogdiana, around Samarcanda on the river Jaxartes, and in Scythia, beyond the Caspian Sea. At the time when the envoys of Henry IV, King of Castilia, reached Samarcanda, the empire of Samarcanda was called Mongolia, a name which is also applied to the regions of Scythia which border on the Northern ocean.

THE MONGOLS ENTER INDIA.

Otthodayus, great Can (*i.e.*, prince) of Darganxus and Emperor of Tartary, was poisoned after a reign of only two years. The other sons of Cinguiscanus, having been driven out of their own provinces, had attached themselves to his armies, and on more than one occasion planted colonies of Mongols and Tartars (which names the invaders still retained) in India. They first established themselves at Mandho[1] and in the province of Malva. The Tarchan Mongols and the Arguni held Sindus up to our own time; and it is only recently that they were reduced and deprived of their kingdom there by Zelaldinus. Long ago they gave their name to the populous district of Mangalor, as it is called by the Portuguese. The natives of those parts pronounce the name Mongolor. However the district of Moghostan, near Ormuz, is not called after them, as some have been led by the similarity of the sounds to suppose. For the name of the region 'Moghostan' does not signify Mongolistan (*i.e.*, the kingdom of the Mongols), but the region of palm trees. For in the local[2] dialect "Mogh" means a palm tree.

It is not long since the Mongols were looked upon with contempt and anger by both the Xacattaei and the Osbequii

---

1 Mandu.

2 Monserrate here uses the Persian (?) word 'Rustani' explaining in a note that it means 'rustic'.

as paid mercenaries in both their armies. They are supposed to support the masters from whom they see hope of obtaining the highest pay. Hence they are not reckoned to be genuine descendants of the same stock as these tribes, but are regarded as foreigners. The Xacattaei resent being called Mongols. A certain learned man pointed this out to the Fathers; but his ideas were incorrect, as he asserted that the name of Mongol was given to those who were neither Osbequii nor Zacattaei, but the descendants of mixed marriages between the two tribes. In reality of course both these tribes are descended from the Mongols.

The Descendants of Jenghiz.

To proceed—Othodayus was succeeded by Cinguiscanus, whose Master of the Horse, by name Cicaltay,[1] sent an embassy to St. Louis, when he was in Cyprus, and announced that the great Can of Tartary had embraced Christianity.

After Cinguis reigned his son Begecanus,[2] and after him his brother Tagondar-canus,[3] who was a Christian and bore the name of Nicholaus. However he deserted the faith and became perverted to the superstition of the Musalmans. He paid the penalty for this impiety, for he was deprived both of his kingdom and of his life by Argon-canus,[4] the son of his brother Bage-canus. Argon-canus is said to have favoured the Christians, though he was not a Christian himself. This shows how important it is that baptism should be administered in infancy, without waiting for the child to attain a more advanced age.

Argoncanus was succeeded by Baido-canus,[5] who incurred the hatred and opposition of the Musalmans by preferring the Christians to themselves and treating them with more marked favour. Cassan-canus,[6] son of Argon and nephew of Baydo-canus, was bribed by these Musalmans with gifts and promises, and thus induced to drive Baydocanus from the throne and to slay him.

1 Kuyuk (Hosten).
2 Abaga (Hosten).
3 Tigudar (Hosten).
4 Arghun (Hosten).
5 Baidu (Hosten).
6 Ghazan (Hosten).

However God so ordained that, after he had been installed as great Can, Cassan-canus began to hate the Musalmans no less than his father and uncle had done, and waged war against them to protect the Christians. For he allied himself and his army of two hundred thousand cavalry with the Armenians and Hyrcanians[1], who at that time were attacking Palestine in order to recapture Jerusalem from the Musalmans. When the King of Babylonia marched to meet these allies with an army of a hundred thousand cavalry and a countless host of infantry, Cassan-canus by reason of superior courage and strategy routed the Babylonians, occupied Syria, entered Jerusalem as a conqueror, and there visited the holy places. Before however the war could be carried to a conclusion, he was recalled to Persia by an insurrection there. He despatched embassies to Pope Boniface the Eighth, to the king of France, and to other Christian princes, urging them to occupy Syria and Jerusalem, which he himself had conquered. Finally he was converted to Christianity in consequence of a miracle. The daughter of the king of Armenia had refused to marry him unless she were free to live as a Christian. This condition he granted, and the marriage was celebrated. The queen however afterwards fell under suspicion of adultery, since she gave birth to an exceedingly ugly infant quite unlike Cassan-canus. Learning that the king intended to have her executed for this, the queen asked permission to make confession to a priest, to receive the sacrament, and to have her child baptized. When the holy water touched the infant, it was, by the grace of God, transformed into a child of distinguished and most beautiful appearance. The king was mollified by this wonderful miracle, became reconciled to the queen, was baptized, and became a Christian.

After his death, Totamixus[2] came to the throne. Totamixus was succeeded by Coramxas the Second. All these are believed to have been Christians; but the carelessness of historians has lost the names of those who ruled over Tartary after them from the time of Temur the Lame.

---

1 Georgians (Monserrate).
2 Takhtamish (Monserrate).

AKBAR'S DESCENT.

Now the mother of Zelaldinus transmitted to him neither royal lineage nor the dignity of descent from Cinguiscanus. For she was the daughter of an obscure officer. Her name was Txoelii[1] Beygum; and before her marriage to Emaumus[2] her parents had given her as wife to Cayacanus.[3] Hence Zelaldinus was only grafted on, as it were, to the royal family of Cinguiscanus through his grandmother or some other famous lady of that line. We could not learn from him how distant the connection was; but we believe he was right in asserting that his relationship to Cinguiscanus was only through a female. However we are clearly quite justified in declaring that the favour which Zelaldinus shows to the Christians is the result of heredity and ancestral descent.

TIMUR'S YOUTH.

Temurus, the ancestor of Emaunus, father of Zelaldinus, rose from a humble origin to the very highest dignity by reason of the qualities of which we shall now given an account.

At the time of the birth of Temurus, the kingdom of Samarcanda was, as has already been pointed out, in the hands of the Xacattaei. The king's name was Ahicanus, who is said to have been the son of an unknown father, though his mother was of noble birth. He governed Persia and Syria under excellent laws and institutions, devised by himself. Temurus was born in the village of Taragoy, near to the city of Quexa,[4] which is also called Xaresabz[5] on account of its beauty and the vivid green of its fields and gardens. His father, whose name was Xacathaeus, was an idolator. He belonged to the equestrian order, and was the leader of four horsemen. The mother of Temurus was of the same rank. Temurus followed his father's example, became like him a leader of four

1 Chuli Begam (Hosten).
2 Humayun.
3 Qaim Khan ? (Hosten).
4 Kesh (Hosten).
5 Shahr-i-Sabz (Hosten).

horsemen, and fought for a time under Ahycanus. Even in his childhood Temurus is said to have been jestingly saluted as king by his companions, the children of his father's dependants and the shepherd-boys of the neighbourhood, so great was the impression made by his early strength and cunning and pugnacity. He made these companions of his swear that they would obey him in later life; and when they reached early manhood and were capable of bearing arms, he called them and bade them follow him to a more manly form of livelihood than sheep-tending. They obeyed his summons, but soon began to find themselves in need of daily food; whereupon they began to maintain themselves by stealing cattle. When the number of his followers reached three hundred, he began to practice brigandage, and hence was denounced before the king of Samarcanda, who gave orders that Temurus and his band should be seized and executed. The king was persuaded however by some Xacattaei to reverse this sentence, to summon Temurus to the court, and to put him in command of a troop of cavalry. Through the malice of his enemies the young man was however again accused before the king, and to save his life was obliged to fly in secret from the royal camp. He returned to his brigandage, and on one occasion looted a rich caravan of traders in Persia. On learning of this the king of Persia sent against him an officer with a body of a thousand men. Hearing of their approach Temurus retired to a stronghold, safe in which he could repel all assaults. Then he sent bribes to the Persian officer, and induced him, by the hope of gaining richer booty under Temurus than under the Persian king, to forsake the latter and to join himself. Thus strengthened, and with a total in all of fifteen hundred mercenary troops, he began to raid the very rich and fruitful country of the Cistani.[1] However, enraged by his depredations, these Cistani attacked Temurus one night when he was driving off a herd of cattle, and killed many of his men. Temurus was wounded in the right leg and right hand, but succeeded in escaping. However, being rendered lame by

---

1 Seistan ? (Monserrate in a marginal note calls the 'Cistani' Sebastani).

the wounds and unable to use his right hand, he was called Temurlang by his men, i.e. Temurus the Lame. When his wounds were healed and he himself recovered from his illness, Temurus collected his band once more.

His Conquests.

Recognising his audacity, the citizens of Samarcanda, who were plotting an insurrection against their king, persuaded him to kill the king by means of an ambush. Accordingly Temurus laid a trap for the king while he was proceeding without his guards from Samarcanda to some other place. Being thus suddenly attacked, and seeing his followers put to flight, the king himself found a hiding-place amongst the mountains, where he entrusted his life and safety to a countryman, to whom he paid a great sum as a bribe. However the peasant handed him over to Temurus, by whom he was cruelly murdered. Thereupon Temurus hastened by forced marches to Samarcanda, seized the city, palace and fort, and secured them with a large garrison. Having forcibly married Cannu, wife of the slain king and daughter of Ahicanus, emperor of Samarcanda, he next summoned the military forces of the Xacattaei to his standard.

After having thus became an emperor, the ex-brigand proceeded to more ambitious undertakings. At that time the throne of Persia was in dispute between two brothers. Thinking this a good opportunity to seize that kingdom, Temurus embraced the cause of one of these brothers and drove out the other. The successful candidate placed complete confidence in his supporter, who, basely abusing this trust, deceived him by pretending to be planning a war against another king. He requested the Persian ruler for auxiliary troops, and meanwhile collected his own mercenaries. When he had thus prepared a great army, Temurus instead of leaving Persia, treacherously turned his arms against his host and protege, finally driving him defeated and beggared from his kingdom.

Wars Against the Turks.

Having secured Persia with a garrison of Xacattaei, Temurus next attacked the Parthians, who paid tribute to the Persians. Hamidus[1] the fugitive king of Persia, took refuge in the fortress of Alinga, where Temurus besieged him for three years. He also advanced into Tartary and defeated the Coramxas mentioned above on his return from a successful expedition against Cusaqhana (*i.e.*, the house of Cusa). A great part of Tartary was subdued, after which Temurus turned his arms against the Hircani, a Christian people whom we name the Georgians. Their chief stronghold, called Tarcon, was captured and Temurus reached the iron gates of Darbentum,[2] which the Turks call Damarcab, on the far side of Iberia and Albania.[3] He then changed the direction of his march towards Armenia, which he subdued. Next followed the conquest of Mesopotamia. Then he turned back, crossed the Euphrates near Arsinga and entered Capadocia. The reason for his attack on Capadocia was as follows :—Zaretanus, the ruler of Arsinga, having refused to acknowledge the claims of Payazitus,[4] who was demanding tribute from him and the surrender of Arsinga, sent an embassy to ask help from Temurus. This embassy came upon Temurus at Alinga, where he was celebrating his final victory over the king of Persia, who had fled into Babylonia. Temurus gave the ambassadors a despatch for Payazitus, in which he warned the latter not to molest Zaretanus, who was a protege and feudatory of his own. No more tribute must be demanded from him. If such were demanded, he himself would see to it. Payazitus, who was of a very arrogant temperament, was incensed by this despatch, and poured contempt on an upstart leader whose very name he had never heard before. He rated the power of Temurus very low, and returned a threatening and insulting reply to his despatch, bidding him at once to cease all dealings with Zaretanus on pain of war with himself, a most powerful enemy.

Temurus was at that time in winter quarters at Qhaterbagus (*i.e.*, the garden of delights), a town in Persia. On receipt of the despatch, he immediately put his forces into motion against Payazitus, in order to avenge the insult

1 Ahmad Khan (Hosten)
2 Derbend
3 Districts of Georgia
4 Baiazid (Hosten)

contained both explicitly and implicitly in the despatch. He pushed ahead with his cavalry, crossed the frontier of Capadocia, first attacked, Sebaste,[1] (the birth place of Saint Blasius), stormed it, massacred the inhabitants, and razed the city to the ground. He left the place at dawn; and at evening on the same day Xelebius,[2] the son of Payazitus, arrived there with an army of two hundred thousand archers. Temurus forebore to contest his advance, deeming it beneath his dignity to do battle with a subordinate and youthful commander. Hence, ignoring Xelebius, he marched into Babylonia. On his way he met with the hordes of the White Tartars, as they are called, who have no fixed abode, but wander here and there fighting everyone they meet. Their number both of men and women was about fifty thousand. Temurus attacked them, captured their leaders, slaughtered great numbers of them, and led the rest off captive. On his entering the territory of Babylonia, the emperor of Babylon offered him tribute in money and military support if he would refrain from slaughtering and burning. He also consented to use the coinage of Temurus, and permitted the latter's armorial devices to be painted up and inscribed in public places. Hence, marching past Babylon, Temurus next arrived at Damascus, which is the richest city in Syria. He sacked it, bécause its inhabitants had imprisoned some envoys who had been collecting tribute in his name. The captives taken at Damascus and Sebaste (who were mostly Christians), and the white Tartar prisoners, were despatched to Samarcanda, in order that the movements of Temurus might not be hindered by their presence. He himself passed the summer months with the army at Alara in Armenia.

Payazitus was enraged by the sack of Sebaste, and in revenge stormed Arsinga, the cause of the whole war. However he gave orders that the wife of Zaretanus, who had been captured, should be set free again, and should be treated with all honour. He also restrained his men from

1 Sivas (Hosten)

2 A name wrongly rendered Cyricoelebes, or Calepinus by European writers. It should be Cide Xelebius. (Monserrate).

burning, slaughtering and sacking on pain of severe punishment. Many writers have put down this leniency on the part of Payazitus to the weakness of his character; for it is clear that he never took a due revenge for the cruel treatment of Sebaste by Temurus. But his real intention was to make odious, by the contrast of his own kindness and indulgence, the cruelty of his enemy, who boasted himself to be the scourge of God, and chose to be regarded as a monster of ferocity. Payazitus was unwilling to resemble Temurus even in the smallest detail.

When his scouts informed Temurus that Payazitus had stormed Arsinga, he advanced as rapidly as possible towards that place and Sebaste from Alara. On learning of his enemy's approach, Payazitus, in order to be able to outdo him in swiftness of movement, deposited all his baggage and treasure at the strong fortress of Angurum[1], and then followed Temurus by forced marches. Learning of this, Temurus turned towards the left, crossed the ridge of Mount Taurus, and for eight days disappeared in the fastnesses of the mountains. Having reached Arsinga and Sebaste, Payazitus even advanced beyond the latter place before receiving at one and the same time the news firstly that his enemy was behind him instead of before him, and secondly that he had stormed Angurum and completely looted the royal treasury. In order to confirm by a clever artifice the advantage thus successfully gained, Temurus laid the following snare for his enemy. At that time there happened to be in his camp an envoy of Payazitus. Temurus gave directions that sulphur and chaff soaked in wine-lees should be burnt near him, in order that the fumes might make him very pale. He next swallowed down an immense amount of warm blood, which he drank direct from the throat of a slaughtered ox. He then lay down on his bed, pretending to be grievously sick: and summoned the envoy of Payazitus by an urgent message. On his speedy arrival Temurus began to vomit, with pretence of terrible distress and most dangerous exhaustion. He brought up a huge quantity of blood, so that the envoy was seized with the deepest pity. Noticing this, and per-

---

1. Angora.

ceiving that his visitor was convinced that he was very seriously ill, Temurus addressed him in broken and gasping tones—"You see how near I am to death. I have lost all the blood in my body. So write to my dear brother Payazitus that I desire to leave in his hands all my property, my children and my army. For no one in the world is as well qualified as he is to protect my children and my property. Let him therefore come hither quickly, before I die: for it will be of great advantage to both armies that he should do so." The envoy replied that, if permitted, he would himself deliver the message to his master. Temurus gave him leave to do so. His intention in laying this snare was to deprive his enemy of all suspicion and to ensure his presence in a condition wearied and weakened by rapid travel. The envoy reported what he had seen and heard to Payazitus at the earliest possible moment. The latter, either because he believed Temurus' assurances or because he promised himself a safe and certain victory over a sick enemy, proceeded to Angurum as swiftly as possible. He arrived there with his army tired out and in disorder, and found himself confronted by Temurus, who was awaiting him in battle-array and with fresh and unwearied troops. Temurus, giving his opponent no opportunity for resting, collecting or arranging his forces, attacked at once, defeated Payazitus, and captured him. The battle nevertheless was long and dubious, lasting for many hours and being marked by fluctuating fortune. Now one side drove its foes in rout before it, and now the other. At times a body of troops advancing to the support of their comrades had suddenly to withstand an enemy who had just received similar reinforcement, and whose defence was thus stiffened. The battle was like a stormy sea, which is driven hither and thither by the fickle violence of the winds, with no fixed motion or direction. At length, towards evening, the victory inclined towards the Tartars, who were vastly superior to their enemies both in numbers and in the strategic skill of their commander. The Turks were overwhelmed by an unremitting hail of Tartar arrows. For Temurus had in his army four hundred thousand cavalry—a force larger then that of Darius or Xerxes.

Elaborate care was taken to supply these horsemen with arms and missiles sufficient for a whole day's fighting. The Tartar charge threw Payazitus down into a pit, from which he could not escape, and so he was captured by Mohammed Sultan, son of Temurus. For he was held down by the weight of the horse he had been riding, and so was unable to rise. Mahammed Sultan spared his life, and conducted him to his father Temurbegus.

This battle of Angurum took place near the frontiers of Armenia Minor, Bythinia and Galatia, and close to mount Stella, a spur of the Antitaurus. There is a very broad plain here called in the Turkish language Cassovassi (plain of the ducks), which is celebrated as the site of Pompey's victory over Mithridates.

Temurus had his royal captive bound with golden chains and shut up in a cage, which was carried in front of him wherever he went. In acting thus he was imitating the example of Sapor, king of the Persians, who did Valerianus Caesar to death with similar grim cruelty. Payazitus quickly sank under the burden of disaster and grief, insult and shame. For they say that Temurus when at table was wont to throw the bones which he had gnawed to the captive Payazitus, as if to a dog; and when he wished to go out riding used to mount his horse from the back of his prostrate captive.

Having thus mastered his enemy, Temurus crossed the Taurus mountains, and hastened into Adiabene[1] with such impetuous speed that every city of that region surrendered, and both Asia[2] and Syria submitted to him. While devastating the kingdom of Payazitus he reached New Paladia, where he caught the few troops which had survived the destruction of the forces of Payazitus, and drove them headlong into Phrygia. They took refuge in the fortress of Quiniscum. Traditian relates that two hundred thousand Turks perished in the battle described above. Temurus pursued his warlike course with unwearying persistence. Following the favouring breeze of victory, he drove the king of Egypt from Memphis, where

---

1 Dierbeca (Monserrate) *i.e.*, Diarbekr.
2 Natolia (Monserrate).

he then had his capital, to Pelusium and beyond. Such however was his care for the well-being of his men that he refused to complete the conquest of Egypt on account of the danger which he anticipated it would involve for his troops in consequence of the desert marches, the lack of water and the poverty of the country; and this although, the king having fled, no further resistance was to be feared, and he would only have to deal with mean-spirited slaves (the word Mamalucus signifies "slave"). Thus he returned from Egypt, reduced to the state of a tributary the king of Trapezus,[1] and then seized Teharanum, a rich and famous city situated in the district of Rhages in Media. He fixed the boundary of his empire at Alangogaca in the district of Arsinga in Cappadocia. He subdued all the countries between the river Tanais and the Nile. Amongst the many famous cities which he captured were Smyrna, Antiochia, Damascus, Tripolis, Alepum, Babylon, Persis, Ecbathana, Susae, and Memphis.

WARS AGAINST THE TARTARS.

He carried on frequent wars against the Tartars, and twice put to rout Totamixus, son of king Coramxas of Tartary, whom also he had conquered. The war with Totamixus took place as follows. Hearing that Temurus had been long absent and was deeply involved in foreign wars, Totamixus made an incursion into Media, Adiabene and Armenia. He sacked Persepolis, Calamira, Susae and other cities, and returned to his country laden with plunder. On learning of this Temurus set off in pursuit of the Tartars with such forces as he had at hand, though these were far inferior in numbers to those of Totamixus. Temurus caught his enemy up near the river Tesina (*i.e.* the Tanais) in Tartary. Totamixus crossed the river and protected the ford with excellently devised earth-works and fortifications, in order to prevent Temurus crossing. The ford in question was the only place in all that region where the river could be passed without boats. Seeing his way thus blocked, Temurus had recourse to guile. He sent envoys to Totamixus announcing that he had not come

1 Trebizond.

there with unfriendly intent, as was clearly shown by the small number of troops he had with him. Hence there was no reason for Totamixus to be afraid of him or to obstruct his passage. Totamixus replied that he was perfectly well acquainted with his opponent's deceitful and treacherous character. Hence he might cease trying to delude him. Temurus then pretended to be about to retreat, and marched away up-stream. Totamixus did the same, and for three days they marched in this fashion. Having thus drawn his enemy three days' march away from the ford and its fortifications, Temurus gave orders for the women in the army to dress and arm themselves like men and remain in camp together with the slaves, whom he also armed, and a guard of several thousand cavalry. His object was to conceal from the enemy the fact that his army had been reduced in numbers. When darkness fell, he set out with all the rest of his forces, giving each soldier two horses so that he might have a second ready when the first was tired. Thus in that one night he covered a distance equal to twice that marched by the army in three days, crossed the river and at the third hour after sunrise fell upon the unsuspecting Totamixus. Having routed him, Temurus sacked his camp, recovered the booty which he had amassed, and carried off also the treasures of Totamixus himself. Totamixus, collecting another army, tried to fight once more and to wipe out his disgrace. However he was again vanquished by Temurus, and as a consequence became very unpopular with his Tartars for his ill-luck. Temurus gave instructions for his booty, captives, and the treasure which he had collected from the various regions he had conquered, to be conveyed to Samarcanda. He conferred kingdoms upon his sons, and entrusted the government of the provinces of his empire to his relatives and connections amongst the Xacattaei.

Description of Samarkand.

Samarcanda is a very large city situated in Sogdiana near the river Jaxartes, not far from the boundary of the country of the Scythians and the Dahae. This city, which has been world-renowned since the days of Alexander, grew to such a size in the time of Temurus as to measure three miles across in a direct line from gate to gate. Its circumference was nine miles. It was surrounded by a great number of beautiful estates, country-seats, parks and pleasure-houses, to a distance of four miles or so from the walls. The approach to the city, which was defended by earthworks and ramparts, lay along roads of great breadth. There were many markets, in which fine merchandise, grain, food, etc., were sold. There were also a great number of striking buildings. Within the city-wall were broad and spacious colonnades and parks, in one of which Temurus had erected the tomb of his mother-in-law, a building of truly regal magnificence. Outside the walls stood four great palaces and parks. By far the finest and largest of these was the so-called Talicia palace, which was three miles from the city, and extended for a distance of three miles more. It was built on a very large artificial mound, by the side of which there was a colonnade extending along the whole breadth of the gardens. The prospect of the city and its surrounding country always gave the greatest delight to strangers, for Samarcanda appeared to be a most beautiful woodland track rather than a city. Moreover so equable is the climate there, that even at Christmas time, when the cold of that district is at its maximum, there is a very plentiful supply of grapes and melons. Abundance of cotton is grown, but flax and hemp have to be imported from abroad.

Temurus despatched confidential servants into Persia, Parthia and Hircania with instructions to bring to Samarcanda all orphans and indigent artisans and farmers, together with their tools and property, however meagre. They were made to bring all their sheep, oxen and donkeys with them. The expenses of their transit had to be defrayed by the inhabitants of the towns and villages through which they passed. Their arrival is said to have added one hundred thousand to the population of the city, besides a great quantity of cattle and sheep. Their labours soon greatly beautified Samarcanda.

The territory around Samarcanda abounds in fat-tailed sheep and herds of cattle and horses. Grain was very cheap in the city; and hence it is still called by the inhabitants 'Cimesquint' (the abode of abundance). "Cimes" means fat or abundant, and "quint" "means a country abode in the Tartar language. The arms of the city and kingdom are a lion standing in the Sun's orb.

OTHER WARS.

To return to Totamixus—the Xacattaean Ediguius, a former officer of Temurus and a bold and unscrupulous man, being ambitious to seize the throne, learnt that the king his master was unpopular with the Tartars, and hence gave them to understand that he himself hated Temurus and was anxious to destroy him: wherefore, if they would support him with an army, he pledged himself to overthrow the tyrant and to fight for them against any enemy they should name. The Tartars readily agreed to this proposal. Whereupon Ediguius laid a trap for Temurus before the Tartar forces could arrive, in order the more effectively to ingratiate himself with them. The plot was detected and frustrated, and the culprit fled to the Tartars, who received him very kindly and saluted him as king in opposition to Totamixus. Temurus, having failed to prevent the flight of Ediguius after the conspiracy had been detected, tried to entice him into war, but in vain. He next had recourse to his wonted guile and caused it to be announced that he would forgive Ediguius for all the past, and would arrange a marriage between his own grandson and the daughter of Ediguius if the latter so wished. To this Ediguius sent the following message in reply:—"I perceive perfectly well the purport of your message, for I have not lived twenty years in your army without learning to see through your wiles. Wherefore I have decided that agreement between yourself and myself shall only be made with drawn swords and on the field of battle. Cease therefore to provoke me, rather than entice me, with your deceitful fraudulent messages."

Totamixus, outraged by the usurpation of his throne and the insolence of the traitors who had betrayed him, met Ediguius in battle. However, having the worst of the day, he was forced to flee to a village near Samarcanda where he placed himself in the hands of the troops of Temurus. His son took refuge in Theodosia, a city of the

Genoese situated near the Black Sea or the Maeotic Marsh,[1] on the Cimerian Bosphorus of the Tauric Chersonese.[2] Its name is now Caffa. Thence he sent a challenge to Ediguius, who in return besieged Caffa and devastated its territory until the citizens, unable any longer to bear the hardships of the siege, besought the Tartar secretly to leave the city. He acceded to their request, left the city in secret, and joined his father and brother at Samarcanda, where they unitedly threw themselves on the mercy of Temurus. Meanwhile the people of Caffa made peace with Ediguius. Forthwith this abandoned wretch caused all the Tartars, who up to that time had followed whatever system of belief pleased them best, to embrace the superstition of Muhammad. Ediguius was content with ruling over Tartary, and dreading the cleverness and treachery of Temurus made no further attacks on him.

After the expulsion of the descendants of Cinguiscanus, Tartary was exposed to the cruelty of many petty tyrants. The line of Cinguiscanus was lost amongst the Xacattaei.

To return once more to Temurus. One cannot sufficiently wonder at his good luck (if such a manner of speaking may be allowed), for fortune never turned her back on him, except in that one reverse when he was wounded and put to flight. With his strong will and his proud spirit he compelled fortune to show favour to him: and he never forsook an undertaking without putting that favour to the proof.

Wars Against the King of Delhi.

In the time of Temurus a Christian king was ruling over that Indian empire which is now held by Zelaldinus. The capital was Delinum. This king fought a battle with Temurus, whom on the first day he put to flight by means of the great number and strength of his elephants. However on the second day Temurus, who had rallied his army and was not in the slightest perturbed by the check he had suffered, rendered unavailing the strength and courage of

1 Sea of Azov.
2 Crimea.

the elephants by loading his camels with straw. As the phalanx of elephants began to advance towards his line, he ordered the camels to be driven towards them. When the two bodies were almost in collision, the straw was fired, and suddenly blazing up, terrified the camels, which rushed amongst the elephants. Now elephants have a horror of fire; and hence they turned and fled in terror, throwing the ranks of the Indian army into confusion. The soldiers, who could not see their enemies on account of the smoke, were slaughtered or put to the rout. The king of Delinum, being thus vanquished, never stopped his flight till he reached the Paharopanisus.[1] Temurus occupied part of Lesser India, which is situated west of the Indus and the Paharopanisus. Lesser India formerly consisted of four governments—Paharopanisus, Aria, Aracosia, and Gedrosia.

The king of India, having rallied his forces, soon started the war afresh. Temurus remained in his camp, wishing to entice the enemy to attack him. However his former defeat had made the king of Delinum cautious, and he refused to be drawn away from the mountains. Battle being thus avoided, Temurus remained in possession of the districts he had occupied, whilst the king of India guarded the mountains to prevent the Xacattaei advancing any further.

The Emperor of China.

Meanwhile Temurus, elated by his numerous great victories, refused any longer to pay to the king of the Serae[2] the tribute which had been paid by former kings of Samarcanda. Now Cambalecum[3], the chief city of the Serae, is three thousand miles distant from Samarcanda, and for a thousand miles of that distance no town or village is to be met with, only the sheepfolds and the tents of the pastoral peoples. With the intention of provoking the king of Serae to war Temurus looted a caravan of eight hundred camels, which was travelling from Tartary to Cambalecum.

---

1 Hindu Kush.

2 North China.

3 Khanbaligh (Hosten), *i.e.* Pekin.

The land of the Serae is in our time known as Cataium.[1] These Serae, or Seres, of Cataium are said to be mainly Christians by religion, though with a large admixture of Jews, heathen and Mohammedans. At the time when the priests of the Society were vising Zelaldinus, the name of the king of the Serae was Emanuel. His ancestors had once lived on the coast of Caucinsyna,[2] but had been driven out by the inhabitants of that region in the course of a war, and had migrated northward and inland. Access may be had to the land of the Serae up the river which reaches the sea near the port of Caucinsyna. It will not perhaps be out of place to mention here that those are wrong who have supposed, in consequence of the similarity of the names, that the people of Cathaium once lived in Cambaia. For there is a race of people who live by petty trading not only at Cambaia, but at Calecutium and along the whole coast of India. They are called Chatini, and are despised as being vile and abject. These are Cathaini and have always been Christians.

In the time of Temurus the circumference of Cambalecum was forty miles. The royal army exceeded one million in number, and was the terror of the Tartars and of all the peoples of Greater Asia. For when the emperor of the Serae led out his army to battle he left behind in garrisons four hundred thousand cavalry, but took with him six hundred thousand. The multitudes in his armies were almost infinite. All the silken goods which are imported to Europe from Syna[3] are said to reach the Syni from the country of the Serae who are supposed to have been the first manufacturers of silken fabrics.

Timur's Army.

Temurus, like his ancestors, always kept his troops in camps fortified as strongly as a well-defended city. In these camps every kind of artisan or workman had his own particular locality assigned to him. Provisions and articles of merchandise were sold in different markets.

1 Cathay.
2 Cochin China (Hosten).
3 S. China

Thieves found no scope in these camps; for if they were caught, their noses were, by imperial decree, pierced with an awl. All roads were very carefully guarded in order to prevent any robbery or violence; and thus an abundance of supplies was assured for the army. Stringent precautions were taken through the agency of the military officers against serious riots and seditions. Whilst Temurus was encamped at Bursa[1] after the defeat of Payazitus, his camp consisted of twenty thousand tents. When at Samarcanda he had thirty thousand more. In camp the emperor used a wooden shrine made with joints so devised that it could easily be moved from place to place. When his purpose was friendly and merciful, he displayed white standards: when bloody and slaughterous, red: when that of total extermination, black. The strictest measures were taken to prevent the soldiers leaving camp. After his capture of Samarcanda, when he was advancing into Persia, a bridge was thrown across the Jaxartes to assist in the crossing of the army; but, when all had passed over, this bridge was cast loose to prevent the Sogdian and Xacattaean troops returning on account of homesickness. After his return to Samarcanda another bridge was destroyed in order to prevent the escape of his prisoners. Orders were given moreover that no one, not even Xacattaei, should be ferried over without a written permit, although every one who was crossing towards Samarcanda was granted a passage without restriction or payment of toll. When he marched against Payazitus, in order to prevent the soldiers from retreating through their desire to see their wives, he first bound himself by an oath not to return to Samarcanda for seven years, and then gave orders that his soldiers should divorce their wives, adding also that if they did not do so he gave authority to the wives that they might consider themselves free from all obligations to their husbands and marry whomever they wished, (a barbarous edict indeed, and one showing Temurus' contempt for all laws, both human and divine). When he crossed the Volga, he ferried over also in his boats a multitude of women and innumerable flocks and herds, so that it seemed

1 Brusa

unlikely that pasture could ever be found for them all. He gave directions that each horseman should give a helping hand to some individual infantryman, especially in crossing rivers. He made his nephew Jansa Ruler of the People and Master of the Horse. This was the man by whose help he had carried out his original violent attack upon the king of Samarcanda.

His Cruelty and Cunning.

It is hard to say whether Temurus was more remarkable for courage, generalship, or guile. He won many battles by sheer trickery. Such trickery is indeed a hereditary trait in the Tartars and those races which have sprung from them, for instance the Parthians, whose warfare consists in flight, as has been so elegantly described by Lucan :—

"Their mode of fighting is easy and gentle; their warfare is to flee away; their squadrons travel far. Their troops are better skilled in retreat than in routing the foe. Their land is stained with guile. Their courage is never enough to permit of hand-to-hand fighting; but from afar they bend their bows, and leave it to the winds to decide whom their shafts shall strike."

In this same fashion Temurus frequently outwitted bodies of cavalry much larger than his own.

I shall now proceed to give instances of the guile which was peculiar to himself—guile to which cruelty and barbarous ferocity were sometimes added. During the siege of Sebaste[1] the citizens sent to him an embassy to propose that they should surrender the city and pay his tribute on condition that no blood were shed. Temurus granted these terms, and summoned the principal citizens to confirm the treaty. When they came, the wretched men were seized and buried alive in pits, which had already been prepared for the purpose in large numbers. The city was then sacked, as has been mentioned above. When he was advancing to the siege of Caffa, he sent on ahead Scythian traders with instructions to sell the furs of ermines at less than the usual price, in order that the

1 Sivas.

citizens might be enticed out of the city to purchase them. By this trick he secured possession of all the money in the city; and moreover, after the town had been stormed, recovered the furs amongst the other booty; for such furs cannot be buried in the ground, as is frequently done with money and treasure.

Occasionally Temurus wreaked his brutality upon his own subjects and upon Muhammadans. On one occasion, in order to test the fidelity of his courtiers towards his sons, he had the report spread that he was dead. On hearing this, many of his subjects, with insults and abuse, repudiated their allegiance to his sons, and were subsequently very cruelly punished by the king. When, in passing through a country district, he found no supplies ready for him, he ordered the rearguard of his army to cut down the crops, lay waste the district, and carry off captive both its inhabitants and their cattle and draught animals. During his invasion of Mesopotamia the white Tartars who had been resisting him, were slaughtered, and a huge pile made of their corpses, by order of Temurus, on the spot where they had been defeated, in order that the sight of it might strike terror into others.

During the war in which he conquered and captured Payazitus Temurus showed great cruelty to the Christians, since the Greeks and Genoese had favoured his enemy. On reaching Arsinga, after the successful termination of the war, the Muhammadans of that place accused before him Zaretanus, the ruler of the city and surrounding district, on the ground that he gave more money to the Christians than to themselves, whence the Christian places of worship were in a more flourishing condition than their own. Thereupon Temurus ordered that the Archpresbyter should be immediately put to death, unless he abjured his faith (which the excellent and truly pious man resolutely refused to do) together with all the other Christians; and that their churches should be levelled with the ground. Zaretanus, who, although a Muhammadan, was by nature gentle and equally well-disposed towards both the Christians and his other subjects, offered a ransom of [1]seven

1 Perhaps about £55,000.

thousand sestertia, and thus succeeded in securing that the lives of the Christians should be spared. He could not however save their churches from destruction. At another city called Pagrixum, in response to a demand of the Muhammadans, Temurus, after accepting a ransom in return for which he had promised not to destroy the Christian churches, nevertheless broke his word, and had them all razed to the ground. In the same spirit of hatred against the Christians, he almost decided to hang the envoys of Catay Canus, *i.e.*, the king of the Serae, who came in their king's name to demand the tribute which had been paid by former kings of Samarcanda.

His Wealth, etc.

Yet had he been willing to pay the tribute, Temurus had abundant resources for the purpose. For he was supposed to be far richer than Croesus ever was. The spoils taken from the conquered Payazitus alone brought so much silver and gold into his treasury that its very doors were made of gold, and it included a store-room, also made of gold, in which were a vast number of gold and silver cups, plates, bowls, basins and jugs. Above, in the door of this store-room, was set a single huge pearl, as big as a walnut, and also other smaller pearls, surrounded with heraldic figures and emblems. Besides this he had a golden table with an emerald of extraordinary size inserted in it, also a most beautiful golden oak-tree, and a great number of other gold and silver vessels. He had countless quantities of hoarded money. All these treasures were greatly increased by the fact that in his dominions lay the mountain from which diamonds are extracted. All his treasure and other property, and all his precious plate and furniture, were stored in a certain camp which he had constructed at a great distance from any inhabited place. At this spot his arsenal also was situated, where a thousand artificers made the arms for his troops.

To turn to his private affairs—as is the custom of Muhammadans he had many wives, by whom he became the father of the following sons, Janguirius, who died before his father, Miramxas, Xarocus and Mahammed

Sultan, who captured Payazitus and died on military service. Janguirius was the father of Pir Mahammed: Miramxas[1] of Ommar, Abobacar and Carilus.[2] These sons and grandsons received kingdoms to govern. Miramxas was given Persia, but was ordered by his father to abdicate that throne, because he had destroyed some important buildings at Persepolis and Ecbatana, and because he had fallen under suspicion of plotting against his father in consequence of an accusation brought against him by his own wife, the mother of Carilus,—so bitterly enraged was the woman against him. Temurus gave directions that his place should be taken by his son Hommarus.[3] Babylonia as far as the Euphrates, Alepum, and Damascus in Syria were entrusted to Abobacar, son of this same Miramxas. Hircania and Parthia were given to Xarocus. Miramxas was long afterwards pardoned in response to appeals from other members of the royal family; but he had to fall at his father's feet with a halter round his neck, and to implore forgiveness for his offence in destroying the buildings mentioned above. Temurus was so fond of Pir Mahammed, son of Janguirus, that he gave him all the lands captured from the King of India. He made his sister's son Jansa commander of the royal guards, and Jansa's brother Sultan Hammedus captain of his personal body-guard.

He had an enormous number of household slaves, amongst whom must be included those runners mentioned above under the name of gelabdares. By the Tartars they are called Anch. The attendants in his palace and court were the same as those of Zelaldinus, who always took the greatest pains to imitate, even in the minutest details, the traditional system of Temurus. Conquered princes were employed as slaves, and were set to feeding the king's beasts and birds, which were brought before him for inspection at stated times. If one of them died,

---

1 Miran Shah (Hosten.)

2 Umar, Abā Bakr, Khalil (Hosten.)

3 Note in this and many other instances Monserrate's carelessness and inconsistency in spelling proper names. He has spelt it Ommar just above.

the wretched man to whom it had been entrusted paid for it with his life. The practice of Zelaldinus was less cruel, but more sordid; for in such a case he merely demanded payment for the dead creature.

Rulers of surrendered and tributary territories were ordered to paint up his coat of arms in public places and to have it stamped on their coinage. This coat of arms consisted of three circles in a three-cornered pattern, one below and two above. These circles were intended to represent his dominion over Asia, Africa and Europe. The badge of his military dignity was a braid of hair arranged in a three-fold plait, which hung down to his shoulders, and was affixed by a golden broach to whatever helmet or other head dress he happened to be wearing.

After Temurus had gained leisure from his wars, he turned his attention to architecture. He built a costly palace at Quexis,[1] where he was born. In the brief space of twenty days he erected a spacious market-hall in the centre of Samarcanda, with store-houses and dwelling-houses attached, an arched roof to keep off sun and rain, and windows on either side to admit the light. This building extended the whole distance from one gate of the city across to the opposite gate. At Samarcanda he also built the tomb of his son Mahammed, who was called Mahammed Sultan because he had captured with his own hand the Sultan Paiazitus. This tomb he at first considered too low, and hence gave orders for it to be improved. These orders were carried out in the space of ten days on a most lavish and ornate scale. The work was executed with the most extreme despatch and diligence, under the very eyes of the emperor, who urged it on both by terror and rewards, and with his own hands supplied food to the workmen. A magnificent facade was also added to the tomb of his mother-in-law in the shortest possible time and the most elegant possible style. He founded Carabacum[2] in Persia, whither he often despatched his troops for the winter season. It was a town of twenty thousand well-built houses.

During his periods of leisure he was devoted to the

---

1 Kesh (Hosten.)

2 Karabagh (Hosten.)

game of chess and to watching the combats, of gladiators and boxers. He held frequent banquets, at which the flesh of horses was served, boiled or roast. His ferocity is shown by the fact that he used to have prisoners slaughtered before him in the course of these banquets. At the games held to celebrate the marriage of one of his officers—games which were attended by a large gathering of all ranks of people from the whole district of Samarcanda—he had a gibbet set up, and announced that at those very games he would reward the worthy and punish the guilty. This threat he abundantly fulfilled; for in the very middle of the festivities he had a certain distinguished officer hung on the gibbet. Another wretched man was similarly punished, who had been a protegé of the first. In this latter case the king's own nephew Burodus, to whom he was much attached, besought him to pardon the offender if he paid a fine of four hundred sestertia.[1] Temurus agreed; but when the money had been paid, he handed the wretch over to torture, in order to extract from him all the rest of his money; and finally, when all his resources had been extorted, he had him hung head-downwards on a cross. Another wretched offender, to whom he had entrusted three thousand horses, and who could not produce them at once when required, was strangled, although he promised to produce six thousand horses if he were given time to collect them. At this same festival the corn merchants were punished for selling their corn too dear, and the shoemakers for exceeding the prescribed price.

When receiving foreign ambassadors he had most magnificent and sumptuous banquets prepared, and entertained them in some fine colonnade, park or country-seat, or sometimes in a well-fortified camp. The object of this was to make a display of his wealth; and for the same purpose gold and silver coins, and jewels set in beaten gold, were distributed to the common people. The Mongols thoroughly approved of the opportunity thus given for lavish feasting; for enormous dishes of horseflesh were set before them. The rest of the army, however, was disgusted by this kind of banquet. On the occasion when the

1 About £3,000.

camp of Paiazitus was sacked, they saw the Mongols fall upon the fat horses, which were wandering in all directions, like an eagle on a hare. A similar savage and horrible practice of theirs is that of drinking without hesitation the blood of horses in order to quench their hunger and thirst, if they have need. For when they are exhausted, they open a vein behind a horse's ear and eagerly quaff the warm blood.

To pass on to the few details which remain to be given about Temurus. His court was frequented by a crowd of ambassadors and notables from almost all over the world, amongst whom were the envoys of Henry the Fourth of Castilia, from distant Spain. He used to pronounce judgment after the manner of the Muhammadans. According to the heathen custom of his forefathers, noble culprits were strangled on a fork-shaped gibbet, and plebeian ones had their heads cut off (the opposite of the European usage), or were impaled.

His laborious and triumphant career was prolonged to an old age so extreme that his eyes could scarcely be seen through the overhanging eye-brows. He became so weak as to have to be carried everywhere in a litter. Finally he died at Samarcanda, his death having been portended—so say those who study the stars—by a great saffron-coloured comet.

In his youth Temurus was active and handsome, and of a very pleasing appearance. His mind was acute, his judgment and decision swift; but his face, after he had grown accustomed to war, was fierce, glowering and terrible. He was tall, broad-shouldered, sinewy and strong. When he joined in the Tartar archery contests, he could draw the bow-string back past his ear, and could pierce a brass mortar with a spear. Those who saw Temerbegus say that his appearance corresponded with the descriptions of Hannibal.

In his childhood he worshipped the sun, moon, stars and fire, as is the custom of the Mongols. As a young man he embraced the superstition of the Muhammadans. He greatly favoured the Darveges,[1] especially those who

1 Darveshes (ascetics)

wander about entirely naked, with shaven heads, exposed to all rigours of summer heat and winter cold, and who sing or rattle castanets, and live by begging for alms.

Temurus was a man of remarkable common-sense and skill in dealing with men. Towards his own followers he was very careful to be both just and generous. It was hard to decide whether he was more remarkable for energy and courage or for prudence and statesmanship. But his drunkenness and innate cruelty cast a dark shadow on all these excellent qualities. With regard to his excessive cruelty, it is recounted (though the very mention of such barbarism arouses one's disgust) that on one occasion he gave orders for a procession of boys and girls, who had come, carrying palms, in order to beseech his mercy on their country, to be trodden and crushed to death by his cavalry. Closely connected with this infernal cruelty was his pugnacity, which on the occasion of the capture of Damascus prompted him to refuse terms to the defenders of the citadel, who had at first resisted but afterwards wished to surrender. Rather than enter in triumph through gates opened by the defenders themselves, he chose to exhibit his warlike courage, ferocity and cunning, and to reduce the citadel by force of arms, by means of building close to it a huge wooden fort or tower.

Temurus was keen-witted and acute both in speech and in action. The city of Egida, situated near the foot of the mountain on which Noah's ark settled, was a stronghold of robbers. He therefore destroyed all the house-doors in the city and took care that they should not be replaced. On being besought by a certain Genoese to show greater mercy to the vanquished, he responded frowningly, 'What? Do you suppose me to be a mere man, and not rather the Wrath of God?' He was highly incensed with another who asked him to have pity upon the sufferings of Paiazittus, replying to him, 'I do not so much punish Paiazittus for his pride and arrogance, as for his unnatural crime in murdering his elder brother in order to secure the throne.' He destroyed a number of houses in order to build that market-hall at Samarcanda of which mention has already been made: and when their owners advised Temurus of their loss, through the mediumship of certain familiar friends of his, who were descendants of Muhammad, (they are called Saiidii and Xarifii by the Muhammadans, and are greatly honoured), he grimly replied to their representations:—'This city is mine. I bought it with my own means. I hold the articles relating to the purchase, and the title-deeds. Tomorrow I will publicly produce them. If you judge the purchase money to have been insufficient, I will pay whatever additional sum you may think right.' It is extraordinary indeed that he did not order the complainants off to instant execution; for he was apt to take such representations very ill. By his own men Temur was called Cushlan, *i.e.*, 'the sword of good fortune.' By foreigners he was known as the terror, destruction and ruin of the whole world. He was wont to call himself by a boastful and terrible name 'the Wrath of God,' which had come upon the earth to punish the wickedness of that corrupt age.

Disturbance after Timur's Death.

Great commotions followed the news of Temur's death. His grandson Carilus,[1] son of Miramxas hastily gathered an army and slew Butodus, the son of Jansa, who, with the help of his brothers, had seized the treasuries of his uncle Temurus at Samarcanda. After the death of Butodus his two brothers fled to Xarocus,[2] the son of Temurus and their own cousin, who was at Helacum in Parthia. Carilus, having possessed himself of Temurus' treasures and gold, first offered a solemn sacrifice in memory of his grandfather, and then sent swift messengers to announce to his father that Temurus was dead and that he himself had slain Butodus, who had usurped the throne and seized the treasury and the city. He urged his father to come to Samarcanda with all possible haste. Carilus was son of that Gansada who had accused her husband Miramxas of treason before her father-in-law Temurus. All this happened at Samarcanda.

At Carabaca[3] in Persia Jansa (the brother of Butodus

---

1 Khalil (Hosten)
2 Shahrukh (Hosten)
3 Karabagh (Hosten)

and grandson of Temurus), who was an intimate friend of Ommaris,[1] the son of Miramxas, (this Ommaris had been governing Persia under the suzerainty of his grandfather Temurus), taking advantage of his position as confidential adviser of Ommaris, stirred up an insurrection in the army, and killed a certain chief who was a favourite with Ommaris. He then hastened to occupy the arsenal, but was driven away by the guard. Finally, hurrying to Ommaris' tent in order to assassinate him, he was in like manner repulsed by the bodyguard, and forced to take refuge in his tent. There was a panic in the army; for the rumour spread that Ediguius, tyrant of Tartary, had made a sudden attack on the camp. Ommaris, to whose tent the whole army flocked together, was at a loss whither to go or what course to pursue. He was afraid of the authority and power of Jansa, whom he had treated as his foster father. Whilst he was in this state of uncertainty, one of his friends ran up and cried "Give me leave to kill Jansa, and this disorder and panic will cease at once." Ommaris replied, "Why then do you delay? Make haste." Forthwith the man, catching Jansa unawares, killed him, cut off his head, and brought it to Ommaris. His death, and the quelling of the wide-spread rumour about Ediguius, soon put a stop to the insurrection and rioting.

Ommaris sent the head of Jansa to his father Miramxas, who was at Babylon in Assyria, and wrote as follows to his mother and brothers:—"Behold the head of my enemy. My grandfather is dead. Come therefore to me, that I may receive my father with royal honours and dutifully embrace him." Ommaris himself remained at Viana, not far from the border of Persis.[2] Miramxas was offended at his son's arrogant message, and advanced with his army from Babylon towards Viana. Learning however that his son had a great force with him, drawn up ready for battle, he sent heralds to demand of him his intentions. Ommaris replied, "I desire to protect the country that was given into my charge, and to strengthen my frontier-guards."

---

1 Mirza Umar (Hosten)
Farsistan

Abobacaris[1], the brother of Ommaris, who was with his father, was enraged by this answer, and asked his father for permission to kill Ommaris. This Miramxas and Hansada, the mother of Ommaris, refused, fearing the anger of the Xacattaei, and wrote to Ommaris not to fight against his father and to leave Persia. Ommaris wrote back to his mother that he would gladly obey. Hence Abobacaris was despatched to confirm the peace. Ommaris seized him, thrust him into prison in the citadel of Ecbathana, and marched against his father. His mother sent an embassy expostulating with him for his treachery and the imprisonment of his brother, and begging him not to put him to death. He replied that he had imprisoned his brother because he was rash, crazy and unbalanced. However, it was quite clear that Ommaris had really imprisoned him because he was strong and brave and a favourite with the Xacattaei, and because he himself was plotting to kill his father. To avoid this fate Miramxas fled to his brother-in-law Sulemxas in the district of Rhages in Media, where he remained until, having gathered a larger force, he marched towards Samarcanda, whereupon Ommaris and his forces followed him. On learning from his scouts that his father's army was stronger and larger than his own, Ommaris asked for reinforcements from his uncle Xarocus on condition that, if victorious, they should divide the empire between them. Xarocus was at Helacum, through which place Miramxas was about to lead his army. On learning what was happening, Miramxas remained in Parthia, and the treacherous Ommaris, in order to avoid the hatred of the Xacattaei, spread the report that he had come to terms with his father.

While all this was going on, Sorsus the Christian king of Hircania,[2] seizing the opportunity of the civil warfare amongst the Xacattaei, attacked Azrun[3] and Aumiana on the border of Armenia, and even invaded Persis itself, devastating the country, and sacking, burning and destroying many towns. Ommaris sent a large detachment of

---

1 Abu Bakr.
2 Georgia.
Erzerum.

Xacattaei against him under the command of Ommaris Toba, a veteran commander who lived on the borders of Hyrcania and thus was accustomed to the style of fighting practised by the Hyrcani. He stationed his army on the frontier of Hyrcania. On learning of this, Sorsus made a surprise attack on the Xacattaei at night, cut down some, and put the rest to flight. They were greatly disgusted at being worsted by Cafarii (by which name the Muhammadans call Christians). They attributed their misfortune to Ommaris, and declared that the good luck of Temurus had come to an end.

Abobacaris, who was being kept in prison at Ecbathanae, killed his guard, rifled the treasury, and fled to join his father. His flight was reported to Ommaris when he returned to Ecbathana from his unsuccessful campaign. He had intended to poison his brother; but hearing of his escape, he sent a squadron to intercept his flight. However Abobacaris hastened to his father, obtained from him an army to act as an advance-guard in the coming campaign, caught his uncle Xarocus unawares at Helacum, and carried him captive to Miramxas. The cavalry and many of the Xacattaei in the army of Xarocus readily transferred their allegiance to Abobacaris. With their support he conducted his father Miramxas safely to Samarcanda, where he occupied the throne of his father Temurus. Ommaris made peace with his father, and by his permission remained at Viana, where he performed the obsequies of his grandfather.

The Line of Timur.

If may be believed that the tradition is true which declares that Pir Mahammed who was styled king of India, submitted to Miramxas; for ancient historians tell us nothing about Pir, and only a single dynasty of kings is mentioned as having reigned in continuous succession over Sogdiana, Bactria, the Paropanisus, and India, down to the time of Zelaldinus himself. Distance and ignorance of the affairs of the house of Timur, as well as the civil wars of his sons and grandsons recounted above, have led European historians to declare that the sons of Timur lost by their sloth and weakness all that their father's valour had gained, and that the line of that great hero soon died out. The true line of succession was, however, as follows: Abobacaris, otherwise Abussaius, succeeded his father Miramxas. After him reigned Ommarxecus.[1] After him Gaumirxas.[2] After him Baburxas,[3] whose son was king Emaumus, father of king Zelaldinus and Mirsachimus. The house of Timur retained their founder's conquests in Media and Asia Minor till the time of king Hossenassanus, which coincided with that of the reign of Baburxas. Hossenassanus deprived the Xacattaei of Persia, Parthia, Adiabene and Susiana.

Zelaldinus did not hesitate either to protect the empire which he had received, or to recover what had been torn from it, or to make new conquests. He is even now fighting a great war with Abdullacanus[4] for the possession of the kingdom of Samarcanda. For Cancanus, on the departure of his master Baburxas to invade India, stole from him, as has been mentioned above, his kingdom of Sogdiana. He did not however live to enjoy his ill-gotten realm for long. For soon afterwards he died and was succeeded by his son Babusultanus, and he by Bosacoras. Abdullacanus, the son of king Osbeqsultanus, and himself king of Balcum, slew Bosacoras and claimed the kingdom of Samarcanda for himself, though by rights it belongs to Zelaldinus. This king of Balcum can put into the field a force of three hundred thousand archer-cavalry. The vanguard of Zelaldinus received a check at his hands in the Paharopanisus, near Chabulum. On that occasion twenty thousand men were lost; and hence the war is still going on, it being even yet doubtful to which side victory will incline. As long as he lived, Abdullacanus supported Amurathes[5] the king of the Turks against the king of Persia, whilst Zelaldinus favours and supports the latter.

---

1 Umar Shaikh (Hosten).

2 Khan Mirza (Hosten).

3 Babur Shah.

4 Abdullah Khan.

5 'Since Abdullah Khan died on Feb. 12, 1597, Monserrate must have corrected the passage above in India between 1597 and 1600, the date of his death' (Hosten). The passage before correction read 'supports' and omitted 'as long as he lived.'

Hence the whole Muhammadan world has been divided into two camps. God grant that His prophecy, which His Son Christ uttered so many centuries ago, may teach these Musalmans the terrible danger to themselves if they are not converted to the true Faith, and the necessity for making peace with the whole Church and all Christendom. I mean the words "Every kingdom divided against itself shall be laid waste, and house shall fall upon house."[1]

The Scythians.

Seeing that Zelaldinus traces the origin of his line to Scythia, it may not seem out of place to add, as a foot-note to this work, some brief account of the origin of the Scythians. They are an exceedingly ancient race. For the ancestors of the Scythians are said to have been Magogus, son of Japetus,[2] Hasarmotus, Diclas and Sebas, sons of Jectanus, who was the brother of Phalegus, a descendant of Sem,[3] the son of Noa. The Scythian race is (and always has been from the most ancient times) so called from their custom of living in tents made of skins; for the name means "hide-men." Their neighbours, the Persians, call them "Aramaei;"[4] for they believe them to be descended from Aramus, a kinsman of their own ancestors.

A very great region of Asia, or rather a region lying partly in Asia and partly in Europe, is called Scythia after them. Some hold that European Scythia, *i.e.*, Sarmatia, with its inhabitants the Sarmatians, is so called from Hasarmothus. The similarity of the names is probably the only reason for this idea. Others, however, hold that these superficial resemblances of spelling and sound, which the Greeks were so fond of hunting up, generally lead to totally wrong derivations.

Asiatic Scythia may be roughly divided into Serica and Tartary (or Mongolia as it is sometimes called). These are separated by the Imaus.[5] The first settler in Serica

1 Luke 11: 17.
2 Gen. 10: 1.
3 Gen. 10: 1.
4 Pliny, Nat. Hist. 6: 13 (Monserrate).
5 Altai or Thian Shan Mts.

is said to have been Sebas, who was the ancestor of the races dwelling beyond the Imaus. The most noteworthy of these races is named the Seres, celebrated for the wool-like substance found in their forests in the form of white foliage. This substance they first moisten with water and then gently pluck, or so says one ancient writer. In our own age it has been discovered that the material here mentioned is silk, and does not grow on trees. It is a similar type of silk to that grown in the district of Tarracona[1] not far from Caesaraugusta,[2] and used for cloth of the finest texture, through which flour is sifted.

Diclas and Magogus are said to have been the first settlers in Tartary. A certain writer,[3] eminent alike for his piety and his erudition, who acted as ambassador of Pope Innocent the Fourth to Tartary in the time of Cinguiscanus, held that the Mongols derive their name from Magogus and are mentioned in the prophecy of Ezechiel.[4]

Amongst the Scythians living on this side of the Imaus the Dahae and Daci used to be included ; and amongst those living on the other side are the Sacae[5] (by which name the Persians used to call all Scythians) and the Messagetae. Amongst the Dahae are included the Aparmi, living next to the Hyrcanians and their Sea,[6] the Xanthii and the Pissuri.

In ancient times the Essedones, who used the gold-decorated skulls of their ancestors as cups, wandered at large over the whole of Scythia, as also did the Ariaci, the Rhimnici and the Appellei, whose race and name has perished, with so many more, in the passage of ages.

All the Scythians have derived their various names from their pursuits and manner of life. They are sometimes, for instance, called Nomads,[7] sometimes Scenitae, some-

---

1 Tarràgona.
2 Sarragossa.
3 St. Antoninus (Monserrate).
4 Ezekiel 38 & 39 (Monserrate).
5 Sakas (?)
6 The Caspian.
7 Wanderers, Tent-dwellers, Cave-dwellers, Wagon-dwellers, Milk-eaters, Horse-eaters, Horse-milkers, Milkers, Lifeless people.

times Troglodites, Amaxobii, Galactophagi, Hippophagi, Equimulgi, Galactaei, and Abii—this last signifying wild, savage, uncouth and uncivilized. Their neighbours still use these same names in describing them. They are called Aymachii, *i.e.* wanderers who carry around with them all their household goods, Carganixtae, *i.e.* tent-dwellers, and Xeroqhorae, because they live on milk.

The Scythians, both those who invaded Europe and their kindred in Asia, have in every age, as also in our own, been famous for their warlike valour. In Europe the Sarmatae conquered the greater part of the Tauric Chersonese,[1] to which they gave the name or Little Scythia. They were called Scythotauri, and are said to have been in the habit of cruelly sacrificing strangers to Diana.

The Asiatic Scythians, or Dahae, founded the Bactrian and Parthian empire, which gave great trouble to the Romans. For the Scythian Atsaces, shunning a contest with the great forces of Callinicus Demetrius, fled for refuge with a little band of Dahae to the Parthians—a people of his own race, who had long before been driven from their home in some civil war, and had settled as exiles (the name 'Parthian' means an exile) in a small and mountainous district. Any who resisted having been overcome, Arsaces established his rule over these Parthians, and thus founded the dynasty of the Arsacidae. His descendants were the following:—Arsaces his son, Pampatus, Pharnaces, Mithridates and others down to Phraates, who made peace with the Romans, entrusted his sons to Caesar Augustus, and gave him also his grandsons as hostages.

The Sacae and Messagetae were named after kings, as is the custom ot their country. They made a practice of deporting large numbers of the inhabitants of conquered territories as settlers into other provinces. One such colony, and the largest of them, was planted between Paphlagonia and Pontus, and consisted of Assyrians. Another, consisting of Medes, they located beyond the Tanais. The settlers there are called Sauromatae, for they have little eyes like lizards (Greek "sauros"). I imagine that Sarmatia gets its name by the dropping of letters

1 Crimea

from this Sauromatia. These same Sacae founded Indo-Scythia, near the Paharopanisas, whose inhabitants are called Patanaei[1] and Delazacquii,[2] *i.e.* 'true of heart.' They speak a mixture of the Scythian language of Bactria and the Median of Parthia, called Pastoum. By the Persians they are called Aufgani. The Bactrians were brought into that region first by Eucratides. Subsequently the Parthians were brought in by Mitthridates, the great-grandson of Arsaces, after he had slain the son of Eucratides.

Whenever they have gone to war, the Scythians, women as well as men, have brought back with them great martial glory. It is remarkable wlth what courage and fortitude the queens, who have from time to time, ruled over them, have carried on their campaigns. For instance Thomyris, the queen of the Amazons, very cunningly entrapped and slaughtered two hundred thousand Persians in the defiles of a mountain range, by means of an ambuscade. She also captured[3] and crucified Cyrus, king of Persia, cut off his head, and had it shut up in a bag full of blood, sternly exclaiming "Drink your fill of that blood, for which you were so thirsty."

I omit many details about the Scythians in order not to digress too much from my subject. I will merely give two striking instances of Scythian valour. They put to flight so ignominiously Uxoris, the king of Egypt, who had ventured to attack them, that he was forced to take refuge beyond the marshes of the Nile, leaving behind him his army and all its warlike equipment. Again under their general Lauthinus, they overcame and routed Darius. They exacted tribute from Asia for fifteen hundred years. They forced the army of the slaves to surrender, and then scourged the prisoners with whips and rods. They drove in rout from their country Zopiron, the generai of Alexander the Great. In short, down to our own time, the Scythians and their kindred races have carried through whatever they have undertaken exactly as they had planned it, and have earned thereby the greatest prestige and glory. And would to God that the whole earth had not found out in

---

1, 2 Pathans and Dilazaks.

3 B. C. 529.

practical experience, with such terrible loss to Christendom, how great is the military strength of the Scythian races. For the Turks, who are Scythians by descent, have conquered by their martial valour almost half the world, under the leadership of their great kings from Ottomanus, founder of the line of Turkish kings, in continuous succession to Amurathes, who now reigns.

INDEX

A

B

H

I

J

L

M

N

O

P

Q

R

S

T

THE END.